IMAGINING
LITERACY

IMAGINING LITERACY

Rhizomes of Knowledge in
American Culture and Literature

RAMONA FERNANDEZ

UNIVERSITY OF TEXAS PRESS
Austin

A portion of chapter 4 was previously published as "Disney's Labyrinth," in Elizabeth Bell, Lynda Haas, and Laura Sells, eds., *From Mouse to Mermaid: The Politics of Film, Gender, and Culture* (Bloomington: Indiana University Press, 1995). Reprinted here courtesy of Indiana University Press.

Excerpts from Maxine Hong Kingston's *The Woman Warrior: Memoirs of a Girlhood among Ghosts* (1977) reprinted here courtesy of Random House/Alfred A. Knopf, Inc.

LIBRARY OF CONGRESS CATALOGING-IN-PUBLICATION DATA
Fernandez, Ramona, date
    Imagining literacy : rhizomes of knowledge in American culture and literature / Ramona Fernandez. — 1st ed.
        p.   cm.
    Includes bibliographical references (p.   ) and index.
    ISBN 0-292-72521-3 (cloth : alk. paper) —
    ISBN 0-292-72522-1 (pbk. : alk. paper)
    1. Literacy—United States.   2. Educational anthropology—United States.   3. Culture.   4. Multicultural education—United States.   I. Title.
    LC151 .F47   2001
    302.2'244—dc21

                                            00-066592

CONTENTS

PREFACE

WHOSE MULTICULTURALISM?

It is easy to forget that the term *multiculturalism* has been in wide circulation for only about a decade. Its origins are suspect, and there is little evidence that it arose first in the discourses of socially conscious theorists. Furthermore, its history outside the United States is not uniformly positive; for example, its Canadian use suggests institutionalized separatism, and South African blacks dislike the term's connection to apartheid. The *Oxford English Dictionary* notes one of its earliest uses in the 1966 British journal *The Economist,* hardly a noted proselytizer of racial justice. Rightist ideologues made the term a bone of contention in the early 1990's when Stanford's "Cultures, Ideas, and Values" course began including non-Western reading selections alongside Western European classics. As the term became part of our everyday vocabulary, it was attacked by conservatives who resist broadening America's school and college curriculum.

What does it name? Often, it seems to be used mindlessly as a mild concession to the many differences around us. While the term seems to challenge established attitudes, it has often been used to depoliticize any effective resistance to those attitudes. Like the melting pot allusions of an earlier era, *multiculturalism* (spelled with or without the hyphen) can mean almost anything, or nothing, depending on who deploys the term. Wahneema Lubiano, Peter Erickson, and the Chicago Cultural Studies Group have published interesting essays demonstrating that this term is being used in ways that ensure that it will *not* contest established injustices and cultural norms. On the contrary, administrative agencies have invented self-serving theories of multiculturalism that only reinstitute historical divisions and oppressions.

Lubiano advocates a radical or "strong" multiculturalism that reconceptualizes education and its relation to power instead of deploying it as a rhetorical device to "'manage' diverse student populations and curricula."

The connection between "weak" multiculturalism and crude identity politics that falsely name individuals as part of "coherent" and "pure" cultural groups is a central problem in American society. We are all of us as individuals already mixed ethnically and culturally; our roots are historically constructed out of subtly mediated cultural strands.

In response to this conservative discourse, Guillermo Gómez-Peña has put into circulation Roberto Sanchez's countercoinage, *culti-multural*. This coinage satirizes attitudes toward multiculturalism that refuse to perceive the historical reality of cultural mixing and instead collect "exotic" cultures alongside one another in a Disneyesque "It's a Small World" cacophony. When multiculturalism is used this way, it indeed reinscribes notions of difference as cultish variants from recognized Western European and North American norms. Collecting artifacts and styles from "exotic" cultures into a collage turns differences into curiosities. Curiosities are denuded of their power to challenge; they are absorbed as decoration.

Rejecting crude models of ethnicity might help us reject culti-multuralism and construct a "strong" model of multiculturalism. Increasing our international focus might also help break open American discussions around these issues. If multiculturalism is to fulfill its implied promise to usher in a more egalitarian era, we must all engage in an extended debate around its meaning and political implications. If culti-multuralism is to become strong multiculturalism, sustained and deep changes must take place in our thinking, institutions, policies, ideologies, identities, and epistemologies.

The purposes and implications of this study suggest that the phrase *mixed cultures* more exactly expresses our present state. "Purity" of culture is a pure illusion. *Mixed cultures* echoes Lucy Lippard's wonderful book, *Mixed Blessing: New Art in a Multicultural America*. Lippard cogently explains:

> *The terminology in which an issue is expressed is indicative of the quality of the discourse, and the fact that there are no euphonious ways to describe today's cross-cultural exchange reflects the deep social and historical awkwardness underlying that exchange. Much has been tried and found wanting. Writing about intercultural art, looking for satisfying ways to describe the groups involved, many of whom are living between cultures, I find myself caught in a web of ungainly, pompous, condescending, even ugly language. (15)*

This thesis begs your indulgence should it descend into ugly language. The term *mixed cultures* is used preferentially and quite deliberately in this text to refer to the borderlands that we all inhabit. I agree with Lippard that "the borderlands are porous, restless, often incoherent territory, virtual minefields of unknowns for both practitioners and theoreticians" (6). May we all be blessed as we negotiate maps of this culturally mixed territory.

ACKNOWLEDGMENTS

I am immensely grateful for the guidance of Donna Haraway, Hayden White, Angela Davis, and Maxine Hong Kingston during the creation of earlier versions of this book. I would also like to thank Jose Limon and Gerald Vizenor for their guidance during my preliminary explorations.

Roz Spafford deserves a special mention for her encouragement and editing advice at key moments. Billie Harris and Sheila Peuse kept me on track throughout this entire process. I am more than grateful.

The Ford Foundation, the Smithsonian Institution, and the University of California, Santa Cruz, all honored me with fellowship awards that made this process possible. I would like to thank Christine O'Brien for her encouragement and all my Ford fellowship friends for sharing their energy and commitment with me, especially Leonard Brown, Matthew Countryman, and Caroline Sinevianna.

My friends and colleagues all over the country and around the globe contributed to my work by encouraging and supporting me time and time again. I would like to thank Bettina Aptheker, Roz Bennett, Camelia Fernandez Eckstein, Evan Eckstein, Carmen Fernandez, Jerry Fishman, Bonnie Ford, Jennifer Gonzales, Lynda and Bob Haas, David Harrington, Donna Hwang, Adrienne King, Katherine and Daniel Kostelec, Judith Pettibone, Gina Polsinelli, Maurizio Rosso, Mia Farone Rosso, Don Rothman, Chéla Sandoval, Susan Schiller-Chainey, Charlie Singer, Xe Yiao, and my students. And a special thanks to Etta Abrahams, who coaxed me through the final manuscript revisions.

My Smithsonian mentors and friends helped with the final chapter. My thanks go to Nancy Fuller, Ivan Karp, Zahava Doering, Lucy Fellowes, Jim Volkert, and Kitty Smith.

I want to thank my mother and her mother and all her mother's mothers back in an untraceable line, none of whom, to my knowledge, has ever been in a position to translate her voice into a written record. I break this silence for the first time.

IMAGINING
LITERACY

Introduction **TO READ OR NOT**

GUARDING THE BOOKS

"The Keeper of the Books" is a haunting poem penned by Jorge Luis Borges about a dozen years after he became the director of the National Library of Argentina and began losing his sight.[1] The increasing inaccessibility of the written word must have affected both his physical routines and his intellectual and spiritual self. "El Guardián de los Libros" can be read as an expression of these difficulties. To be installed in his position as director of the library just as his ability to read was receding must have created special ironies. Hence, it is not surprising that Borges's work is filled with meditations on libraries, books, and the ephemeral and eternal qualities of the written word. The library as universe is a recurrent theme in his work.[2]

"The Keeper of the Books" reflects these obsessions and has inhabited my imaginings about literacy and knowledge since my undergraduate days. It is no accident that this poem rooted itself in my consciousness. I am a child of literate but unschooled working-class parents. For them, even a high school education was impossible, and when my attraction to books surfaced early, it was more a curiosity to them than a path they could lead or encourage me down. Borges's poem speaks from this outsider position, for those who are locked out of literacy and thus locked out of something more: our cultural record of human life on this planet.

"El Guardián de los Libros" is narrated by Hsiang. He has inherited guardianship of an ancient library from his grandfather, who rescued the books from the fires of Mongol invaders. Borges located this library in an imaginary China of his own construction, an ancient China that is rich in the written word, rich in scholarly traditions and the arts, a China fascinating to literate Westerners schooled in, by comparison, a youthful culture. "The Keeper of the Books" begins by representing the universe of knowledge as containable. Located in a tower surrounded by ruin, the books fill shelves too high to reach, recording everything worthy of representation, "gardens and temples and the reason for temples . . . the harmony of the world." And although Hsiang has dutifully accepted the burden of his inheritance, he confesses that he has never learned to read.

> The truth is that I never learned to read
> But it comforts me to think
> That what's imaginary and what's past are the same
> to a man whose life is nearly over.

This canon towers over him, visible but impenetrable. To whom does Hsiang confess his illiteracy? Whose voice speaks this poem? Surely Borges, a man of enormous literacy, was not inhabited by Hsiang. Surely Borges's erudition placed him above and beyond any anxiety about his own literacy. Surely.

The knowledge represented here is secret, eternal, holy. As keeper of the books, Hsiang dreams of deciphering wisdom and lettering "characters with a perfect hand." Envisioning Chinese calligraphy as art and wisdom encoded in ideographs whose subtle iconography recalls to the subconscious a delicate representation of the world, Borges suggests that literacy itself opens the door to a humanist ideal of harmonized perfection approaching the transcendent. For Hsiang, imagining that he can decode these books allows him to envision himself in the image of a traditional scholar, wise, accomplished in arts and letters, a man of right conduct. In China, such a scholar would possess economic and political power. Such a scholar would advise the emperor "whose perfect rule was reflected in the world." For Hsiang, imagining he can decode these books and can letter with a perfect hand gives him the keys to action in the world, the keys to re-creating himself as another person inside another social contract, one of elevated class and status and with access to a wide social discourse. At the end of his life and isolated here in this tower, he knows this is a futile dream, but these books in their materiality are the signs by which he measures his loss. Here in his tower, his imaginative rememory[3] competes for ontological status with the library as a sign of what is past.

In an inversion of the Buddhist and Taoist injunction to live in harmony with nature, the perfect rule of the emperor causes the natural world to mirror his rule "so that the rivers held their banks." Right conduct enables the world. The emperor's right conduct creates the harmony, and right conduct can be shelved here in this tower. Metonymically, the emperor's perfect rule is shelved here and *is* knowledge.

Into this delicate universe ride the Mongols, "innocent as animals of prey." Reversing the previous inversion of culture ordering nature, the barbarians *as* nature undo culture. Hsiang's isolation in his tower and his illiteracy metonymically place him outside culture, outside social discourse. The past he imagines projects him into a history within the social fabric, a history he never had. This imaginative projection is central to his dreams of literacy and central to the thesis of this study.

In this poem and many other works, Borges frames reading and writing within the context of memory, imagination, dream, desire, possession. For Borges, reading and writing are not merely functional skills. They exist to give humans access to the universe of knowledge, a universe representing the universe of experience. That experience is one key to transcendence. Like William Blake, Borges envisions a trembling but powerful relationship between the written word and movement toward other states of being. Despite this library's materiality as paper and ink, the canon of what might be known is represented as unattainable, as total, transcendent, eternal, and secret, but paradoxically, also as vulnerable to destruction and disintegration, for the pages disintegrate before Hsiang's eyes and under his fingers. Throughout Borges's work, there is a pervasive sense of the receding quality of letters. Abstractions are encoded in ink on paper as concrete objects, which, nevertheless, are ephemeral. They disintegrate before our eyes and under our fingers, just as concepts and information often recede in the memory. Hsiang lives in a tower that is disconnected from the larger social discourse because of social disintegration, not because of the betrayal of the intellectual or the artist. In Hsiang's tradition, the intellectual was an artist and a politician. And as all three, the intellectual created law and culture. Perhaps Borges dreams of a Western tradition that never was, one in which intellectuals and artists are consistently at the center of cultural power.

As keeper, Hsiang has become isolated because of the violent destruction of his community, and his illiteracy has further enforced his isolation from his communal history. The books he guards are severed from their connection to the son of heaven and the empire, but no evidence is presented to suggest that the emperor failed in his duties. The books and the emperor have not committed error. What has happened is cataclysmic: barbarians— that is, humans as nature—have undone human culture. Hence, Hsiang's metonymical isolation within this dusty tower seems total, the result of his lack of access to the acculturation of the written word. Without a mediator between the material world and the written word, without an emperor's perfect rule, the city outside the tower turns to dusty wilderness, "leagues of dust and sleep surround the tower." Before this disintegration, the word had alchemized nature and the emperor's perfect rule into harmony. This trope attributes supernatural powers to the written word, but there is nothing unusual in such an attribution. The mystical traditions of many cultures make this connection. In Borges's poem, the empire is destroyed by an inexplicable agent: barbarians who are themselves the agents of a nature filled with rivers that will not hold their banks. Without the alchemy of the written word, culture unravels.

Throughout this poem, Hsiang's dreams of literacy are expressions of his longing to live within a human community. His apparent physical isolation reiterates his banishment from his community's encoded collective memory, the library. The books on these shelves hold the keys to the spiritual self and physical sustenance. And Hsiang seems starved for every kind of sustenance. In Borges's formulation, literacy/illiteracy is tied to the making and unmaking of culture; and humans live either in culture, that is, within a written semiotic system, or like Hsiang in tragic isolation.

Hsiang's illiteracy disconnects him from a viable community and the "ceremonies, which are the only wisdom the Firmament accords to men." Indeed, his discourse has shrunk to a silent exchange with silent books. He can only dream of possessing all that literacy promises, and literacy promises both material and spiritual wealth. Without literacy, Hsiang's fate, like the empire's fate, is dismal.

But Hsiang's dreams of literacy are powerful and give him comfort because they suggest the possibility of another life. Like Hsiang's dreams, our dreams of literacy comfort us because they seem to offer the same possibility. My own dreams of literacy certainly seemed to offer me another life.

THE POLITICS OF LITERACY DEFINITION

The covert debates around literacy recognize few, if any, of our dreams about the power of literacy. Examining the structure of various representative definitions of literacy can give us a sense of the confusion and contention that shape this debate and help reveal how the discourses around literacy control and disenable our thinking. Imagining literacy is rarely fostered in these competing definitions; rather they address not the preliterate, semiliterate, or even functionally literate but those who police literacy. This study does not deny that the phrase "a literacy crisis" names something significant and dire. This phrase is dangerously unhelpful, however, because it is fostered by various groups that have everything to gain if they can retain the right to police literacy.

The earliest definitions of literacy in the United States referred to an individual's ability to write his or her name, often termed *signature literacy*. Gradually, literacy was redefined as something more than the ability to make identifying marks on a document. Various researchers have pointed out that literacy crises have been manufactured whenever structural economic changes have required a more literate workforce and political uncertainties have driven nations into anxiety. Certainly, signature literacy is not considered literacy in any contemporary society, and neither are basic decoding skills now considered acceptable literacy in most. Even the ability to read literally is no longer taken to be adequate literacy. In the twenty-first century, minimal standards for literacy insist on the ability to make inferences, to carry out complex comparisons, and even to think critically and creatively.[4]

What this might mean in practice is often defined by those who create literacy tests. The sophisticated language skills of contemporary rappers are not valued by the educational establishment, the news media, bureaucratic and corporate organizations, or Middle America. Instead, rap is portrayed as universally pornographic and violent, while Hollywood films produced by white male Republicans such as Arnold Schwarzenegger and Bruce Willis are held up as models for right conduct. Transnational high-tech, high-status professionals like software designers are recognized for their sophisticated language skills because of their obvious value to late-twentieth-century corporate culture, but rappers also display well-developed language skills. Our inability to honor a wide variety of language skills impoverishes our cultural practices and invalidates our pronouncements.

If it is true that standards for literacy have increasingly escalated, then the media-fostered notions of declining literacy are manufactured and dangerously misleading. Increasing standards, not declining performance, can be pointed to as the root cause of the literacy crisis. The discourses of declining literacy imply personal and national disaster, as any cursory examination of numerous governmental reports will make clear.[5] Ironically, although the statistics can be cited from hundreds of reports, and although the mass media suggest that the case for declining literacy is irrefutable, the factoids in circulation regarding levels of literacy in the United States are by no means universally negative. One report based on the largest study of its kind indicated that United States ninth and fourth graders were among the best readers in the world.[6] While the 1992 *National Educational Goals Report* mentions this fact, it does not cite the relevant statistics supporting this conclusion. Instead, it points out that studies of this kind focus on basic literacy skills. Since basic literacy skills translate into functional *illiteracy* in the current climate, the report, perhaps appropriately, deemphasizes these findings. The report's authors make it clear that American students must perform at a higher standard in reading, writing, mathematics, and science than they have to date. More than three hundred pages of charts and graphs in the *National Educational Goals Report* reinforce the notion that the United States is in trouble because it is losing the literacy war. Our level of achievement in math, science, and engineering is measured against the level of achievement in selected countries that are our economic competitors, like Korea, Taiwan, Japan, Germany, and Canada. But literacy levels in countries like Belgium and Hungary, countries that are not our economic competitors, are cited only in passing. It may be true that our educational system has adjusted less rapidly than those of other developed nations to the demand for an increasingly educated workforce, but a great deal of our discourse surrounding this issue is ahistorical. This helps to foster condemnatory and reactionary policies.

With this in mind, it is no surprise that for the members of the National Commission on Excellence in Education, headed by David P. Gardner, a former president of the University of California, literacy is nationhood, and illiteracy threatens that nationhood. The "Mongol" barbarians sweeping down on us are resistant to our civilization.

> *Our Nation is at risk . . . eroded by a rising tide of mediocrity that threatens our very future as a Nation and a people. . . . We have, in effect, been committing an act of unthinking, unilateral educational disarmament. . . . Knowledge, learning, information, and skilled intelligence are the new raw materials of international commerce. . . . Learning is the indispensable investment required for success in the "information age" we are entering. . . . All, regardless of race or class or economic status, are entitled to a fair chance and to the tools for developing their individual powers of mind and spirit to the utmost. This promise means that all children by virtue of their own efforts, competently guided, can hope to attain the mature and informed judgment needed to secure gainful employment, and to manage their own lives, thereby serving not only their own interests but also the progress of society itself. (A Nation at Risk 1983:5–8)*

The commission goes on to recognize obliquely that changing standards and conditions, not failing schools, are the cause of the literacy crisis.

> *It is important, of course, to recognize that* the average citizen today is better educated and more knowledgeable than the average citizen a generation ago—*more literate, and exposed to more mathematics, literature and science. The positive impact of this fact on the well-being of our country and the lives of our people cannot be overstated. Nevertheless* the average graduate *of our schools and colleges today is not as well-educated as the average graduate of 25 or 35 years ago, when a much smaller proportion of our population completed high school and college. (11)*

Notice that "average citizen" is opposed to "average graduate." A series of social revolutions have led to radically changed demographics in our schools and colleges. A higher proportion of our population graduates from high school and college because women from all social groups, working-class Europeans, and people of color gained political power and access to education in record numbers in the past two decades. Statistically, these groups are often blamed for the decreased standards in higher education. These groups are the metaphorical Mongol hordes. They are not genuinely qualified and/or prepared and/or capable. But as we will see later, literacy discourses are recursive; they circulate in a closed semiotic system that is infected with Enlightenment ideology. This makes it simple to blame those who have had little or no access to economic and social advantages, and it becomes easy to ignore any evidence suggesting that the former "best and brightest" are neither as bright as they used to be nor as bright as we thought them to be.

Reports like *A Nation at Risk* tie our imaginative projections regarding literacy to national security issues embedded in a new cold war discourse—the cold war of global economic struggle. Just as the old cold war was tied to jobs in the defense industry and its many corollaries, so too is the new cold war, the literacy war. But what exactly are the new "defense" industries in this literacy war? We conveniently ignore the fact that there is no ready answer to this question.

What we have done historically is to focus on a literacy defined by the minimal skills needed to assure an adequate workforce. This is a serious error, for we cannot say what our future work will be. Postmodern society requires a flexibility of mind that does not rely on decoding and calculating skills but rather is capable of traveling across a constantly shifting terrain of knowledge and weathering many storms in the process. We can only say, as Bill Clinton and many others have, that work will change and change again in each person's lifetime; we cannot say precisely how it will change.[7] Elspeth Stuckey in her discussions of the inherent violence of literacy issues has insisted that in America "work has changed, and the nature of the change is probably as complex and contingent as any change in history . . . the change in work is literacy. The change, in fact, is a change *in* literacy" (1991 : 12).

This change in literacy is driving great social dislocation. Retraining individuals for new jobs that are themselves doomed to extinction is a mistake. The 1992 *Educational Goals Report* is subtitled *Building a Nation of Learners,* meaning lifetime learners.[8] But how many times can people recycle themselves through an educational system that is expensive in dollar and psychic cost to themselves, their families, and society? President Clinton's proposals called for increased on-the-job retraining, requiring substantial investment in the private sector. The glib discourses concerning retraining largely ignore the disruption that formal schooling both inside and outside of the workplace causes in an adult's life. Extensive periodic retraining will require still more lifestyle adjustments and will strain families and communities to the breaking point. And current prescriptions for retraining ignore the reality that no one is able with certainty to point to which jobs will be available in the future.[9] Clearly, general liberal arts training supplemented by strong math and science instruction is one place to begin building contemporary literacy, but our technical schools, colleges, and universities are not structured around such goals, despite general education requirements. College majors lead individuals toward training in specific professions, often with little competence outside narrowly defined disciplinary limits. In such an environment, students often have little sense of the value of general knowledge and more often than not demand to be told how they will use what they are learning. Working- and middle-class Americans have consistently viewed education as preparation for jobs, i.e., as an economic ticket to a better material life, not as general intellectual training. Simultaneously, the elite class has valued general education, often equating it with a cultured lifestyle, a lifestyle it viewed as reinforcing an assumption of its intrinsic superiority. Ironically, it is the skills embedded in general liberal arts training, the ability to make inferences, think critically, call upon literature and historical reference, understand the basis of rational thought as defined by the Enlightenment, and so on, combined with economic placement, that enable the elite class to maintain its power. This circle is one variation of the reiterative logic surrounding literacy discourses.

Traditionally, the most economically lucrative and politically powerful professions begin their training with a good liberal arts foundation. The typical training that lawyers and physicians received a generation ago was, and still is, considered an extravagance that only the privileged or the very intelligent can use to advantage, but it is the appropriate basis for continual intellectual growth. It produces a mind ready and able to retrain itself continually throughout life. This is precisely the sort of cultural literacy we need to foster if we are to have a workforce able to confront the radical transformations facing us in this millennium.

What happens when an electronics technician, from the average middle- or working-class family, who knows how to produce computer chips is thrown out of a job because American manufacturers no longer make computer chips or, worse, because computer chips have been replaced by another technological innovation invented and patented in a competing country? Often, his or her general education has not fostered flexibility of mind and spirit. Nowhere in our culture or educational establishments do we emphasize or value the kind of intellectual training that would have given this technician what s/he really needs to move through a series of professions.

It is no small irony that current government and business proposals regarding increased literacy call for teaching masses of individuals critical and creative thinking skills and giving workers increased power in the workforce. These are precisely the skills that the bureaucracies of education have denied to the masses. Certainly, if the majority of Americans possessed such skills, our entire culture and politics would be rewritten after a period of great social disorder. So we are caught between fostering a functional literacy that is inadequate and a deeper and broadened literacy that very few value and, worse, that would imbalance the power structure of our pseudodemocracy. Increased decision making at the level of the worker requires a freedom to think creatively and to problem-solve. Our schools, tests, and training are not designed to foster such skills. The authors of proposals to revamp our corporate bureaucracies seemed convinced that our future work environments will require redesign, but they do not clearly describe these environments. One wonders if we are wise enough to transform ourselves, no matter what the risks of stagnation.

Even a cursory review of literacy proposals suggests that what is needed is a completely new understanding of literacy as a complex and constantly evolving skill, embedded in interwoven sets of knowledges, deployed in innumerable settings, and using existing and yet-to-be-invented technologies. But literacy discourses very rarely move in this direction; rather, their discourse is confused and confusing.

The discursive space around literacy is rigorously ideological and nationalistic, and it is virtually always extraordinarily narrow in scope. Further, it is impossible to point to a stable, authoritative definition of either "basic" literacy or more "advanced" forms of literacy. And because there exists no canonical definition of literacy, alternate definitions rarely feel obliged to make gestures of recognition toward one another. Each definition fails to recognize the existence of alternatives, not to mention their validity. That is to say, the debate regarding literacy and literacy standards is covert even as it progresses. The problematic sentence "Literacy is . . ." appears everywhere in the literature concerning this subject. Even the most insightful studies fall into this trap. Such reductive discourse is dangerous and narrows our thinking, pedagogy, research, and vision. As Elspeth Stuckey has reminded us, the discourse itself constitutes the crisis because it constructs the literacy discussion in disenabling language (21).

Stuckey is correct. The change in work *is* a change in literacy. The state alliance with corporate power and the elite class is imbalanced by this change. The scramble both to increase standards for literacy and simultaneously to expand economic opportunity comes to a head in regressive proposals for a national testing system. Goals 2000, the reform program supported by the Clinton administration, had the stated purpose of improving education by stimulating pedagogical change via test scores. The distinction between teaching and testing is never mentioned in any of these proposals. In fact, teaching is rarely mentioned at all. Neither is the fact that such a testing system would eat up billions of dollars over the coming decades. The profits from such tests would accrue to the very groups proposing the development of them. And the classic pedagogical problem of teaching to the test raises serious questions about the totally unsubstantiated assertion that such tests will drive pedagogical changes, thereby raising literacy standards. The dismal results of current standardized testing and the existing infrastructure of remedial college classes in California is a case in point. Burgeoning enrollment in remedial classes driven by eligibility requirements tied to standardized testing has created a backlash against the concept of open enrollment in California's community colleges and admissions practices in its state universities. In 1995 the regents of the California State University system moved to abolish remedial classes and deny admission to students who could not pass standardized tests. Their stated intention was to force K–12 education to improve student preparation. Despite increased efforts focused on improving elementary school preparation, standardized test scores continued to drop across the state.

The trajectory of "The Keeper of the Books," from imagination to possession, is the trajectory of this study. It accepts that the discourse around literacy is unstable, recursive, maddening in that it seems all-inclusive while it produces numerous covert debates. Literacy presents a moving target. Literacy is consequential. Lives depend on it. Civilizations rise or fall with it and with them their semiotic systems. In the modern world, national policy, personal and collective investment, business prospects are tied to it. Indeed, the sentence beginning "Literacy is . . . " will be among the most problematic sentences written in this study. Likewise the question "What is literacy for?" elicits a series of cascading disputable assertions.

Like the keeper of the books, we frame our discussions of literacy within the context of imagining, desiring, dreaming, possessing, and remembering. "What's imaginary and what's past are the same" at the end of a life. But on the way to the end of a life, imagining literacy enables us to dream that we might letter "characters with a perfect hand" and open our past to our future. Imagining and literacy are inextricable because it is only through the imagination that we can create other possible selves, as Hsiang does. The founding trope of this thesis owes much to Elaine Scarry's *The Body in Pain: The Making and Unmaking of the World*. A reading of chapter 3, "Pain and Imagining," stimulated for me a cascade of associations regarding the imagination and literacy. Not the least of these can be summarized by examining Scarry's final statement about the imagination: "The imagination is self-effacing, and often completes its work by disguising its own activity" (325). It is clear that the imagination shapes literacy by disguising its own activity. "Pulling the covers off" literacy requires sleight of hand and clarity of purpose.

Imagining literate selves allows us, whoever we may be, to envision community, nation, and ultimately world. Indeed, *imagining literacy is central to the many necessary acts of making ourselves and the world*. Imagining literacy allows us to define what literacy is and what it is for, what it offers and what it enables. Sometimes imagining literacy allows us to see what literacy causes us to lose, but that anxious thought is usually quickly repressed. Imagining literacy allows us to project a future self with yet-to-be-acquired skills and a yet-to-be-defined professional life.

Through these projections we can come to understand what and how to be. We can acquire the motivation to become literate to a lesser or greater degree. What Henry Louis Gates Jr. has named "the trope of the talking book" describes a collection of these imaginative leaps recorded in the autobiographies of early African Americans. My construct, mixed cultural literacy, names another imaginative leap that allows individuals to aspire to layered literacies. Imagining literacy allows us to use it to continue to make and remake self, work, community, and nation, enables the creation of our future selves and our future lives in the form of work in a postindustrial economy and in the context of our communal selves.

Even though there are aspects of postmodern society that provide spaces for the making of self outside of literacy, print literacy remains key to our self-agency. It is possible to remain outside print literacy in the postmodern moment, but usually at a tremendous economic and social cost. Examining the ways in which this is possible and the differences between postmodern orality and traditional orality can provide fascinating and important illumination on this subject.

In the not-so-distant past, literacy may have fostered the power of the Christian church and the power of the state. It may have been the technology that structured the ancient Chinese bureaucracy. But in democratic states with democratic notions of literacy, literacy should enable the construction of new selves based on a profound impulse toward social equality. The evidence of this sort of transformation abounds in the literature of literacy, but we need to place a literacy of social equality at the center of our discussions, not at the fringe. The celebrity status of a few individuals whose literacy skills are either minimal or made to seem minimal obscures the dire situations of many confused Hsiangs who idolize them.

Illiteracy threatens late-twentieth-century North America in the form not of Mongol hordes but of undereducated people of color and working-class European Americans, ignorant barbarians within our midst. The "nation is at risk" because of these hordes.

But in Borges's poem, those who destroy literacy are outsiders who are cruel and "innocent as animals of prey." By cathexis, we can equate the Mongols with Borges's paternal cultural ancestors, the Spanish conquistadors. The Mongols threatened Hsiang's library; the conquistadors destroyed the libraries of Central American civilization. Borges's New World grandmother and grandfather did not rescue those great libraries, which are estimated to have been the most extensive on the planet at the time of their destruction. They are forever beyond our reach. Perhaps they are imaginary, but Borges tells us that "what's imaginary and what's past are the same." The imperfect destruction of other knowledges and the inevitable multicultural exchange resulting from that imperfect destruction are repressed in the Western history of knowledge. But rememory is at work recovering and reinventing these knowledges.

Native Americans, other peoples of color, and women have begun documenting their influence on our collective histories. For example, Paula Gunn Allen and other Native American scholars have noted that Benjamin Franklin's visit to the Iroquois Nation probably influenced our Constitution, and through it, constitutions around the world. Even a cursory review of the Iroquois Confederacy confirms the obvious similarities. And in "Who Is Your Mother? Red Roots of White Feminism," Allen describes how Native American women taught European women many Native American practices. Innumerable "American" cultural practices can be traced to Native American culture: frequent bathing (hardly a European practice), social informality, relaxed attitudes toward children, the value of leisure, and feminist attitudes all have their roots in Native American culture (Allen 1988:11–27). Because we refuse to recognize this history of cultural mixing, our cultural literacy is damaged and damaging.

We believe that literacy or the lack thereof leads to profound consequences. Intense debate swirls around this moving target, much as intense debate swirls around an entire series of signifiers: race, crime, gender, feminism, sexuality, government. All are contentious. Add literacy to this list, and it becomes easier to see how it replicates confusions and debates along a chain of signifiers. The features and structures of the debates surrounding these signifiers are often dramatically similar. It is not just that all these debates are dualistically constructed, as in *race* equaling *white/black* or *gender* equaling *male/female*. But rather those who are termed illiterate in the *literate/illiterate* construction are also often black, female, and/or criminal. That is, those who have been marked by illiteracy have been marked negatively again and again within a series of dualistic pairs. It is as if the crises of the postmodern world are all of one fabric at the discursive level; each debate echoes another. Each of these terms seems central to a reorganization of the contemporary world.

The statistical correlation between literacy and socioeconomic class is constant across cultures and time. This relationship is so obvious that it hardly seems worth repeating; nevertheless, it is consistently repressed in discourses of power concerning literacy—and all discourses regarding literacy are discourses of relative power. For example, the annual reporting of the nation's SAT scores consistently laments their decline over the past three decades in an echo of the accusations regarding literacy that have been discussed above. The initial norming sample, collected in the 1950's, was white, male, and middle to upper class. Those scores reflected the economic and cultural privileges of that group, including their access to superior elementary and secondary schools. Since then, the SAT scores have declined as those who took the test increasingly diversified. When the Educational Testing Service (ETS) recalibrated the scores to reflect a demographically changed norming group, many protested that they were cooking the results. But those same critics did not protest changes in the test that were the result of women sometimes outscoring men. For example, when Navajo women outscored Navajo men on the mathematical aptitude section of the test, the ETS questioned the test and the Navajo community. Then the ETS responded by modifying the test in order to erase the statistical difference. This kind of manipulation of tests in order to stabilize a set of norms that uses the white male as a standard is universally glossed over.

The discourse and debates around literacy run the gamut of a continuum of control versus liberation. In order to counter political and economic oppression, individuals like Paulo Freire imagine literacy as a resistance tactic. Discussions, like Freire's, of the need to introduce students to critical thinking stand in direct ideological opposition to other concepts of literacy like "workplace" literacy[10]—usually without recognition of that disparity. Rarely does a literacy theorist counter earlier theories, even if those theories are dominant and explicitly oppositional. This curious silence preserves the covert nature of the disagreements and reinforces the logjam in our thinking about literacy.

It is no accident that "The Keeper of the Books" represents literacy as painful, illusory, and elusive, though a prize worth a lifetime's obsession. Hsiang's pain is our pain. Hsiang's voice is Borges's voice because there is no safety or mastery in literacy. Our literacy constantly threatens to fall away into illiteracy, as Borges's sight fell away into blindness. The sense that whatever one knows is not sufficient shames many of us into relative silence and humility. Our literacy disintegrates under our fingers, like Hsiang's books, as what is known quantitatively and qualitatively on this planet explodes. No amount of education seems to be enough at the outset of the twenty-first century.

An individual can never be adequately or safely literate, since standards for what is acceptable change. And worse, our notions of literacy imply a transcendence to a perfectible state that we are forbidden to attain. Borges's work echoes this notion. A transcendent, omniscient, total literacy has always been not only impossible but also blasphemous. In Borges, the mystical attempt to push literacy toward totality results in the undoing of the universe.[11] This ultimate literacy equates to the Word, God, as represented in the Old Testament. The desire to be literate parallels the desire to be godly, but aspiring to acquire a transcendent literacy is blasphemy.[12] In this equation, *contemplating* literacy lands humans in a state of imperfection, a state of sin, as it were (Freire 1985). Indeed, the exhortation to know is balanced by the equally insistent exhortation not to know too much, lest one blaspheme.

Caught on the twin horns of this paradox, an individual's literacy constantly threatens to fall away into illiteracy. The virtuous are exhorted to continue to increase their knowledge. The expectation that we will know enough but not too much is complicated by the pressure to know more, to be constantly "retrained," or lose our livelihood. Under this rubric, it is inevitable that literacy becomes a site for anxiety and obsession on a personal and group level. Hence, the current governmental, business, and personal obsession with the subject.

In this context, desiring literacy depends upon a complex series of projections in which the individual first imagines what literacy might be and then what it might offer. The consequences of literacy must be imagined before literacy has been acquired, and the effort required to attain more than minimal literacy skills is substantial, relative to other skills.

The first projection of what literacy is and what it offers is often the result of exposure to literate persons as they live their lives engaging with the written word. If those literate persons are central to the preliterate's life—that is, if they are parents, siblings, teachers, employers, or whoever—or even if they are not, the way the preliterate views literacy will depend largely on his/her emotional ties to the individuals who are modeling literacy. If these models are viewed with respect, affection, admiration, even love, imitating them is an act of emulation tied to our desire for them, a desire to be more fully what they are, to exist more completely in their space. *If those who possess literacy are cruel or exploitative, then literacy becomes associated with those qualities.* Desire for literacy, if it can be awakened at all in those who have almost consciously rejected it, will have to be rooted in the desire for freedom from exploitation. More often, desire for another literate self is never awakened or is deadened in many whose negative associations with the literate come to dominate their experience. Hence the many interesting educational programs that seek to pair students with mentors outside of schools who can serve as admirable role models for literacy and work.[13]

This can help explain why it is necessary that teachers be admirable role models who do not alienate their students. Alienation from learning is often alienation from learned individuals and their personal behaviors. And if the literate's socioeconomic position seems unattainable, then literacy seems analogously so. In the case of African Americans under slavery, this was a legally enforced injunction not to read so as not to threaten the stability of the economic institution. Under such conditions, literacy becomes revolution. Literacy as revolution echoes through the work of theorists like Freire and Stuckey alongside discourses that seek to control and limit. Literacy as rebellion and revolution seeps through the discourse of many theorists and is explicit in many testimonials of writers who describe their acquisition of literacy.[14]

All of these projections surrounding literacy in even its most basic forms are dependent upon the ability of an individual to imagine a different self without knowing precisely what that difference might be. This vision is tied to projections that humans make about other humans and the conscious and material lives they lead. A vision of a possible self enables the preliterate child to say, "Daddy reads the newspaper. I want to read the newspaper." Such an imaginative projection implies love and the desire to possess qualities that Daddy embodies, absent explicit knowledge of those qualities. The possible scenarios for such a projection are as numerous as there are possible models. Imagining other literate persons as models for self can be tied to those close to us, or to those we never meet, or even to those who are no longer alive.

For Hsiang, such projections are tied to some knowledge he has of the historical place of the literate in his culture. His dreams of "lettering with a perfect hand" imply that his imaginative projection is tied to a model from his culture that honors the literate as wise, artistic, accomplished in the social graces, and connected to power, both earthly and heavenly. At the beginning of the twenty-first century such models are almost nonexistent. Rarely does literacy earn honor in the mass imagination.

The potential self we can imagine through literacy is a potent driver. Childhood games that mimic various writing and reading activities are imaginative projections during which the child imagines what literacy might confer.[15] For the very young, the connection between literacy and work is tenuous, but as we mature, literacy becomes the icon by which we can imagine work in a postindustrial society.

Students are aware that they must read and write well in order to succeed in the professional world. This does not mean, however, that they value reading and writing. The connection between imagining self, imagining literacy, and imagining work is broken in many children long before they are old enough to prepare seriously for a profession. If, because of social injustice, literacy's potential rewards cannot even be realistically imagined, then acquiring literacy seems not worth the effort.

Ironically, "stealing" literacy certification is worth the gamble for some students, and some educators are complicit in this. Any English teacher can describe for you how this manifests itself in the classroom; students will declare in all sincerity that they want to improve their "English," but often what they really desire is to be inoculated with "English" certification, erroneously believing that certification alone leads to degrees and degrees lead to work and the "right" work leads to the American dream. The notion that they themselves might change as a result of what happens to them in the classroom never occurs to many students. When it does happen, they are often overwhelmed by the unexpected challenge this change represents and the extraordinary bonuses it affords.

If we pass this first barrier to acquiring literacy, the one that allows us to imagine another self, a literate self, and that self in the world, we are poised to acquire ever more sophisticated forms of literacy and with them their imagined rewards. Literacy, then, becomes intrinsic to self-definition, self-construction, and the reception of that self by the world. Literacy allows the making of self and work and the continual development of that self, the work produced, and the world created by that work.[16] Through this we can continue to build the world around us; we can imagine and construct community, nation, and finally intercommunal, intercultural, international selves.

ETHNOGRAPHY AND LITERACY

The skills that literate persons possess give them personal, economic, and social power. Though these skills are describable, they cannot be reduced to a fixed collection because they vary from person to person, circumstance to circumstance, era to era. What is clear from the historical record is that such skills change and change again under the pressure of cultural, social, technological, and political change. Basic reading and computational skills were sufficient for a number of blue-collar jobs in the first half of the twentieth century. Those same jobs, if they have not been made obsolete by new technologies, now require much more sophisticated skills, including the ability to interact with computers, to make decisions formerly made by managers, to problem-solve, and to work closely in a team. And all of these require more-advanced reading skills.

Discussing literacy then becomes a matter of ethnography, a matter of describing what is needed in a particular time and place by a particular person who is part of a particular community. In fact, much research into the writing process that has then been applied to new writing pedagogies involves research into and description of the processes of competent writers. In other words, this contemporary research around the teaching of writing has become ethnographic description of writers writing. A great deal has been revealed to educators about the nonproductive nature of their traditional pedagogies, which have often inculcated destructive habits in students.

Ethnographic studies of competent writers revealed that they commonly use different techniques than supposed by both teachers and students. For example, professional writers routinely edit far more than has been allowed for within traditional classroom practice. It is not surprising that students edit hardly at all when pedagogies require them to produce texts under conditions that virtually preclude editing.

What skills have individuals used to good effect? What skills can be identified as evolving as a response to current conditions? At what level must we read, write, and compute? What scientific notions are necessary to understanding everything from the medicine that applies to our bodies, to the computers that many of us use every day, to the ecological crisis? Describing those skills is one way of imagining literacy. Describing those skills is one way of imagining ourselves and the world as we transform ourselves and it. We can never define an evolution as it happens, but we can describe it as it proceeds. We can describe what it is that we do, how we came to know something, what skills we have. Even though we can do this, we rarely do. This tendency not to describe our own processes contributes to the covert nature of literacy. In this sense, literacy definitions serve to deflect our attention from literacy narratives. Those who know, know what it is they should know. The rest are unsure. Silence in these arenas keeps us from recognizing that alternate literacies exist alongside dominant literacies, that alternate literacies are re-creating our culture. Describing what we do as culturally literate individuals contextualized within communities is crucial to demystifying our literacy definitions.

EMERGING LITERACIES

Our notions about literacy must change so as to enable the global transformations under way today in nearly every field of knowledge and experience. Only then can we imagine a literacy that enables us to make ourselves and the world. The literacies we need are being created right now. They are being lived in the bodies of individuals who use their literacy to consequential effect. We cannot prescribe a fixed canon of knowledge or even a canon of skills, because we are in a time of radical transformation and while the culture around us is in metamorphosis, *we cannot know what we need to know.* Our best chance of meaningful discussions about and policies concerning literacy needs to examine what successfully literate individuals actually do as they live their lives. Hence the portion of this study that concentrates on the literacies of specific individuals or groups. We can uncover a series of literacies, each valid and useful within its appropriate context. In this way, we can better understand the possibilities of and for literacy. What this study will later call trickster literacy is only one model for imagining literacy.

When literacy is conceived as a collection of ever-expanding skills, it creates choice and flexibility. It enables invention. Imagining literacy points toward the acquisition of many existing but not described skills and also to skills that are not yet required but soon will be—sending a computerized fax, surfing the Internet, deciphering a menu composed of California's multicultural cuisine. Literacy, when understood this way, comprises any number of skills in a grab bag collection. This collection is added to and subtracted from as needed. We are all *bricoleurs*[17] of literacy.

Our imaginings regarding literacy should be liberated to include a whole range of repressed and rejected elements, including the visual literacies required to "read" video and film, the literacies required to negotiate the postmodern architecture of our cities and suburbs, the literacies required to interact with multiple cultures around the globe either directly or indirectly. If we think of the term *literacy* as a semantic field of contradictory and repressed notions, opening that semantic field and revealing its structure, revealing what has been devalued and repressed, will help us to understand how the ideologies of literacy have limited us and how breaking open the discourse around literacy offers constructive promise. Like all dualisms, literacy/illiteracy traps us in self-defeating loops of meaning that reinscribe us more tightly within the dualism even as we seek to interrogate it.

Multiculturalism (or what I prefer to call mixed cultures) is one place to begin opening up the dualistic thinking about literacy. Issues concerning the repression of the knowledges of women is another. Including not just reading and writing but looking, speaking, viewing, traveling while viewing, manipulating artifacts (photographs and other sign/symbol systems not limited to written texts), video, film (perhaps even singing and dancing) is inevitable if the ideologies of literacy are seriously questioned. But if the notion of literacy is extended to all these fields, what do we have except an expression of what it means to live as a human in culture? Like Borges, we have made literacy and the world equivalent to the universe of experience. Elspeth Stuckey reminds us that it is widely accepted that "literacy confers special power, the power to be human. To be wanting in literacy is to be wanting in human fulfillment" (67). This is exactly what Borges's poem seems to suggest. Is it true?

This study postulates that literacy will remain what it has always been but has not been recognized to be: a trope for vastly differentiated and differently valued collections of skills deployed by individuals who have invented technologies that suit their needs and desires. It will insist that oppositional literacies have always existed in tension with the literacies defined by those who possessed hegemonic power within education, government, and business. These oppositional literacies express the desire of those who have been denied access to standardized, valorized literacy. Capturing the imagined literacy of the dominant group both for economic purposes and for the status that attaches to the position of literate, and translating that back into economic enfranchisement is a dream that is at once embraced and rejected by those like Hsiang who imagine that they can "letter with a perfect hand." Chapter 3, "Reading Trickster Writing," attempts to describe this process relative to Zora Neale Hurston, Maxine Hong Kingston, Gloria Anzaldúa, and Leslie Marmon Silko.

How can our concept of literacy be reconceived so as to enable rather than disenable? *The ideologies of literacy are cruel; their social results are deadly.* All the more reason to enter this dangerous terrain.

One

THE SEMIOSIS OF LITERACY

The terms of the literacy debate in Western culture have been set by a range of theoretical discourses produced by academics, governmental agencies, and business interests. Each theorist—and there are hundreds—proposes a notion of literacy from a specific location in time and space, imagining it differently, according to his or her origins, interests, goals, and expectations. In the process, a narrative is constructed within the closure of a complex ideology, within a semantic field. Examining three discourses produced by Walter J. Ong, E. D. Hirsch Jr., and J. Elspeth Stuckey can help illustrate the nature of our collective imaginings about literacy. Ong imagines that literacy will bring him and others to a state of grace, not a surprising conclusion for a Jesuit priest and, of course, not unlike Borges. Hirsch imagines that literacy will foster democratic equality within the Enlightenment tradition, a value held by the liberal academic community of which he is a part. And Stuckey imagines that escaping the violence of literacy will lead to liberation, a dream developed as a teacher on the front lines of literacy projects.

These three theorists construct their narratives out of a complex cloth of situated knowledge infused with high personal stakes. Nevertheless, this examination reveals these theories to be ideologically caught within a single circular discourse. Despite ostensible differences, Ong, Hirsch, and Stuckey construct narratives that consistently inscribe a familiar set of dualisms about literacy. In *Orality and Literacy: The Technologizing of the Word* (1982), Ong suggests this himself:

The elements out of which a term is originally built usually, and probably always, linger somehow in subsequent meanings, perhaps obscurely but often powerfully and even irreducibly. Writing, moreover, as will be seen later in detail, is a particularly preemptive and imperialist activity that tends to assimilate other things to itself even without the aid of etymologies. (12)

Let it be clear that much *is* valuable in these three works. However, these characterizations and the ones that follow are necessarily reductive because the purpose of this discussion is not to mine these three theories for their insights but rather to demonstrate that discourses of literacy circulate within a closed circle of assumptions and agendas, guaranteeing to lead us in a circle, despite their sophistication and no matter how well intended they may be. Each of these theories appears to occupy a different ideological space within the discourse(s) surrounding literacy; however, because the suspect binary *literacy/illiteracy* underpins all three, they fail to lead us out of the thicket of ideology. Successive examination of these theories illustrates how they echo one another down a long hallway of illusory difference.

Despite the fact that E. D. Hirsch's *Cultural Literacy: What Every American Needs to Know* was produced by an academic, it captured the popular imagination regarding the literacy crisis in America and remained on the *New York Times* best-seller list for twenty-three weeks in 1987. Walter Ong's 1982 *Orality and Literacy: The Technologizing of the Word* was produced as part of an academic series that seeks to provide a forum for current literacy theory. Its audience is necessarily narrow, but the book is in fairly wide circulation among academics interested in these issues. J. Elspeth Stuckey's 1991 *The Violence of Literacy* was published by a press specializing in practical pedagogy. It targets literacy educators, but it is not likely that it will be well received even within that narrow market since it asks a series of anxiety-producing questions.

Hirsch's notions of curriculum reform define nation and culture from within an educational system that represents and fosters cohesive control. His discourse seeks to imagine literacy as nation making, administered by authorities whose control is benignly directed toward humanizing citizens in the interests of the common good as defined by those same authorities. His position is clear. "I imagine literacy this way," he tells us. "If you agree, we can save ourselves. The problem is that we have imperfectly understood what it is we are doing. The problem is an error of pedagogy."

J. Elspeth Stuckey agrees that there has been an error of pedagogy, all pedagogy. Stuckey's position is that pedagogies of literacy are based on a violent notion of authority, a violent notion of who enjoys what within our nation's culture. Her radical discourse imagines that literacy should be fostered not to form a more perfect union, as Hirsch suggests, but to question the state of that union. It is no accident that these two theorists' discourses can be glossed in such a way as to situate them politically on the one hand to the right and on the other hand to the left. Taken together, Hirsch and Stuckey illustrate how literacy discourses inhabit positions that reflect more about larger political struggles than about skills and knowledge.

On the other hand, Walter Ong's discourse suggests that literacy inevitably leads to consciousness of self and world and, ultimately, to redemption. Hirsch's goal is a humanistic nation-state; Ong's is spiritual grace. Ong's musings place literacy and orality within a culturally comparative context, but his stakes in this discussion as a Catholic who is committed to the Word predetermine his ideological bias.

A. J. Greimas's semiotic square can help us see how discourses of literacy are trapped in this thicket. The semiotic square is a maddening and fascinating little engine for discourse analysis. Greimas is responsible for beginning its circulation in French structuralist circles, but Frederic Jameson introduced it to U.S. academia. It helps deconstruct the hidden ideology inherent in any discourse built around a founding dualism. That which is presented as a logical category is revealed to be a covert ideology without logic. In the process, the square makes us conscious of that which is excluded from the surface of a dualistic text. The semiotic square helps bring dualistic hierarchy to its knees by destabilizing one dualism at a time. Once the relationships between the positions on the square are denaturalized for a particular dualism, it becomes nearly impossible to think, speak, or write as if that dualism were anything but a fiction invented for the purpose of furthering oppression.

Frederic Jameson, in his foreword to Greimas's *On Meaning* (1987),[1] describes the square as a kind of "discovery principle" that can be called upon "to map thoughts and interpretations arrived at in other (seemingly less technical) fashions," claiming that it can be used "to articulate a set of relationships that is much more confusing, and much less economical, to convey in expository prose. The square is a "'black box' through which narrative is somehow 'converted' into cognition and vice versa" and takes the visual form shown in figure I (xiv–xv).

In the figure s_1 and s_2 are the founding dualism of a set such as *white/black* or *male/female*. These dualisms are binary oppositions expressed in the

$$S$$

$$S_1 \qquad\qquad S_2$$

$$\bar{S}_2 \qquad\qquad \bar{S}_1$$

$$\bar{S}$$

FIGURE I

language of philosophical logic as a "contrary." Inserting any founding dualism into the square immediately implies the existence of a series of slots already preexisting in a conceptual and logical process generating a semiosis, a cascade of meanings built up through unconscious logical opposition.[2] The square reveals the invisible semiotic engine of ideology.

As the negatives of s_2 and s_1, $\bar{s}_2$ and $\bar{s}_1$ include far more than either: thus "non-white" includes more than "black," "non-male" more than "female." Simultaneously, S and $\bar{S}$, two compound or "synthetic" positions implied "above" and "below" these founding four, offer the possibility of exit from the logic of the square. S is a "utopian" term, implying that the contradictions might be transcended, that there might exist a path out of this logic, and $\bar{S}$ is a neutral term somehow implying that this logic might be negated (xiv). Redrawing this schematic, we might understand the semiotic square as represented in figure 2. By extrapolation, a semiotic square for the field of gender might appear as shown in figure 3.

The contraries *man/woman,* occupying the first and second positions, are paired with the contraries *non-woman/non-man,* occupying the fourth and third positions. While the left side of the square, the side occupied by positions one and four, is generally valorized, the right, the side occupied by positions two and three, is generally the position to which the "other" is relegated. And while Frederic Jameson declares the fourth position to be the most difficult to identify, it is the position closest in hierarchy to the first, occupying, as it does, the valorized left side. Because of this, it is possible to recuperate position four; that is, movement from four to one is possible, e.g., a boy is not a woman but will grow to become a man. But movement

IMAGINING LITERACY

from the right to the left is impossible. In other words, if you are a woman, you cannot become a man without violating the semiotics of the square and the ideology of masculinity. Even more important, the third position is always the least visible, always part of the subtext, the place where the oppression gets covered over. Hence this is the most critical position to interrogate if we are to deconstruct oppressions. Awareness of the third position destabilizes the dualism because it demonstrates the illogic of the square. The third position is often referred to as "the third term." Repressing the third term is central to the stability of all static dualisms. Understanding this helps us explain the vigorous resistance to, for example, a gay/lesbian agenda. The validation of this "third term" radically destabilizes the static dualism male/female.

A compound utopian term

1. +	2. −
4. non- −	3. non- +

A compound neutral term

FIGURE 2

Gender

1. (+)	2. (−)
man	woman
4. non (−)	3. non (+)
non-woman	non-man

Genderlessness

FIGURE 3

THE SEMIOSIS OF LITERACY

Color

1. (+)   2. (−)

    white   black

4. [non- (−)]   3. [non- (+)]

    non-black   non-white

Colorless

FIGURE 4

Similarly, for the founding dualism white/black, the square generates figure 4.

Jameson inserts *mestizo* in place of *color* as the utopian term, but this example is meant to outline the abstraction white/black quite apart from racial definitions. Not that there is not an inherent relation; there is. Jameson's *mestizo* is itself a slippage between the semiotics of color and race. This is what the term *infinite semiosis* suggests, that each position on a square opens up to another square of refracting meanings. The following discussion attempts to chase racial categorization through the logic of the semiotic square. It is an aside, but since all squares implicitly suggest all other squares, it helps clarify why the debates surrounding literacy are structurally similar to the debates concerning other controversial signifiers like *race* and *crime.* Each of these debates echoes the semiotic logic of the other, thereby reinforcing the illusion that these logics are, without question, statements of Truth.

Remember: discourses that create a founding dualism do so not out of a transcendent logic but out of ideology. For example, in the discourse of race, *white* is opposed to *black,* but the logic in such a system is founded in racism. The contrary of *white* is not *black* when we are referring to humans unless we are within a racist discourse (figure 5).

Further, the founding dualism *white/black* "hides" the third and fourth positions, *non-white* and *non-black,* from conscious awareness. Semiotically, these positions reinforce the categories *white* or *black,* precisely because they are not overtly present in *white/black* discourses. In fact, obscuring the other two positions of the square helps reinforce the dualism by *not* complicating it with shades of "gray," signifying mixing that is a logical impossibility within the square. Suppressing awareness of the other positions on the square forces a choice between the two sides of the dualism. In racist discourse, this forces a *linguistic* choice: each individual must be categorized according to the rigors of this dualism, *white* or *black,* and by extension *good* or *bad, human* or *not human.* Even if common sense tells us that humans cannot be categorized according to this nonsensical rubric, it persists, partially because the alternatives, all shades of "color," are unspeakable within the discourse of race itself.

Choose *white* or *black.* There are no alternatives, declares the dualism. The structure of the square enforces a series of ideological choices and enforces a suppression of the alternatives even within that ideology. Consciously entertaining positions three and four makes the erroneous logic of the founding dualism more obvious and subject to question. *Non-black* and *non-white* are messy categories. These positions are semiotically occupied by "other" people of color, including African Americans of various shades, some of whom might "pass" for "white," and all people of mixed "race." The dualism *white/black* implicitly denies that any "mixing" is possible and *makes miscegenation an unspeakable crime even within the linguistic structure.* The dualism forces "nominals" such as "octoroon" and "mulatto," which describe precisely these unspeakable mixings, into the subconscious and into position three. It also forces into the subconscious all the other "races" and their "colors."

Under the logic of the square, those "races" that are non–white ultimately may be recuperated in the same way a boy becomes a man from the fourth position. For example, semiotically, Asians may occupy position four when they are constructed as *non-black.* Sometimes accorded the status of honorary whites in the popular media, Asians are often referred to as a model minority. The opposition *yellow/black* becomes possible once this discourse

mestizo

1. white	2. black
4. non-black	3. non-white

racelessness

FIGURE 5

is in circulation because some Asians have semiotically moved to the fourth position. In 1992, media depictions of Los Angeles following the initial Rodney King verdict relied on this covert dualism for the force of their representations and in doing so reinforced it.

Insofar as Latinos can be seen to be *non-black,* they too may be recuperated. When because of class, education, culture, religion, they can be sorted into categories approximating middle class, educated, culturally North American, secular, they attain this status. When they are sorted into the categories working class, uneducated, culturally Latino, Catholic, they remain more *non-white* than *non-black.* Similarly, Native Americans can be assimilated into the *non-black* category by leaving the reservation and acquiring modern civilization in the city, thereby giving up connection to community and native culture. If they remain on reservations and/or are openly Native American in practices and style, they are associated with the *non-white* position. Whether you are sorted to the left or the right makes all the difference.

This analysis helps make clear why the popular media in America construct their narratives of racial issues in black and white language. No matter how many times journalists are taken to task and corrected by members of the other "racial" groups, who point out that racism in this country cannot be understood, much less corrected, if an analysis does not address the other groups involved in the semiosis of racist language and acts, journalists continue to create narratives consistent with a dualistic logic. This in itself reinforces racism, but it also demonstrates how entrapment in dualisms enforces a damaging ideology and seriously cripples our understanding of the semiotic process that is our historical reality. What is not said in such discourses is at least as unsettling as what is. In this way, the semiotics of race echoes the semiotics of literacy. What is not said controls and damages our understanding of the nature of literacy. And race and literacy are inextricably tied to each other in our nation's imaginary; for peoples of color are, by definition, uneducable barbarians sweeping down on our libraries of culture, "slaughtering the wicked and the just."

Deploying this technology of analysis can help us to see how the dualism *literacy/illiteracy* is founded on a bedrock of similar Western ideological constructs. The relationship between *literacy/illiteracy* and all the other signifiers embedded in complex layers of meaning around it can help us understand how discourses of literacy do not enlighten but rather continually recirculate us through a closed ideological system, remystifying this subject.

What this method of analysis cannot do is provide a complete discussion of each theorist's argument. But through its reduction, it can provide one method for exploring how the language around literacy is layered, self-

literacy

1. reading   2. writing

4. not-writing   3. not-reading

illiteracy

FIGURE 6

referential, and self-defeating. By giving us perspective, if only for an elusive moment, outside the discourse itself, it allows us to imagine a point outside this ideological entrapment.

By examining the founding dualism, *literacy/illiteracy,* and the various alternate versions of this hierarchy, we can similarly begin to understand what the debates surrounding literacy raise to consciousness and what they suppress. One version of the square can yield the following opposition in relation to literacy within our system of schooling—*reading, writing, not-reading, not-writing* (figure 6).

The founding dualism of this version of the square, *reading/writing,* dominates the structure of curriculum design. Elementary school pedagogy commonly emphasizes reading over and against the teaching of writing. Reading is de facto primary, and reading is taught first because of this unconscious hierarchy. Because of this opposition, reading is constructed as passive absorption; writing is constructed as active production. To read is to consume; to write is to create. This follows a rigorous historical logic. Literacy instruction for the masses has its origins in religious training, and religious reading usually concentrates on the passive absorption of sacred text, not its active interpretation, certainly not its creation. Because of this hierarchy, literacy programs such as IBM's "Writing to Read," which teach writing first, seem counterintuitive and revolutionary.

Within the discourse of schooling, *not-writing,* occupying as it does position four, is relatively valued and encouraged. What could not-writing imply in this scheme? How would one read without reading text? Viewing might be one answer—as in "Watch the teacher," "Look at the map," "Examine the object." Viewing carefully is a sanctioned activity within school, and a student "looks" in order to "read" non–print.[3]

Not-reading is quite another matter. If a student is not viewing, looking, and observing in silence *and* is not reading, s/he is probably speaking. To speak in the classroom, when not sanctioned to do so, is to commit a criminal act. The result can be a form of incarceration: detention. This version of the square demonstrates the close alliance between the pedagogy of reading and writing and discipline and control, a correlation obvious to any student.

Semiotically, speaking out of turn is structural rebellion against literacy training. Ironically, the complicated primal struggle to attain an effective speaking and writing voice as a student and scholar is counterpointed against the exhortation to remain silent, to obey textual authority. This initial semiotic square in relation to literacy is illustrative of others.

VALID INTERPRETATION, OR "READ AS I DO"

For E. D. Hirsch, "To be culturally literate is to possess the basic information needed to thrive in the modern world" (Hirsch 1987: xiii). Competent readers possess a vast network of information, stored in their minds and accessed as they decode the written word. At first glance, Hirsch's founding dualism seems to be the most conventional of the three examined here. We might identify it as *cultural literacy/natural literacy*. According to Hirsch, cultural literacy is the literacy of shared civilization, one civilization, Western civilization. Natural literacy might be understood to be literacy stripped of a cultural context. This would have to be an impossibility in his system. But a more interesting semiotic square constructed out of Hirsch's discourse uses a different founding dualism—*(valid) interpretation/ (naive) decoding*, creating a very different square (figure 7).

For Hirsch, *valid interpretation*[4] is founded in the common cultural knowledge embedded in our literature. Encoded in standard written English, this knowledge is largely monocultural; it does not admit alternative knowledge except around its edges. *Naive decoding* is precisely what is often taught in schools—recognition of phonemes and morphemes without comprehension of complex meaning. Without that common knowledge, reading comprehension is not possible. Naive decoding might also be understood as reading and interpretation confined to the literal.

In 1978 Hirsch conducted experiments that compared the reading comprehension of university and community college students. The community college students demonstrated the necessary reading skills involving memory, eye movement, basic vocabulary, and reading strategies. That is, they could "naively decode." Nevertheless, they interpreted passages less well than the university students, who possessed broader background knowledge of a recognized mainstream American culture. An experiment involving a passage

1. (valid) interpretation   2. (naive) decoding

4. reading   3. misreading
   not-(naive) decoding   not-(valid) interpretation

FIGURE 7

about Ulysses S. Grant and Robert E. Lee and another about friendship revealed the nature of this problem. The Civil War passage was difficult for the community college students who did not recall enough about Grant and/or Lee to place them in context; they could not make inferences beyond the specifics supplied in the paragraph itself. However, the community college students decoded the friendship paragraph with fluency equal to that of the university students, despite its advanced vocabulary, because both groups possessed roughly the same background knowledge about friendship (Hirsch 1987:41–42). They could follow the semantic logic of the passage because their cultural knowledge of friendship was adequate. Hirsch concludes that possessing reading skills absent adequate associative knowledge results in unexpected reading problems. His cultural literacy prescription is simple and straightforward: instruction should supply the appropriate background knowledge in a revised curriculum. Hirsch's pedagogical claim is that those who possess basic reading skills can be taught cultural literacy through the medium of a curriculum that concentrates on cultural markers.

The paired contraries *(valid) interpretation/(naive) decoding* yield the secondary dualism: *not-(naive) decoding/not-(valid) interpretation,* which can be understood to signify *reading/misreading.* Those who can read literally without the ability to draw inferences are reading without interpreting; their decoding is not entirely without context, but they have not learned a key academic skill. Even though the educational establishment generally assumes that such students can be taught to read for inference, often they do not attain this level of comprehension. This inability to draw inference is dependent, in part, on background knowledge, and it is one reason why community college students can "read" the Civil War passage but cannot interpret it. Hirsch's theory claims that those who can read in this formalistic sense, those who can follow the syntax, can be recuperated into cultural literacy if the curriculum is reformed, and this claim is consistent with his square's logic because those who can read can be taught to interpret.

The ultimate result is that Hirsch's overt discussion focuses on the ideal of monocultural literacy, a literacy enabling valid interpretation, because it is only through deep and broad exposure to background knowledge that interpretation becomes possible. Hirsch assumes that knowledge of many cultures must necessarily be superficial and could not possibly supply a foundation for valid interpretation. Inference is impossible without deeply structured systems of vocabulary. The ability to decode or even to read absent the ability to infer does not result in valid interpretation.

Hirsch is concerned with the pedagogical and political problems of getting readers to increase their skills so that they can digest the texts in front of them. In his discourse, naive decoding is not worthy of mention, but understanding its place within the history of education can illuminate a great deal about our ongoing literacy crisis and what Hirsch misses about the implications of his theory. And examining his secondary dualism, *reading/ misreading*, can help us understand the criticism that he endured for the monocultural bias of his theory.

NAIVE DECODING, OR WHAT LITERACY WAS

Only recently has literacy come to be understood as more than simple decoding. The first complete system of writing in the West dates to Sumerian Mesopotamia around 3100 B.C.E., a system that was later to influence Egyptian writing. Prompted by the need for inventories, Sumerian writing was needed for the administration of an expanding economy producing agricultural surplus and increasing its store of manufactured products. Bureaucratic systematization required the recording of tribute, war booty, rations, and taxes (Goody 1977:82; Graff 1979:18; Hoskin 1981). Comprehension was based on a literal one-to-one correspondence between sign and concrete referent. These decoding skills did not require syntactic interpretation, never mind valid interpretation. Literal correspondence was the goal. Lexical lists, that is, lists that existed outside the immediate necessities of enterprise, were less common and represented "the first steps in the direction of an Encyclopedia" (Gardiner, quoted in Goody 1977:83).

Early lexicons may have led to the first catalogs, or "textbooks," lists of hundreds of trees, reeds, wooden objects, and birds. In fact, the necessity for this listing may have itself led to the development of the alphabet (Goody 1977:84). In any case, both sorts of lists, those that were necessary for record keeping and those that existed to make catalogs without explicit connection to inventory items, required reading skills that were clearly in the realm of minimum decoding. At this point, reading did not require a knowledge of syntax. Decoding lists required simple skills, skills far less complex than understanding a passage about friendship. Comprehension did not require the correlation of items or concepts.

For five thousand years, simple decoding skills defined acceptable literacy. Reading with comprehension did not become the minimal standard for literacy until the nineteenth century. In the twentieth century, simple recitation without comprehension remained the definition of minimal literacy in some parts of the world. Keith Hoskin relates the history of an eighteenth-century Scot who describes learning to read the Bible in English without comprehension (Hoskin 1984). Brian Street describes the literacy practices in northeast Iran in the 1970's similarly. Some Iranian students in the traditional religious schools or "maktab" learn to "read" Arabic letters or even simply recite passages as part of their religious training. This process is completely rote and involves little or no digestion of the material. The words might as well be nonsense syllables. Perhaps they seem so to these "readers." Nonsense full of spiritual sense. "As Muslims would themselves say, the Koran is the Word of God and so there is no need for interpretation. To many students in 'maktabs' over the ages, recitation by rote of the Holy Word was itself sufficient" (Street 1984: 134–135, 158 ff.).[5] Pronunciation is its own reward. Prayers or mantras do not require understanding. One should not presume to know too much.

Similar practices were common in England well into the twentieth century. Indeed, the alphabetic method of teaching reading was still in use in the 1950's in parts of England. This method requires memorization of the alphabet in sequence and its oral repetition. This exercise is followed by memorization of all possible two-letter combinations, then three-letter combinations, and so on. All of this drill proceeds without connecting phonemes to morphemes, without connecting meaningful sounds to meaning. This method drains all comprehension out of early reading lessons and concentrates on simple deciphering (Hoskin 1984). Knowing that these definitions of and assumptions about reading and pedagogy are still in circulation is critical to understanding the dimensions and politics of the literacy crisis. Because examples like this are rarely circulated in literacy discussions, our perspective regarding "a nation at risk" is distorted.

Obscuring the rapid change in standards for literacy over the past century in itself enables the construction of literacy as a problem needing aggressive intervention and allows the outrage of report writers, politicians, and the media to seem reasonable. Understanding that schools are not failing because they are accomplishing less than they historically have but because expectations regarding literacy standards are escalating is crucial to solving the real problems of undereducation and miseducation. This realization is complicated by the fact that elite populations have historically been educated to very high levels, while the schooling of the masses has never attempted to educate every student to the limit of his/her potential. Highly developed intellectual skills hardly foster contentment with twenty-first-century assembly-line production, bureaucratized lifestyles, and consumption of useless and tasteless products. To this point in history, there has been no economic advantage to educating large numbers of people to high levels.

Awareness of the escalation of literacy standards is exceptionally difficult because our consciousness of what we know is solipsistic. As individuals, we are unaware of what others around us know or do not know until a disjunction occurs in our exchanges. College professors can provide ample examples of this phenomenon. A colleague once described a student who had never heard of an ox and therefore was mystified by the plural, *oxen*. According to the Gallup polls, many United States citizens apparently believe Canada and Mexico to be states in the Union. But how would we ordinarily realize this? Often, discrete instances of miscommunication are our only cue that differences of this sort are common. Those who are well educated assume that others around them, while not necessarily trained to specific professional standards, share in the general knowledge of the culture. But well-educated individuals were supplied with background knowledge as a precursor to their professional training, usually in educational tracks and informal settings, which separated them from others at an early age. Researchers are just beginning to understand how this happens, and there is important evidence that much of this background knowledge comes as a result not of school instruction but as a result of social experiences within the family and community (Heath 1983). Those lucky enough to have had formative experiences that have positively contributed to their cultural knowledge are largely unaware that others have not. Most often from the middle or upper class, they do not realize how their class placement has formed a critical foundation for their general knowledge.

The importance of class placement to literacy skills is supplemented by what may be the cardinal American myth: hard work can overcome economic disadvantage. Class defines family, social, and community experience, and that experience enables wider cultural knowledge within a literate context. This knowledge is key to literacy skills. If this is true, the problem at the heart of pedagogy is class. Hirsch claims that the lack of a coherent national curriculum has locked the underclasses into a disadvantaged position because they have not been given a systematic introduction to key cultural markers, and his point is well taken. Schooling, as our culture has heretofore constructed it, may be irreducibly tied to class. Hirsch insists that this class gap may be overcome, but what if this is not possible? What if class equates to cultural difference no matter how brilliantly conceived new curricula may become? The academic success of disadvantaged Asian American students is cited as proof that class can be overcome through hard work, but this success is largely based on an academic superiority in math and the sciences, disciplines that rely very little on cultural knowledge. Even "model minority" Asian Americans often do not excel in those disciplines and professions that require sophisticated language skills.

Reading without cultural literacy is Hirsch's named evil. But by omitting naive decoding from his overt discussion, he obscures the astonishingly recent elevation of our literacy standards from naive decoding and reading for literal meaning to cultural literacy. His prescription is the absorption of general knowledge contained in a canon that he aggressively defines in a series of "dictionaries" of cultural literacy.[6] He sets this general knowledge (very largely contained in the great books of the Western tradition, beginning with the Bible, but not limited to them) against current textbooks that intend to inculcate skills (literal reading and naive decoding) rather than content (cultural literacy). In this formulation, reading instruction seeks to transmit basic skills; "real" literacy, cultural literacy, however, requires exposure to content. Without general knowledge of the Western tradition, (valid) interpretation is not possible; reading remains literal, tied to simple syntactic logic or even rote memory.

MISREADING MULTICULTURALISM

The third position implied by Hirsch's ideology, *misreading,* provided the political flash point for his most vociferous critics. For if (valid) interpretation can take place only as the result of cultural knowledge and cultural knowledge is contained largely within the great books of the Western tradition, semiotically, non-Western traditions implicitly occupy this third position. If valid interpretation is the result of knowledge of the Western cultural tradition, misreading must be the result of a misapplication of other cultural knowledge. (Clearly, all persons have cultural knowledge of some sort—or would Hirsch argue that some individuals have no culture at all? In fact, a case could be made for *class constructing itself as culture,* especially in multiple American subcultures that produce distinctive mixes of ethnic and regional influences in the context of economically isolated enclaves.)

In an early essay on cultural literacy, Hirsch uses another reading study as an example of the cultural basis of comprehension. In this study, an American and an Indian wedding were described in two separate letters. The letters were presented to an American audience and an Indian audience. Predictably, the American audience interpreted the letter about the American wedding accurately but misread the letter describing the Indian ceremony.

The Indian audience displayed similar difficulties with the letter describing the American wedding (Hirsch 1982 : 164). Each group somewhat misread the letter from the alien culture. Such findings reinforce common sense. What does not appear as common sense to Hirsch and many others is that America is and has always been multicultural. Our multicultural reality has created parallel misreadings within American culture and continues to do so. It is not just that diverse groups often do not understand each other's codes and values. Groups not steeped in a monocultural European American tradition are at a structural disadvantage in American schools if cultural literacy is defined as monocultural knowledge. If literacy skills rely on wide-ranging, real-world experience in a single culture, defining that culture narrowly guarantees disadvantage to those whose backgrounds and experience are culturally mixed. The literate population that controls our English language schooling has been able, until now, to maintain the illusion of a monocultural society because it dominates the political structure, the educational establishment, the publishing networks, and the popular media.

That the United States has always been multicultural has been carefully and systematically obscured by the omission of the histories of people of color, non–Northern European ethnics, and women from our scholarship and our curricula. When based on monocultural knowledge, the concept of cultural literacy is flawed; its illusion can no longer be maintained because political power is shifting as the United States becomes increasingly culturally mixed.

Advocates of multiculturalism immediately identified Hirsch's bias when they examined the lists he included in *Cultural Literacy,* his 1987 book. Its omissions of key cultural markers from the knowledge of people of color and women created a backlash against his program. His insistence that his theory did not necessarily exclude these knowledges was probably in vain. The semiotics of his argument proves that his theory valorizes the Western tradition over other traditions. While he makes a practical argument for European American culture as primary—insisting that because our written materials reflect that tradition, students should be trained primarily in that tradition—such logic will continue to inscribe a circular problem. For if students are not trained in many cultural literacies, how will written materials calling on other cultural literacies be produced? Those who insist that this is not a necessary project are justifying ignorance of other cultures under the guise of expediency.

In Hirsch's defense, he insists that his lists are partial and invites his critics to suggest inclusions, but not only do the semiotics of his theory preclude equality on this score, his self-construction as the authority in control of these lists reinforces the elitist and authoritarian nature of his prescriptions. In his scheme, Hirsch and his appointees are validated as the arbiters of knowledge. He invites his readers and critics to suggest inclusions to his lists, but he controls their publication. What qualifies Hirsch for this status? Only his position within the educational hierarchy and his access to publishers who did not hesitate to produces numerous versions of these lists. Literacy justifies itself, as Stuckey tells us. Hirsch's position as a professor at a major university and as a best-selling author reinforces his authority to determine the content of these dictionaries, which declare explicitly in their titles that they are what *we* need to know, i.e., *What Every American Needs to Know.*

Hirsch's monocultural emphasis led, on one side, to his appropriation by William Bennett, Lynne Cheney, Harold Bloom, and conservative commentators and, on the other, to his condemnation by multicultural advocates. Though he proclaims insistently that his notions do not lead to a rejection of the knowledge of the non-Western and non-masculine, and in fact can lead to a methodology for their inclusion, the structure of his discourse, when examined semiotically, can predict that multicultural knowledge will be excluded, except as footnotes to Western knowledge. Chapter 2, "Whose Encyclopedia?," will examine Hirsch's notions of encyclopedic-based curricula and their possible effect on individuals' "outsider knowledge."

GUILTY LITERACY

J. Elspeth Stuckey, a graduate of the University of Southern California's doctoral program in rhetoric, linguistics, and literature, currently runs the South Carolina Cross-Age Tutoring Project. She has written another infuriating book, *The Violence of Literacy* (1991). But while Hirsch's book alienated multiculturalists, Stuckey's book questions the literacy establishment itself. Since the overwhelming majority of literacy theorists are professors or professional writers who do not make their living from actual instruction at the basic literacy or even the advanced literacy level, Stuckey's book is a lonely voice from the ranks of the silent majority of front-line literacy professionals. Clearly, she intends the major portion of her audience to be English teachers at all levels. At the heart of her book is the question "What to do with a world whose literacy pampers us but targets those we teach?" (124). *The Violence of Literacy* is riddled with covert self-recrimination. Her audience is not likely to find it attractive. It should haunt all of us.

Stuckey's book implicitly promises to help us escape the recursive discourse of literacy but never quite succeeds. At those moments when the book almost breaks free, it descends into a kind of incoherence. It is attractive to those of us who are deeply troubled by the ironies of literacy instruction; repellent when she displays her anger openly. This book breaks the cardinal rule of civilized literate discourse: that it appear dispassionate and therefore logical. By displaying her confusion, her split alliances, her ambiguous emotions, Stuckey adds to our confusion and turmoil.

Her book is infuriating because she draws the equation *literacy training* = *violence*. Literacy education equals violence because the correlations between illiteracy and race, income, gender and language and cultural diversity are frighteningly consistent. Literacy instruction functions as a gatekeeper, closing down opportunities for success for marginalized groups (97). We have to see that "literacy is a weapon, the knife that severs the society and slices the opportunities and rights of its poorest people" (118), and that "our current approaches to literacy corroborate other social practices that prevent freedom and limit opportunity" (vii). Every day, literacy education at all levels severs our most vulnerable citizens from the protection of a middle-class standard of living. It is all too easy for educators to "overlook the incremental, daily violence against those not favored by the system" (127). This violence is not metaphor; vulnerable human bodies absorb it.

The violence inherent in education is obscured by the good intentions of educators like herself who began their careers with sincerely held beliefs about the democratic and humanizing nature of literacy education. (Are those who are not literate, not human?) Stuckey's anger at the system is probably rooted in her realization that, as a literacy educator, she has participated in the violence. Her belated realization is that mass education in the United States does not liberate or equalize. Rather, it reinstitutes a class system based on mythologies of opportunity. Class determines educational level. There is no substantial exit from this formulation. Literacy education enacts the violence of class warfare because it suggests that opportunity is provided for all while doing nothing to challenge a system that does not provide meaningful opportunities for those without economic power. The mechanisms by which this is accomplished are diffused throughout the curriculum and the political agenda. Those who control this agenda maintain their economic privilege by setting the standards for literacy—precisely what Hirsch has done. Stuckey writes:

> In the United States we live the mythology of a classless society. We believe our society provides equal opportunities for all and promises success to those who work hard to achieve it. We believe the key to achievement is education, and we believe the heart of education is literacy. In a society bound by such a mythology, our views about literacy are our views about political economy and social opportunity. (vii)
>
> The violence of literacy is the violence of the milieu it comes from, promises, recapitulates. It is attached inextricably to the world of food, shelter, and human equality. When literacy harbors violence, the society harbors violence. To elucidate the violence of literacy is to understand the distance it forces between people and the possibilities for their lives. (94)

Despite American mythology, it is impossible to point to consistent evidence that the acquisition of literacy improves class placement. Rather, there is a preexisting circle of literacy and class position. Those who are educated earn higher wages; those who earn higher wages pass on economic, social, and educational advantages to their children under such a system. Literacy recapitulates inherited wealth. The prevailing lie, of course, is that literacy indicates intelligence and worth and that compensation flows properly from this. The best guarantee that a person will acquire adequate literacy is socioeconomic class, and the best guarantee that a person will not do so is also socioeconomic class. Education does not necessarily improve class position, even for successful students.

In fact, there is ample evidence that those who are disadvantaged because of class, race, and/or gender will remain relatively disadvantaged even though they acquire education. They may do marginally better than those disadvantaged who remain uneducated, but the overall statistics are sobering. For example, college-educated women still earn less than men with a high school diploma, and college-educated African American men still have higher unemployment rates than college-educated Anglo American men.

Various studies of the relationship between literacy and social mobility have been largely ignored. In *The Literacy Myth* (1979), Harvey J. Graff fully explodes the notion that education confers social mobility. In nineteenth-century Canada, the concept of literacy was normative. Like Hsiang's Mongols and twentieth-century barbarians, illiterates were and are considered dangerous to the social order, alien. Graff contends, like many others, that the teaching of literacy had to be controlled so that the underclass knew enough to work productively but not enough to take control of economic and political processes. Certain ethnic groups remained disadvantaged, whatever their literacy rates, while other groups continued to hold "skilled" jobs, despite their relatively higher illiteracy rates (198). Even more surprisingly, "illiterates" filled certain higher commercial positions—e.g., as storekeepers and tavern keepers—*if* they came from an advantaged background (5). Because of their socioeconomic status and the social networks that were part of that status, individuals were able to gain employment and own businesses despite their illiteracy. Any secretary who corrects her executive's documents understands the principle in operation here. In nineteenth-century Canada, "the relationship of education to work and earnings was quite complex . . . complicated by other determinants, usually ascriptive social ones: ethnicity, social class, race, age and sex. . . . Education and literacy did not reduce the role of class or status" (198, 200).

The skills expected for some occupations were social skills learned in the home and through the network of associations that a middle- or upper-class family would naturally have. Shirley Brice Heath's analysis of contemporary American class and its relation to the acquisition of literacy reinforces this correlation.

In *Imagined Communities* (1991), Benedict Anderson points out that relationship between literacy, class, and political power worked similarly in medieval times. Anderson points out that for centuries communities of sacred readers were "tiny literate reefs on top of vast illiterate oceans" (1991 : 15) and the many lords and barons of medieval times were illiterate administrators. Similarly, Michael Clanchy, in *From Memory to Written Record: England 1066–1307* (1979), describes a medieval England in which the written word slowly supplanted a vibrant oral tradition. Literacy spread as a result of government records validating property ownership and tracking commerce. The Normans conquered the British Isles and became eager bureaucrats who used written records to deny Saxon claims to land and buildings formerly held on the efficacy of oral records and iconography such as seals, rings, and other physical objects. For the Normans, the literate "mentality" was a deliberate construction used for political and economic purposes by a conquering people over the conquered. Since seals and symbols were more difficult to forge than written documents (it was clearly more difficult to reproduce an artifact and pass it off as authentic than it was to produce a forged document), it was to the conqueror's advantage to validate written records over oral records and objects. The Normans called upon the Anglo-Saxons to produce written records in order to prove ownership of property. In the process, the clergy played a key role in this bureaucratic theft, since, as scribes, they forged many of the necessary documents so as to support Norman claims. It was only after this systematic transfer of ownership through false paper documentation that an ideology of the superiority of literacy gained force in Britain.

The result: literacy legitimated itself. *The Domesday Book*, listing the assets of landowners, including every ox, cow, and pig in the land, and requiring a history of the ownership of every piece of land, was compiled in 1086 as part of this process (Clanchy 1979:21–28, 231–251; Street 1984:111–121; Hoskin 1981; Anderson 1991). Like the ancient Middle East, inventories in England were a key technology in the transformation of an oral culture into a literate one. Property and literacy are inextricable, a realization that Stuckey places at the center of her discussion.

Once we understand that Stuckey's book is about class and literacy, it is easier to see that her founding semiotic dualism is an *x*, which remains unnamed, versus *violent literacy*. Let us call this unnamed *x* radical literacy or, alternatively, *conscientization,* after Paulo Freire's concept. Perhaps radical literacy remains unnamed in Stuckey's discourse because imagining literacy, when one is acutely aware of the discourse of ideology surrounding it, becomes highly problematic. At any rate, her discourse has the puzzling effect of valorizing an unnamed position over and against violent literacy. Indeed, all of Stuckey's semiotics is under the surface, except for violent literacy. This might be a good strategy for escaping the ideology of the semiotic square of literacy if it were conscious and carefully teased out. Refusal to name a valorized term problematizes its valorization. But Stuckey seems unaware of the implications of what she is doing, so her discourse remains murky, creating confusions for the reader. Assuming that *radical literacy,* occupying position one, does indeed lurk under the surface of Stuckey's logic, it yields the test square shown in figure 8.

In each chapter of her book, Stuckey insists that no form or ideology of literacy escapes reinforcing class warfare. But the subtext of her book suggests that there must be some other sort of literacy: "In schools and in other literacy programs, we can foster a literacy that fosters change" (95).

Implicit in this notion is the belief in a literacy that would raise our consciousness so that we might foster that change. This is Stuckey's *conscientization,* a consciousness-raising that actually changes the terms of literacy. Stuckey never explains what this literacy might be, although she does de-

1. radical literacy   2. violent literacy
   consciousness-raising
   conscientization

4. non-violent literacy   3. non-consciousness-raising literacy
                                non-radical literacy

FIGURE 8

clare that "literacy is an idea our society has not yet finished with." This idea
we are not yet finished with is the unnamed *x* of Stuckey's argument, what
this discussion calls radical literacy.

Current approaches to literacy are allied with other social practices that
prevent freedom and limit opportunity. The United States, anything but a
classless society, has an entrenched class system so tied to unconscious humiliation that the working class will not even identify itself (3). Postcapitalism's
economic restructuring has further obscured class placement. When middle-
class, blue-collar workers (really the working class who for a time earned
middle–class wages) lose their jobs and their status, they are labeled undereducated, noncompetitive. Indeed they are, when measured against many
standards of functional literacy, which presuppose a citizenry able to handle
complex information and radical transformation of knowledge systems. But
these same people, less than a generation ago, were led to believe that they
were responsible citizens, fulfilling civic and community expectations.

Stuckey describes key literacy researchers as ignorant of their ideological
frameworks. This discussion is meant to recapitulate that observation. She
believes that pedagogy based on their findings is doomed to replicate the
violence of the system. Stuckey points out that when major researchers like
Sylvia Scribner and Michael Cole "discover" that literacy cannot be found
to produce anything of value, they do not abandon their awe of literacy, they
simply retrench by declaring that the literacy they have been examining is the
wrong form of literacy. She insists that advocates of literacy, English teachers, the above researchers, even critics of the literacy "flurry," all ultimately
fail to question the violence of literacy in meaningful and useful ways. Relatively few within these professions foster radical literacy or manage to help
others toward critical consciousness. Many of the best literacy educators are
angry; many are isolated by their colleagues and their institutions. Even
when they rise to prominence, their views are squeezed out of the discourse.

Since Stuckey's founding dualism is *conscientization/violent literacy* or
radical/violent literacy, she predictably has no kind words for *non-consciousness-*

raising literacy, the third term on our square. Liberal literacy educators, she believes, promote the dangerous illusion that literacy will produce equality. But literacy that is non-consciousness-raising is mystifying; those who do not promote violent literacy directly continue to uphold it implicitly by not challenging it. They do this from within standardized curricula that explicitly state the beneficent goals of literacy education while refusing to acknowledge its dismal results. Many English teachers are philosophically and pedagogically and semantically stuck in this position. This is an embarrassment to a profession composed of many otherwise sincere individuals.

Stuckey takes every opportunity to point out that the persistent refusal to address the reality of continuing class stratification, despite generations of educational "reform" and "progress," leaves liberal literacy educators unconsciously allied with the violence of literacy. They believe that literacy will change work instead of the opposite.[7] Evidence to the contrary is never even examined. Indeed, evidence to the contrary is not even considered to be the business of literacy educators. Their business is to inculcate literacy. If the end result is not a better life, that is none of their business. Their delusion that literacy is a necessary first step perpetuates continued violence under the rubric of liberal policies.

Stuckey's implied fourth term, *non-violent literacy,* is the literacy promoted by such theorists and practitioners as Paulo Freire. Stuckey's critique of Freire offers some insight concerning the participation of literacy theorists and workers in this violent system. Stuckey considers Freire a revolutionary, but because he embraces an idealism that fails to acknowledge fully the materiality of literacy, his radicalism ultimately fails to become her unnamed, valorized *x*. The point of literacy, for Freire, is to give individuals power to grasp the truth of their reality with their minds. The mythologies of literacy keep both literacy and reality "opaque." Piercing this mythology results in what Freire calls *conscientization.* Conscientization happens when individuals become literate; paradoxically, they explode the myth of literacy by becoming literate. Within Freire's formulations, all of this happens in the minds of the newly literate. Stuckey considers this an unfulfilled promise, Freire's dodge, because for Stuckey, literacy is enacted in the material world, in social and economic systems. Consciousness does not undo materiality by itself. Freire's *conscientization* is a dream unrealized in his system.

For Freire, literacy is a precondition of and a catalyst for revolutionary action. Stuckey insists that improvements in material conditions are inextricably linked to increased literacy. For Freire, the literacy comes first. It will lead to social justice. For Stuckey, the literacy without the material change is a dubious reality with even more dubious advantages; it leads to continued social injustice. Decades of social and educational reform in institutions such as the University of California provide ample evidence for Stuckey's conclusions. The best that affirmative action is able to deliver at UC-Berkeley is a body of African American and Latino students, who, while qualified for the UC system, are economically more advantaged than many of the white students denied admission.

Non-violent literacy theorists like Freire recognize the viciousness at the heart of literacy and seek to coerce the preliterate to reject violent literacy. But Freire's pedagogy represents a coercive liberation; this is why the heart of his theory falls short of radical literacy. The preliterate cannot choose to adopt Freire's pedagogy and his assumptions about the necessity for liberation, or those of any other literacy educator; they can inhale Freire's lessons and acquire literacy, or they can refuse and remain powerless. In any case, they must imagine it to be worth the effort. Once again, literacy justifies itself. In Freire, literacy becomes a method of fostering a philosophical revolution, a revolution at the level of the mind. This is not the worst alternative. At least it allows for the possibility of a material revolution.

Violent literacy is a self-justifying system in which literacy definitions are used as weapons against those who have the least defenses and resources. The violence of literacy is inherent in that it promotes one sort of person, just as Hirsch's cultural literacy promotes one culture. The violence of literacy is inherent in that it supports an entrenched class system, one in which those who have the economic advantage are precisely those who have the power to define literacy.

Our educational establishment has strongly suggested that students do not want to learn. Teachers are especially fond of this observation. It is impossible to teach for long without concluding that this is true for many students; the resistance that teachers encounter is often extraordinary. This observation defies logic. Since one must be literate to work in virtually any desirable profession, why would individuals choose to remain illiterate? As an educator, Stuckey has encountered both the resistance and the observations about it. She asks, "Why would so many people choose to disqualify themselves from the possibilities of labor?" (17). What teachers miss when they are embedded in liberal ideology is that many preliterate students, even with their limited experience, subconsciously realize the game is fixed. The classroom enacts the closed equation of class warfare. Liberal exhortations to sort humans into winners and losers in the education game can result in only so many winners. And our system does nothing if it does not sort winners and losers. Only those who can imagine themselves as winners are likely to participate with enthusiasm. Stuckey's observations echo what this study claims about the imaginative leap that literacy requires:

> *It is possible that a system of ownership built on the ownership of literacy is more violent than past systems. . . . Though it seems difficult to surpass the violence of systems of indenture, slavery, industrialism, and the exploitation of immigrant or migrant labor, literacy provides a unique bottleneck. Unlike a gun, whose least precedent is literacy, literacy legitimates itself. To be literate is to be legitimate; not to be literate is to beg the question. The question is whether or not literacy possesses powers unlike other technologies. The only way to address the question is to be literate. What more effective form of abuse than to offer clandestine services. (18)*

Stuckey is echoing the notion at the heart of what this text calls "imagining literacy." The only way to attain literacy is to imagine it and what it can do. The only way to be literate is to become literate, despite your inability to know the ultimate results of the project and despite any misgivings you might have before or after the process. Clandestine services, indeed. Once you attain even minimal literacy, there is no going back. You cannot unlearn your literacy. Looking backward to a time before literacy is explicitly what the next theorist we turn to attempts.

SILENCE, SPEECH, AND LITERACY

For Walter J. Ong, who is concerned with the shift from orality to literacy, writing is a technology that restructures consciousness. In this, he echoes Freire. "Writing is consciousness-raising" (1982a:179). In *Orality and Literacy: The Technologizing of the Word,* Ong claims that he wants to undo the literacy/orality dualism because it has caused us to misunderstand the nature of the connection between orality and literacy. Nevertheless, *literacy* is clearly this Jesuit priest's valorized term; literacy is a technology that brings us closer to grace. Literacy is Christian, clerical, civilized, and finally consciousness-raising. Orality is non-Christian, pre-Socratic. Without writing, human consciousness cannot achieve its "fuller potentials" (14).

Ong succeeds in undoing the literacy/orality dualism by subordinating orality to literacy instead of opposing the two. For Ong, historical orality is

1. literacy	2. silence
4. orality	3. non-literacy

FIGURE 9

not simply that barbaric time before writing and history. This is his central realization: orality is not literacy's opposite; rather, it is its precursor. Orality *becomes* literacy. But if orality *leads* to literacy, it clearly occupies the fourth position on our square (figure 9).

And if the fourth position is *orality,* the second must be its contradictory, *silence.* This makes Ong's founding dualism *literacy/silence,* an interesting duality for the meditative life. If his founding dualism contrasts *literacy and consciousness-raising* with *silence,* his secondary dualism necessarily contrasts *orality* with *non-literacy. Orality* leads inevitably to *literacy,* but the *non-literate* are those who make meaning outside of language. Theirs is the world of gesture, of sound without articulation of a singular meaning. A howl, after all, might signify any number of contradictory states: joy, agony, excitement, even boredom. Ong has semiotically created a discourse that circulates within the circle *literacy—silence—non-literacy—orality.*

> *Oral speech is fully natural to human beings in the sense that every human being in every culture who is not physiologically or psychologically impaired learns to talk. Talk implements conscious life but it wells up into consciousness out of unconscious depths. (82)*

Talk originates in the unconscious, in silence. This is an interesting notion. Ong is building a trajectory that moves us from silence to nonlinguistic communication to orality to literacy.[8] "Orality needs to produce and is destined to produce writing" (15). The movement from orality to literacy is inevitable. Orality is a mode of action. Socrates had to produce Plato. The boy is destined to become the man.

That Ong subordinates silence in this way, his silence about silence, is curious given its place within the religious life in general and Catholicism and Jesuit life in particular. Ong's attempt to undo the literacy/orality dualism, in the name of uncovering human destiny, ironically leads him to ignore the creative silence that has been noted with reverence in literate and religious traditions. Religious silence is a deliberate silence, but what of the many, many involuntary silences around us? Ong's only discussion of silence is in relation to Laurence Sterne's use of blank pages in his novel *Tristram Shandy*: "Space here is the equivalent of silence" (128). Whiteness on the page is an artifact of literacy and of print. Space becomes a method for inscribing meaning and allows for the greater legibility of texts, which "makes for rapid, silent reading" (122). From this silence can come understanding of a different sort. Interestingly, Ong even admits that some typographic manipulations can lead to different ways of constructing meaning. Citing e. e. cummings's untitled Poem No. 276 about a grasshopper, he notes how the words of the text are scattered across the page, suggesting "the [grasshopper's] erratic and optically dizzying flight" (129). The sounds cued by the letters are present in the auditory imagination, but something more happens. The space activates our visual and kinesthetic perceptions, making meaning out of absence and silence.[9] This analysis gives us clues we might use to construct a notion of the relation between written and spoken texts or other semiotic systems encoded in, for example, visual art, music, dance, body language in humans and nonhumans, and so on.[10] And it provides a bridge to Ong's third position.

This position, *non-literacy,* can be occupied only by a silence that is outside language. Gestures are semiotically meaningful but outside language. Body language is human, but it is also nonhuman, as in the intricate flight patterns of bees, which signal the location of pollen or the direction to migrate.[11] The gestural is meaningful, as any pet owner can attest, but it does not raise consciousness. It maintains interaction. Humans who cannot speak are locked into a level of communication that does not seem to lead past silence into interaction within culture.

EXITING THE LITERACY MAZE

Ong's discussion is perhaps the most thoughtful of the three examined here. And interestingly, his dualisms *literacy/silence, orality/ gesture* are the most evocative. They at least point to other ways of making meaning outside the written word. When approached this way, Ong's discussion opens up the possibility of debate about other ways of knowing, one of this study's major goals. If literacy legitimates itself, as Stuckey insists, clearly Ong's discourse accomplishes that handily, but it also gestures delicately to other worlds of experience outside print literacy. Those other worlds surround us at every moment. What if we opened our understanding of knowing to include these other worlds of experience as valued and valuable?

> *Literacy has never, in Western history, been concerned with providing a grounding in skills that were expected to be developed into higher, self-advancing critical tools. Serious questions should be addressed to the consequences that might follow from such abilities' becoming common. That would constitute a powerful "new" literacy. A literacy that sought to interrelate, integrate, and coordinate different communicative modes and abilities would be more powerful again. . . . Any approach to literacy must be flexible and dynamic, and alert to the powerful roles of continuities and contradictions. This flexibility is one of conceptualization as well as action; it may move us from the limits of literacy for the many to the potentials of a newer literacy for all. Recognizing that there are many kinds of tools, many competencies, and many varieties of achievement is a requisite first step. Speech, sound, and visual sights surround us; communication and media reinforce them. They are more pervasive than print. Recognizing that need not diminish the sometimes exaggerated powers and import of alphabetic literacy. . . . What is needed is a broader view of reading and writing that integrates and emphasizes the many human abilities in a context of a changing world that requires their development and use. . . . Questions of class, culture, opportunity, equality, and increasing demands for new skills must be considered. (Graff 1987a:397)*

Imagining literacy this way could lead to something powerful and self-empowering. But, as Graff has noted, this had never been a consideration in Western history. Wrenching literacy loose from its self-defeating dualisms seems nearly impossible when we examine literacy discourses closely. But conceiving of flexible and dynamic approaches to literacy might well lead us to political action that is at its root democratic and optimistic in that it recognizes no limit to what we may, as humans, bring to bear when attempting to make meaning and exchange that meaning with others.

Despite their superficial differences, what ties together the semiotics of the three theorists examined here? For each one of them literacy raises consciousness. This is an explicit declaration in Ong's work, an unnamed value in Stuckey's, and a strong implication in Hirsch's. Hirsch's consciousness-raising is tied to the awareness of culture. The higher one's awareness of "our" cultural tradition, the greater one's literacy. At the other extreme, they all would agree that if one cannot interpret well, one will misread, that mystification is the result of misreading, and that the further one lives outside of written language, the more susceptible one will be to misreading and mystification in all realms of communication. In this way, all three theorists validate print literacy over all other forms of communication. The semiotics of their superficially different discourses trap us within the same circular maze. Nothing better illustrates the confusion at the heart of literacy discourses. Nothing better illustrates how we have been limited by the terms of the debate. Speaking from radically different positions, all three of these theorists cannot escape dualisms that reiterate one another's positions in complex, sometimes inverse, equations.

It is to be hoped that this mapping helps us to understand discourses of literacy as layered and multireferential. That is, each theorist founds his or her argument regarding literacy on some version of the dualism *literacy/ illiteracy.* Sometimes the primary dualism is understated to the point of absence on the surface of the text; nevertheless, these terms exist within the unstated semantic field of the discussion. Debates surrounding literacy have multiple covert agendas because of the unstated relationships between overt and repressed terminology.

This complexity is enhanced by the intertextuality of the discourses surrounding literacy. That is, as one theorist founds a dualism, e.g., *literate* versus *illiterate,* the repressed elements of that dualism, *non-literate/non-illiterate,* take up positions on the square and reinforce meaning not only within the logic of that square *but within the logic of all the other similar squares in related discourses.* So it is that when Walter Ong, for example, begins a discussion of orality and literacy, all other similar discussions are in circulation both in the author's mind and in the readers' minds as they struggle with the immediate text. Literacy discourses, like all consequential discourses, are laminated over one another, each layer mirroring the others but making meaning within a plane of its own.

The semiotic square employed as a heuristic can provide a useful engine of analysis because "it maps the limits of a specific ideological consciousness and marks the conceptual points beyond which the consciousness cannot go, and between which it is condemned to oscillate" (Jameson 1987:47). Jameson urges us to bricolate [12] the Greimassian code, "to steal the pieces that interest and fascinate us, and to carry off our fragmentary booty to our intellectual caves," acknowledging that the square is both static and dynamic (1987:viii, xvii). The semiotic square reveals an enforced closure in the discourses just examined; this closure guarantees that notions of literacy will continue to disable rather than enable. The construct "imagining literacy" is a conscious attempt to escape this closure. From one perspective, deconstructing literacy from within is an impossibility. This problem is familiar. It is the paradox at the heart of structuralist theory: deconstructing language with language exceeds logic.

Reconstructing literacy from within the discourses of literacy leads logically into a maze without exit. The trope *imagining literacy* is a utopian term, suggesting a possible exit, opening a crack in this closed discourse. If, however, one assumes that the human imagination does not operate outside a language system and that meaning can be expressed only linguistically, such a leap is theoretically impossible. This author does not accept that equation. One old saw of writing pedagogy insists that an individual must write in order to know what s/he is thinking. Once again Stuckey's observation comes to mind: literacy legitimates itself. But examining Ong has already given us a hint that there are other possibilities. Whiteness on the page points toward meaningful silence. Gestures point toward meaning-making outside of language. If human destiny is tied to literacy and this is one and the same as consciousness-raising, and all three theorists examined here clearly are making that claim, then literacy has everything to do with the most ambitious human goals. It makes no sense to insist that the technology of the word is the beginning and end of the discussion. The five-thousand-year history of the written word does not warrant such a conclusion. We have barely begun to examine and consider other modes of communication as relevant to systems of knowledge. Extralinguistic modes of communication abound around us. Clearly, they encode systems of knowledge. Our inability to remember this is a reflection of an ideological trap. If dolphins could use human language, they probably would not choose to unless it was out of courtesy to us. If aliens visit, they are as likely to sing with the whales and dance with the bees as they are to write humans a missive.

Two

WHOSE ENCYCLOPEDIA?

Ideological partisanship on the subject of national literacy is both unfortunate and pointless, for the central issues of literacy are more empirical than ideological.
— E. D. HIRSCH JR., "A POSTSCRIPT"

Literacy always comes with a perspective that is ultimately political. . . . A text is a loaded weapon. The person, the educator, who hands over the gun, hands over the bullets (the perspective), and must own up to the consequences. There is no way out of having an opinion, an ideology, and a strong one. Literacy education is not for the timid.
— JAMES PAUL GEE, "THE LEGACIES OF LITERACY"

BACON'S TREE

Within Western culture, the universe of knowledge has traditionally been imagined and constructed by the creation of lists that became encyclopedic. Hsiang's imaginings of his library are dreams of access to an encyclopedia that mirrors the universe. The origin of the term *encyclopedia* reverberates down halls of learning and tells us something about imagining literacy. Its modern spelling is the result of a mistaken transcription of the Greek *enkuklios paideia*, meaning "general education," into *enkuklopaideia*. It is derived from *encyclical*, meaning "general or wide circulation," and *paideia*, meaning "education and training" and is related to the root for *child*. Hence it came to mean "the circle of learning; a general course of instruction" and was used in English as early as 1632 in reference to the *J. H. Alstedii Encyclopedia*. It came into general usage in the eighteenth century in reference to the French *Encyclopédie, ou dictionnaire raisonné des sciences, des arts et des métiers, par une société de gens de lettres*[1] created by a group of scholars and scientists under the editorship of Diderot and D'Alembert, respectively a philosopher and a mathematician. Successive volumes were completed between 1751 and 1772; when fully collected, it finally comprised seventeen volumes of text and eleven volumes of plates. The *Encyclopédie* provided a positivist program for human progress and was the central document of the era; Voltaire, Montesquieu, Rousseau, and Turgot all contributed essays.[2]

Planned to mimic Bacon's classification of knowledge, it provided access to information on every conceivable subject—religion, law, literature, mathematics, philosophy, chemistry, military science, and agriculture. Implicitly empirical in its conception and execution, it collected the trades and the sciences for the first time together with the humanities. "Its purpose was to show the interconnectedness of all knowledge." It was to be a foundation onto which succeeding generations would add and "whose very existence would be a guarantee against ignorance, bigotry, and superstition" (Hankins 1985:163–170). Like Hsiang's library, the *Encyclopédie* was a meditation against barbarism.

Taking Bacon's tree of knowledge as a starting point, D'Alembert was conscious of the implications and limitations of this project. He recognized that knowledge is more effectively represented and negotiated by a map, but his encyclopedia was necessarily limited by its structure. Umberto Eco, whose theories inform this analysis, notes this in his technical discussions of dictionaries and encyclopedias:

> *The eighteenth-century encyclopedia was not necessarily different from a tree. . . . It . . . presents itself as the most economical solution with which to confront and resolve a particular problem of the reunification of knowledge. . . . The encyclopedist knows that the tree organizes, yet impoverishes, its content, and he hopes to determine as precisely as he can the intermediary paths between the various nodes of the tree so that little by little it is transformed into a geographical chart or map. (Eco 1984b:82–83)*

D'Alembert states without equivocation that the general system of knowledge is a labyrinth, "a torturous road which the spirit faces without knowing too much about the path to be followed." He imagines the philosopher who mediates this system to be elevated above it, but presents no justification for this claim. The encyclopedia as an impoverished world map represents local knowledges as individual nodes on an enormous theoretical map. A global vision is not possible, only various cartographical projections from various imposed perspectives. D'Alembert continues: "[The] . . . form of the encyclopedic tree will depend on the perspective we impose on it to examine the cultural universe. One can therefore imagine as many different systems of human knowledge as there are cartographical projections" (Eco 1984b:83). It is this tension between the encyclopedia as tree and the encyclopedia as implied theoretical map that points to alternate imaginings of literacy, alternate cultural knowledges.

Imagining literacy often results in the manufacture of an encyclopedia of one sort or another, which becomes an outline of one possible circle of learning, one local or cultural knowledge. This outline, while clearly an empirical project, defines nation and national curricula. It enables shared literacy within a defined context, simultaneously fostering dissemination of knowledge and enforcing limits on the outlines of literacy. These limits are based in culture and the ideology of culture. Indeed, encyclopedias are structurally trapped in the ideologies of their creators. Encyclopedias may be said to be controlled by the crude ideology of recognized politics and the subtle ideology of the communicative process out of which meaning is made. This is inevitable; however, it becomes the source of conflict and controversy when the outlines of nations and cultures become unstable, as they almost always are. Nation and culture are dynamic, but encyclopedias are frozen in the moment of their creation.

Not only are encyclopedias frozen in a moment, they are also structurally trapped by the demands of listing and definition, which necessarily limit or omit overt discussion of context. But without context, meaning is obscured and understanding necessarily impeded. The paradox at the heart of the encyclopedia is that while it is created by those with expertise in a certain context whose goal is to produce a material map of a mental territory, it is sometimes the recourse of those who possess limited expertise within that context, those who are without a map. In other words, the philosophers, whom D'Alembert identifies as the mediators of the encyclopedia, create a tree out of an internalized and unconscious conceptual map. This map is the result of their perspective and even their secret knowledge. The bifurcated tree that is the encyclopedia is a reduced version of a multidimensional map the philosopher of knowledge possesses but fails to adequately translate. But the tree that is the encyclopedia is often consulted by those who have no such privilege, perspective, or secret knowledge.

Those without knowledge of a specific context sometimes choose or are forced to consult the lists produced by others, but without sufficient familiarity with context, comprehension is incomplete. In short, an encyclopedic entry, appearing as it does as part of a list that is a kind of mental address for a nugget of knowledge, is a poor substitute for a map, for context, for a multidimensional system of associations. The encyclopedist attempts to transform the tree into a multidimensional map, but the encyclopedia's structure necessarily limits this. Even so, curricula and tests often are organized according to the logic of the list, not the map. Or to put it another way, an address without a map is useless to a stranger in a strange land.

A list, comprising single lexical items, implies, in the same way that the semiotic square implies, a universe of semiosis, but *semiosis is a process occurring in a matrix of associations, which a list cannot trigger.* The global competence of the individual triggers semiosis at the moment of interpretation at an embodied moment in a time and place. At the moment of interpretation, the individual possesses a map that represents her semantic competence in a specific context. If the implications of any single item exceed the semantic competence of the individual who is required to interpret that item, communication and comprehension suffer. The ironic goal of the encyclopedia is to provide a semiotic map by means of the construction of the list, but a list cannot supply semiosis. A list *invites and sometimes demands* an interpretative act of semiosis by an individual. Only an individual can supply deep and broad semantic competence. No dictionary, encyclopedia, or other text can supply such competence. That is, the text has limits, but these limits do not constrain the individual. The text can only supply a surface; the individual supplies depth by calling on deep semantic competence that reflects the individual's knowledge of context.

Individuals come to encyclopedias much as Marco Polo traversed Khan's kingdom, without context but eager to acquire it. The stranger in a strange land can acquire context—indeed does—by virtue of visiting the strange land. After a time, the newly acquired context becomes the ground upon which semiosis takes place. The encyclopedic list is replaced by a conceptual map rooted in context and experience in the strange land. This conceptual map is not two-dimensional. It is multidimensional. It exceeds the representational limits of the written text. The encyclopedia's ironic goal, the transformation of the aggregate entries into a two-dimensional and then a multidimensional map, cannot fully succeed because the encyclopedia cannot supply the deep and broad semantic competence that enables semiosis; it cannot supply context. Multidimensional context can be experienced but not represented as a totality. The philosopher encyclopedist, an expert who creates the boundaries and selects the items for collation into a whole, creating a list, has this context; the reader often does not.

The encyclopedia, frozen at the moment of its creation and by definition failing to supply context, has still another limitation: it is structurally limited to a local cultural representation. That is, it exists as a transitory collation of knowledge from a particular perspective. The map that the encyclopedia attempts to provide is necessarily restricted to the experience of the philosopher encyclopedist and, therefore, is biased and limited. The local organization of knowledge, which the encyclopedia represents, allows for common understanding between individuals who are in the process of making meaning within a common context. Those who share overlapping maps constructed out of common experience can share information more easily. This may be stating the obvious, but what is not obvious is the difficulty of constructing maps that include multiple local knowledges. Arrogance generally has led the encyclopedist to deny the local nature of his collection and to suppress revealing its systematic bias; it has led the encyclopedist to declare his local collection to be global and representative of all that can be considered important. But Eco insists that structured knowledge cannot be organized as a *global* system in the form of an encyclopedia because any defined "circle of learning" can be contradicted by alternative and equally transitory and/or local cultural organizations (84). Encyclopedias necessarily encode the ideology of the local. This is not a fatal flaw. It is simply a limitation that must be recognized if an encyclopedic project is not to suffer from hubris.

In contrast to the list that becomes the encyclopedia, multidimensional maps are constructed out of experience, and this is ultimately the domain of the human interpreter. Travel across domains is possible, albeit ideology travels too.

The universe of semiosis *is* the universe of human culture. But global representation of human culture is a semantic impossibility. The collection and connection of potentially infinite local maps can mediate against the ideological bias of the encyclopedia as list.

If the global view is theory, is postulate, and is only a regulative idea that fosters the construction of the local into organized but limited sets, the organization of these limited sets allows the isolation of a portion of the whole of human culture in order to interpret certain discourses and texts. Believing that it is possible to create a map from one of those limited sets, one of

WHOSE ENCYCLOPEDIA?

those lists, allows encyclopedists to imagine the encyclopedia to be a route to literacy. This happens because the encyclopedist is unconscious of the semantic force of his interiorized map. At each moment, he is convinced he has supplied adequate context (or he suppresses the realization that he has not). Over time, the encyclopedist has forgotten his earlier, tentative maps of knowledge, has forgotten what it means not to know. But what seems simple to the encyclopedist, the collation of lists into interrelated maps, is in fact enormously complex. The encyclopedist believes he has created an aid to understanding, but he has also created a riddle. The encyclopedia is an unconscious cryptograph. The encyclopedist has created a literacy problem by encoding his personal secret system of knowledge and implying that it is universal and therefore accessible and useful. It is the belief that the encyclopedia aids literacy, not the inherent limitations of the encyclopedia, that is the fatal mistake.

This is E. D. Hirsch Jr.'s mistake: the idea that the list can supply the semiosis. He would deny that he means for the list to organize curricula or pedagogy, but it cannot help but do so given the history of its use and the inherent implications of its structure. The metonymic force of Bacon's tree of knowledge reaches into our present. Mass media debates about Stanford's "Culture, Ideas, and Values" curriculum were illustrated by a cartoon of a contemporary tree of knowledge torn apart by agents of "multiculturalism."

This study will go on to examine three technologies of literacy, E. D. Hirsch's dictionaries of cultural literacy, Disney World's EPCOT center, and the Smithsonian Institution. All three collections are manifest encyclopedias. Each of these inventions is representative of a complex process of collection and collation of an imagined universe of knowledge from a particular perspective. Umberto Eco's analysis of the semiotics of encyclopedias can help us understand how these collections must of necessity be trapped in ideology and that encyclopedias necessarily obscure understanding.

Lists can be created and collated only by those who are already adept. As prescriptions for those who are not, they have dubious value because they cannot supply semiosis. Instead they foster a crippled literacy, an awkward and tentative understanding that will only serve as a first step. The next chapter will contrast the encyclopedic impulse with its counterpoint: the impulse to travel across local knowledges, making a map as you go, weaving a net of connections as you meander and discover. The literature and literacies of authors like Maxine Hong Kingston, Zora Neale Hurston, Leslie Marmon Silko, and Gloria Anzaldúa provide examples of this impulse.

DISGUISED ENCYCLOPEDIAS?

Umberto Eco's theories can help us understand the relationship between encyclopedias and literacy and the problems surrounding the construction of literacy curricula, especially E. D. Hirsch's dictionaries of cultural literacy. Eco's discussion of dictionaries and encyclopedias is highly technical, involving abstract notions of how an ideal dictionary might be structured. Beginning the chapter in *Semiotics and the Philosophy of Language* concerning these issues with the question "Is a definition an interpretation?" Eco demonstrates that existing theoretical models for constructing definitions are untenable on several counts. Attempts to construct models for dictionaries based on the notion that a dictionary should store a finite number of bits of information about a particular lexical item and inventory a finite list of entries fail.

Dictionaries theoretically rely on the idea of a list of semantic primitives (the simplest concepts that can be identified—e.g., *human* is simpler to identify than *mammal*). This list is devised in order to conceive of a dictionary-like competence free of any commitment to world knowledge; i.e., *human* is identifiable only as a result of experience. In other words, the dictionary attempts to make a list of primitives that can be understood without world experience. But if one believes primitives are rooted in world knowledge, then dictionary competence is dependent on world knowledge.

The Porphyrian tree is the model upon which dictionary definitions are built. Porphyry, a third-century Phoenician, elaborated a theory of division based on Aristotle's *Categories*. While only suggested verbally in Porphyry's *Isagoge,* medieval tradition built the idea of a tree into visual representations tied to logical analysis (Eco 1984: 59). Bacon's tree begins here. This analysis forms the basis for the construction of dictionaries with a finite list of entries and bits of information about those entries. Eco's claim is that the Porphyrian tree upon which such models are built ultimately yields not a finite list but an infinite list, because the semantic primitives upon which a finite list are built remain rooted in world knowledge. His conclusion: it is impossible to construct a dictionary that is free of a commitment to world knowledge. Attempts to limit dictionaries to a list must fail.

Definitions that take the Porphyrian tree as a model rely on dualistic division of the qualities of any item. Thus *man* comes to be defined by the division of the corporeal (body) into *animate* (living being) or *inanimate* (mineral); *living being* into *sensitive* (animal) or *insensitive* (vegetal); *sensitive* into *rational* into *mortal* (man) or *immortal* (God). Each level of division supplies *differentia*. Differentia are qualities and are expressed by adjectives. Differentia belong to infinite sets, not finite sets. The Porphyrian tree appears to be finite and ordered, but it is, in fact, infinite because the number of differentia needed to distinguish any item from any other is unknowable. Each node on the tree requires that we infer other differentia, which are not named. Bacon's tree and then Diderot's encyclopedia grew according to this logic. For example, *sensitive* (animal) implies a contextual knowledge of the category *animal* that has experienced animals as sensitive versus plants as insensitive (a debatable point that also reveals the ideology of local knowledges). This contextual world knowledge necessarily draws on numerous associative networks. Eco makes clear that such networks are a priori infinite. Recent artificial intelligence research has attempted a solution to this problem by constructing semantic models that draw on world knowledge and by inventing the notion of "frames" and "scripts" that enable interpretation based on context. Computers are, of course, trapped in the binary logic of the Porphyrian tree. It seems unlikely that they will be able to break free of it as long as they remain binary "thinkers."

Eco continues his analysis by emphasizing that a dictionary attempts to be highly ordered, to include in its definitions the minimum needed to differentiate between signifiers. In order to hold together, a definition must ultimately rely on concrete and finite differentia. Paradoxically, a definition must explode into a multitude of differentia because the logical exclusion of entries and bits of information about those entries fails in the real world of semiosis. The necessary result is the *illogical exclusion* of differentia. So Bacon's tree grows through systematic *exclusion,* not just at the level of the limits of the primary list of definitions—that is, at the level of what gets chosen for the list—but also at the level of the differentia needed to sort one entry from another. The excluded bits point toward the world knowledge, which is assumed to be unnecessary for interpretation. The result is that we are forced to *infer* the essential differences between entries based on our world knowledge; i.e., we must use world knowledge to interpret dictionary entries, but the dictionary represses our consciousness of this.

> *The tree . . . blows up in a dust of differentiae, in a turmoil of infinite accidents, in a nonhierarchical network of qualia. The dictionary is dissolved into a potentially unordered and unrestricted galaxy of pieces of world knowledge. The dictionary thus becomes an encyclopedia, because it was in fact a disguised encyclopedia. (1984b:68)*

If the dictionary dissolves into an "unordered and unrestricted galaxy of pieces of world knowledge," these pieces require a background encyclopedic knowledge rooted in world knowledge in order to be interpreted. Attempts to create dictionaries that require the semantic competence of an ideal speaker will fail because they are actually disguised encyclopedias that require pragmatic competence, a competence based on interaction with the world. No bidimensional tree can represent the global semantic competence of a given culture. No finite list can represent the universe of culture. An encyclopedic competence requires world knowledge.

But what *are* encyclopedias, and what kind of literacy do they require and enforce? Eco tells us that since dictionaries are theoretically impossible, *all dictionaries are disguised encyclopedias.* We must assume that a more global knowledge is necessary if language is to be interpreted. How can global knowledge be represented so as to be discussed and theorized? All such representations are postulates and take the format of a multidimensional network (68).

The representation that Eco chooses for this network is a rhizomatic labyrinth. Rejecting first the classical labyrinth of Crete—one in which you cannot help but reach the Minotaur at the center—and, second, the Manneristic maze[3]—a labyrinth that gives you choices, some of which lead to dead ends—in other words, one in which you can make mistakes, one in which "the Minotaur is the visitor's trial-and-error process"[4]—Eco chooses a third type of labyrinth, the net, a labyrinth in which you *cannot make mistakes,* since the point of such a net is to meander, to discover, to make connections. "The main feature of a net is that every point can be connected with every other point, and where the connections are not yet designed, they are, however, conceivable and designable. A net is an unlimited territory" (81).

Further, Eco tells us that the best image for such a net is the rhizome suggested by Deleuze and Guattari (1976). Such a net is like the rhizomes of the vegetable and fungal world. Some of its characteristics are (a) all points can and must be connected to all other points; (b) it is anti-genealogical; (c) it has neither an outside nor an inside because it makes another rhizome out of itself; (d) it is susceptible to continual modification; (e) one cannot provide a global description of the rhizome, not just because it is complicated but because it changes over time; (f) there is the possibility of contradictory inferences because every node can be connected with every other node; (g) it cannot be described globally; rather, it must be described as "a potential sum of *local* descriptions"; and (h) since it has no outside, it can be viewed only from the inside. A labyrinth of this kind is necessarily myopic, since no one can have the global vision of all its possibilities, only the local vision of the closest ones. Because of this, every local description of the net is a hypothesis, "in a rhizome blindness is the only way of seeing, and thinking means to *grope one's way*" (82). Thinking means feeling our way along a local path that can change and change again at any moment. Instead of a static tree that disallows growth, we find ourselves in a universe of knowledge subject to continual revision and expansion. The tree is impoverished knowledge; the rhizome infinite possibility. Which matches our imaginings of literacy best?

Finally, Eco tells us that "the universe of semiosis, that is, the universe of human culture, must be conceived" to be structured like the rhizome's labyrinth. Every attempt to codify local knowledges as "unique and 'global'—ignoring their partiality—produces an *ideological* bias" (83–84). Such local knowledges have the potential to "be contradicted by alternative and equally 'local' cultural organizations" (84). And each of these knowledges claims that it represents Truth. In other words, paradox becomes a familiar part of such a net. When local knowledges meet one another, paradox pops up. This can drive an individual into neurosis or start a war. But an acceptance of paradox as a condition of life can lead not to an interruption of ideology within its system but to a kind of truce between local knowledges, an agreement to disagree.

Such a net represents an alternate to the dictionary and encyclopedia as a method for imagining literacy. It is the net to which this study later turns. Rhizomes are a powerful representation for an alternate conception of literacy, but for the moment, we are caught in a Porphyrian tree.

DICTIONARIES WITHOUT IDEOLOGY

Once we begin to understand the impulse behind the creation of encyclopedias, we are ready to understand why E. D. Hirsch begins his prescriptions for the reformation of American education with a list that becomes a dictionary, which is in fact an encyclopedia.[5] His list reflects how he imagines literacy from within his own interiorized map of knowledge, a map based on what he has learned and what he values. What follows is not a comprehensive critique of Hirsch's claims; the reaction to his book has been intense enough to provide many analyses, which, when taken together, do an adequate job of covering that territory.[6] Robert Scholes has called Hirsch's proposals "voodoo[7] education," and while I do not entirely disagree with the implications of that accusation, I also find myself in agreement with Patrick Scott, who finds Hirsch's central thesis fascinating and who considers the profession's negative response to Hirsch intellectually shortsighted and politically inept. Hirsch doggedly defends his proposals by repeatedly publishing detailed and strident refutations of his critics. One of the most interesting and thoughtful of these critics is a former student, Gregory G. Colomb, whose summary takes his professor very seriously indeed. Even so, Hirsch cannot resist responding immediately and testily.[8] Despite sustained criticism, Hirsch's work continues; with the help of very influential policymakers like William Bennett and Diane Ravitch, he continues to propagate his proposals.

Hirsch's main claim is that the current educational "crisis" can be traced to specific pedagogical errors that are replicated throughout the American primary and secondary educational system. Because of an educational formalism based on the flawed philosophies of Rousseau and Dewey, American public schools have concentrated on developing skills in isolation from "facts." This has led to cultural illiteracy. Educational failure results from the lack of a common vocabulary rooted in a common cultural matrix. Without this common vocabulary, comprehension is limited. Hirsch posits an ideal reader, or rather he accurately describes how texts are written with an ideal reader in mind. Those who possess this vocabulary are culturally literate; those who do not are crippled. He defines *cultural literacy*[9] vaguely, as possessing "the basic information needed to thrive in the world" (Hirsch 1987:xii) or

> *the network of information that all competent readers possess.*
> *It is the background information, stored in their minds, that enables them to take up a newspaper and read it with an adequate level of comprehension, getting the point, grasping the implications, relating what they read to the unstated context which alone gives meaning to what they read. (2)*

This is a possible definition of what Eco terms world knowledge, but Hirsch misses the implication of his own discovery. Understanding in context is a result of complex associations rooted in semiosis, not in listing. He tells us that such knowledge is hazy, "information essential to literacy is rarely detailed or precise" (14). But it is not so much hazy as it is deeply structured at an unconscious level. Unfortunately, his definition of cultural literacy is hazy precisely because he does not grasp the most important implications of his discovery: that semiosis is at the root of understanding.

Inserted around his description of cultural literacy is a running string of persistently undefined terms, such as *mature literacy, true literacy, common knowledge, background knowledge, high universal literacy* (for which he provides the wonderfully precise definition "learning a wide range of things"), *national literacy, traditional information, core knowledge,* and *specific broad knowledge.* These terms resemble advertising slogans more than educational theory.

Hirsch's notions appeal to nationalists who imagine America as a coherent entity; he devotes an entire chapter to the relationship between common cultural knowledge and the development of the modern nation-state. Clearly, his imaginings of literacy rely on his interiorized map of knowledge and are tied to a classic dream of progress and unity outside of religion or specific politics. Hirsch sincerely dreams of escaping factionalism through the construction of common knowledge. Unfortunately, he seeks to diminish uncommon knowledge in order to accomplish this goal. His method for canonizing the vocabulary of cultural literacy rests on his own experience as an intellectual and as a participating member of a particular body politic. Imagining the important work of any citizen to be analogous to his own in that it requires reading newspapers "of substance" and books and periodicals of a general nature, he cites Jefferson's pronouncements regarding the importance of newspapers as evidence that democracy cannot succeed without a citizenry that remains attuned to the civics represented in news. Schools are a crucial site for the transmission of the common cultural vocabulary of the nation-state. This vocabulary enables civics.

Despite the inherent importance of this common cultural vocabulary to the building of a modern nation, Hirsch believes the politics of the American educational system is such that a unitary national curriculum is an impossibility. Such a curriculum could foster a common vocabulary, but Hirsch believes it would never be adopted. For this reason, he invents the idea of a list of "what every American needs to know." This list, which appears at the end of the 1987 book, immediately becomes a singular media curiosity and a major point of political dissension. In 1988, it becomes *The Dictionary of Cultural Literacy,* which Hirsch wishes will somehow be translated into varied local curricula across the nation. Hirsch and his foundation are the arbiters of this list. Declaring by fiat that 80 percent of the vocabulary needed for cultural literacy remains stable, that scientific terms account for another 10 percent, and that cultural changes account for a final 10 percent, Hirsch leaves little room for alternate cultural input, despite the fact that he invites it.

The list is gleaned from the vocabulary contained in a body of classical works represented by the canon of great books, including the Bible, Shakespeare, and key cultural documents like the Declaration of Independence. The vocabulary included in these works forms the stable core of Hirsch's list. As to the elements of this list that change, Hirsch has decided that "although the terms that ebb and flow are tremendously important at a given time, they belong, from an educational standpoint, at the periphery of literate culture. The persistent, stable elements belong at the core" (29). In other words, all elements of the culture that are not part of this canonical vocabulary are peripheral. This banishment of cultural diversity and change has marked Hirsch's work as inherently hostile to progressive and radical social change. The notion of a dynamic culture is consistently given only lip service in his analysis.

Hirsch's earlier articles on this subject did not mention the concept of a cultural literacy dictionary. Neither did they emphasize the consequences of cultural illiteracy for "minorities." But on page 1 of the preface to *Cultural Literacy,* Hirsch explicitly declares cultural literacy to be "the only sure avenue of opportunity for disadvantaged children." He is convinced that schools, by themselves, can break the cycle of poverty and illiteracy.[10] Early in chapter 1 (10), Hirsch quotes Harvard historian and sociologist Orlando Patterson at the 1980 memorial conference for Mina Shaughnessy, one of the most innovative and influential literacy scholar/teachers of the 1970's. Patterson seconded Hirsch's ideas but was particularly concerned with the importance of shared knowledge for "blacks" and other "minorities." He emphasized that the "wider culture" is not static, that the accurate metaphor for this "wider literacy" is not domination but dialectic between groups. In other words, culture changes, but nowhere in Hirsch's subsequent discussions does he seriously address this crucial observation: culture is dynamic.

One wonders if he has looked around lately. Hirsch does not see American culture as a mélange or salad or bouillabaisse, as others have; he does not even imagine it to be a melting pot. Instead, "local, regional, ethnic" cultures are somehow severed from "mainstream culture" (1987:22). Terms from "local" cultures enter cultural literacy as accessories after the fact.

It is Hirsch's easy erasure of the knowledges of "local" cultures that has given him the most clout with conservatives. And it is this erasure that has caused him the most trouble with those who are conscious of living in a world Hirsch refuses to acknowledge, a world in which the many cultures of the planet are colliding with increasing frequency, a world that is at once cacophonous and filled with lovely harmonies. The response to Hirsch's program has led to the publication of alternative lists that take this reality into consideration. In 1988 Graywolf Press answered both Hirsch and Bloom by publishing *Multicultural Literacy: Opening the American Mind.* Thirteen essays described the ground of our culture as already multicultural. The collection's appendix began to list items not included in Hirsch's list that are commonly omitted from U.S. educational texts, political thinking, or social planning. It begins with the *100,000 Songs of Milarepa* and ends with *Zulu*. Similarly, in 1997 Kwame Anthony Appiah, Henry Louis Gates Jr., and Michael Colin Vasquez produced *The Dictionary of Global Culture,* which takes as its premise that the West cannot remain the cultural and intellectual center of the world, that Europeans and North Americans know too little about world history and culture, that "European culture is increasingly influenced by American popular culture; and the true roots of the culture of the United States run deep in the soils of many continents," that Western culture risks becoming (remaining) parochial and narrow, that "we have lost that peculiar sense of wonder about the world and its diversity that characterized the European Renaissance and Enlightenment." The central focus of this work is not North American cultural literacy but global literacy resting on common knowledge among the literate citizens of the world. *Global Culture* attempts to gather together "the common knowledge essential for the creation of an international culture, in which the Western tradition is seen as one strand in a complexly woven tapestry of cultures."[11] It is not surprising to note that not only do the editors of *Global Culture* make explicit the methods they used to compile their list, they remark that the cultural experts they consulted surprised them with lists that did not conform to their own biases and that they structured their methodology to elicit these surprises. Further, they warn their readers that no book, no encyclopedia, no dictionary could be comprehensive or exhaustive and that the most complete dictionary would not suffice, that you need to know much more: the grammar of a language, how to read its poetry, how objects and ideas fit together in the lives of the people whose ideas and objects they are. And finally they warn: "A dictionary can never represent the whole range of culture, just because a culture is a whole as well as a collection of parts" (xiii).

Hirsch insists that inculcation of the items on his list is the only reasonable route to greatly increased literacy for the "disadvantaged." This raises the stakes of the debate. If he is wrong, he is fostering practices that will continue to reinforce social injustice. I am convinced that while his insight into the relationship between vocabulary, knowledge, and reading comprehension is correct, his prescription, his list, is flawed at its root, no matter what is included and no matter how the curricula surrounding the list are modified.[12] All dictionaries and encyclopedias must be flawed, but this should not concern us unless we look to them for what they cannot supply. The idea that the list can be neutral and comprehensive is the real problem.

While it may seem obvious that reading well is a function of acquired vocabulary and the development of a broad vocabulary is crucial to intellectual skills in general, American elementary and secondary schools, and perhaps even colleges and universities, have not translated this rather obvious realization into successful pedagogies. As a college professor, I observed the same phenomena that Hirsch describes in my classes. That is, students who had little knowledge of the cultural markers that my fellow teachers and I took for granted were fatally handicapped despite test scores that indicated they read reasonably well.

The similarities between Hirsch's conclusions and my own are striking. About the same time he was conducting research in Virginia, my teaching practices in Northern California were uncovering identical evidence. In 1978 the Gallup organization conducted a survey of 1,000 seventeen- and eighteen-year-olds to determine their knowledge of civics. The results were widely reported in the mass media. High school graduates knew frighteningly little about history, geography, and civics. This and other surveys were part of the impetus in the 1980's to reexamine American educational policy.

As a result of this and other similar reports and my own hunches about what was going wrong in my classroom, I decided to survey my students. Using some of Gallup's questions and adding others based on my experience in the classroom, I collected similar statistics over several years, even some identical wrong answers, e.g., that Mexico and Canada were the last two states to enter the Union. To the examples often cited by Hirsch, Gallup, and others, I can add the following hilarious and horrifying nuggets. Twenty-five percent of my students could not locate the Middle Ages anywhere within its approximately thousand-year time span; Auschwitz and Dachau are noted for their beer; George Bush's name is spelled "Busch" after Anheuser; and Martin Luther (a trick question) was a "black panter." Imagine trying to read anything that dealt with the Middle Ages when you cannot place it historically except in the vague preindustrial past. I am not sure that some students even understood the Middle Ages to be part of the preindustrial period. They associated it with knights, swords, and horses, but Civil War soldiers also rode horses and brandished swords.

When I discussed these anonymous survey results with my students, they were depressed, and often it reinforced the negative self-image they had accumulated from a lifetime of school-based testing and judgment. Even so, they found humor in the situation. As a nation we have developed a laissez-faire attitude toward our own ignorance. In the 1970's, knowing less became chic. But when the discussion deepened, the revelations were sometimes heartbreaking. Many had simply given up trying to absorb the tremendous amount of information that saturates our environment, creating a cacophony for those who are without an adequate foundation. One sincere young woman admitted that she could not understand the evening news because it mentioned many countries and issues that were beyond her experience. It was painful to hear her describe how her good intentions only led to reduced self-esteem and confidence. Another student denounced the absorption of "ugly facts"; after all, most of the news around political and social events was negative. It was depressing to pay attention to these "ugly facts." He had a point.[13]

As I continued to teach more than a hundred students each semester during that decade, I became increasingly convinced that my students' academic success or failure hinged greatly on their lack of cultural literacy. The term became part of my private pedagogical vocabulary at this point. No matter what reading assignments were made, collective and individual vocabulary gaps guaranteed very spotty comprehension. The learning problems that many of my students had were clearly tied to what both Hirsch and I had come to call cultural literacy.

Despite the attention I gave to cultural literacy and a great deal of experimentation, it never occurred to me that the solution to this problem might be a vocabulary list. Having read Hirsch's earlier articles on cultural literacy, I was astonished when his 1987 book unveiled the list as the solution.[14] To any thoughtful person working on the front lines of literacy education, it is obvious that although cultural illiteracy is very real and very deep, a vocabulary list represents a very strange approach to a complicated problem.

Gregory Colomb and I agree: Hirsch is making crucial points about skills and knowledge. "The evidence is increasingly clear: skills cannot be learned apart from knowledge" (Colomb 1989a:413). Reading comprehension is rooted in world knowledge, and many do lack this knowledge. Colomb exhaustively describes recent reading research, including artificial intelligence research, as does Eco in his discussion of encyclopedias. Colomb's conclusion:

> *The knowledge needed for reading and writing is more complex than any list or even network of propositions and . . . literate persons are vague about their knowledge because producing isolated propositions is a poor way to access that knowledge. (420)*

Further, we have little or no evidence as to how readers construct meaning from their knowledge, but we know that they do. The most promising theory suggests that memory is distributed over many intricately connected units without a central controller, just as Eco's rhizomatic theories would suggest.

> *Many other studies suggest that the knowledge that counts most is richly organized and hierarchical—organized by plans and goals, organized into scenarios, organized by being understood and so connected to everything else we know . . . it is not enough for readers to know the requisite facts: they must understand them. (Colomb 1989a:424)*

In other words, individuals are compelled to organize what they know into webs of association. And although it is clear that readers use world knowledge to understand texts, texts can help them to understand entirely new information if the discourse structure leads them through "the web of new information" (Colomb 1989a:432). In other words, reading theory points away from lists toward the construction of webs of meaning. Meaning is made out of a complex and deep process that we do not understand, but we can tentatively imagine it to be analogous to the rhizome or a net of associations. It is interesting to note that the World Wide Web and the Internet are probably ironic tropes, since even "experts" on the Net are groping around in more than semi-blindness. Still, the potential for the Net to be more than a maze of the unknowable seems real. How this might be accomplished is something else. The Net could be just another technology for violent literacy.

Hirsch's claim that the systematic inculcation of a "common" cultural vocabulary can be the solution to our educational problems reflects his investment in a notion of encyclopedic knowledge and the problems inherent in such a notion. His conception of a vocabulary list mirrors a long Western intellectual tradition that imagines knowledge as an artifact that can be represented concretely (and therefore collected) and tested empirically. It is widely accepted that it is possible to possess a fund of knowledge, comprising discrete elements, that then becomes enabling to the individual who deploys this knowledge in the material world. This is clearly the assumption behind the development of curricula composed of a number of subjects organized by discipline and then further organized by topics and subtopics. The idea that what humans know can be organized and transmitted in an organized set is contradicted by Eco's claim that the semiosis of human culture cannot be globally collected. All such attempts result in an ideological bias because the universe of human knowledge cannot be represented as a totality; every attempt to codify local knowledges as "unique and 'global'— ignoring their partiality—produces an *ideological* bias" (Eco 1984b:83–84).

Hirsch's attempts to codify one local knowledge, European American cultural tradition, ignores the partiality of that vision and *structurally* produces a bias. There is nothing intrinsically negative about local knowledges; it is just that they are rooted in a perspective. It is their presentation as unique and global that produces the problem. Instead, they should be presented as tentative visions from a particular perspective. Gates's global literacy project attempts to address this issue by placing the Western tradition in context as "one strand in a complexly woven tapestry of cultures." As it addresses one problem, it presents another: it imagines it can make a global description by exiting the Manneristic maze and providing a bird's-eye view. But Eco points out that a bird's-eye view is possible only as a *postulate*. In practice, meaning is made by groping one's way in semi-blindness through a maze, a net, a rhizome. Learning to tolerate that semi-blindness is one skill we all need to cultivate.

In Hirsch's defense, he does state clearly that "cultural literacy is shallow; true education is deep." But Eco would insist that comprehension of *any* lexical item on Hirsch's list demands deep knowledge, knowledge that Hirsch seems to admit is outside his definition of *cultural literacy*. So Hirsch's list necessarily fails because it attempts a global representation of what cannot be globally represented and because it assumes that exposure to individual lexical items can produce sufficient comprehension to be of use. It assumes that vocabulary knowledge can be fostered outside of deep contextualization.

Describing Hirsch this way results in an insight regarding the encyclopedia. Eco, Colomb, and I are positing cultural literacy as requiring a kind of omnivorous search for the connections between elements, between seemingly disparate nuggets and disciplines. From Diderot's project forward, encyclopedias have attempted to do just that. But individuals require mental maps rooted in their experience in order to interpret encyclopedic entries. Such maps are only temporary postulates, necessarily myopic and rooted in the particular experiences and locations of the individual, which necessarily change over time. Comprehension of the universe of human knowledge requires factual knowledge rooted in mental maps, which are themselves rooted in experience. All understanding is hypothesis and subject to change because these maps must change as experience changes. Comprehension also requires the ability to travel between many local knowledges as someone who not only observes but participates as a responsible member of a community, someone who is at once citizen, traveler, and spy.

Donna Haraway's notion of situated knowledges and Nancy Hartsock's notion of "standpoint" are useful analogs of this observation. "Standpoint" represents an achieved wisdom that is the result of struggle and engagement with oppressive material and social conditions. Hartsock claims that "there are some perspectives on society from which, however well-intentioned one may be, the real relations of humans with each other and with the natural world are not visible" (1983:285). Hartsock considers

> *the ruling group's vision [to be] both perverse [and partial] and made real by means of that group's power to define the terms for the community as a whole . . . The worker as well as the capitalist engages in the purchase and sale of commodities, and if material life structures consciousness, this cannot fail to have an effect. (288)*

We are all at once citizens, travelers, and spies on an infinite rhizome of interlocking situated knowledges.

Hirsch would have done far better to examine the motivations that move individuals to curiosity and to commonality, to examine what motivates them to travel through the rhizome of human semiosis, how they negotiate alternate standpoints and situated knowledges. Literacy requires not the list but its opposite, collation and re-collation across communities of knowledge. This vision of literacy does not make a simplistic division between skills and facts, a division underlying Hirsch's analysis. It recognizes that within a rhizome "thinking means to *grope one's way,*" making connections. Making connections is precisely the point. Remember. "The main feature of a net is that every point can be connected with every other point, and where the connections are not yet designed, they are, however, conceivable and designable. A net is an unlimited territory" (Eco 1984b:81).

Colomb has no trouble seeing this:

> *We need also to stop pretending to teach common readers and to face up to what students know perfectly well: that to move easily from one community of knowledge to another, from one discipline to another, requires not only a lot of knowledge but also the skills of an ethnographer and the flexibility of a spy. We could do a great deal toward creating a new kind of common reader by foregrounding for students the differences between communities of knowledge, by being explicit about the communal*

> *basis of our knowledge, and by helping them to understand the*
> *process of joining a community of knowers. (1989a:461)*

Why is this insight so difficult for Hirsch and many others?

By including a list without definitions as an appendix to *Cultural Literacy,* Hirsch creates a test. That is, the reader is implicitly encouraged to scan the list, trying to identify as many of the items as possible. Presumably, those who read the book could feel encouraged by their ability to identify most of the items. As Stuckey tells us, literacy legitimates itself. Those who could not identify most of the items probably did not read the book; they certainly would not be inclined to buy it. *Cultural Literacy* creates its own validation by positing a common vocabulary among culturally literate Americans— the only Americans likely to read the book. Hirsch develops support for his notions by speaking to the educated group that stands to benefit the least from his proposals.

The circular nature of Hirsch's reasoning persists throughout his discussions of cultural literacy. Nations are nations because citizens have a common vocabulary. A common vocabulary creates a nation. A list is an authentic representation of what literate Americans know because a literate American creates the list.

Despite all that Hirsch has written about his proposals, he remains completely silent when it comes to describing the method by which he and his collaborators constructed the list. He invites suggestions for additions from his critics and supporters, but *he* remains the arbiter of the list. How are items selected? How are suggestions for inclusion accepted or rejected? These sorts of questions are at least as important as the theoretical justification for the list.

Neither does Hirsch give instructions for the use of his list. He is defensive about what he calls caricatures of his program, but he provides no explanations of how these lists will be turned into curricula, and the lists themselves can be seen as a caricature of the universe of knowledge. The lists should not be a guide to memorization, we are told. How, then, should they be used? What is the necessary relation between the list and the dictionary that followed it? How are the dictionaries to be used? Should they be read cover to cover? If not, when should they be consulted? In what ways can the entries aid comprehension *during* the reading process? To what extent do ordinary dictionaries help the reading process? What is the advantage of Hirsch's dictionary over an ordinary dictionary? How does the list, the dictionary, become a curriculum? Responsible educational policy requires that such questions be addressed.

Eco's claim that dictionaries must explode into encyclopedias is played out on the surface of both *The Dictionary of Cultural Literacy: What Every American Needs to Know* and *A First Dictionary of Cultural Literacy: What Our Children Need to Know* (curiously titled to alienate the children who are meant to use it). In "How to Use This Dictionary," the reader is told:

> The Dictionary of Cultural Literacy *is a departure from all other reference works in its attempt to identify and define common* cultural *knowledge rather than to present a lexicon of words or topics. Nonetheless, for the convenience of our readers, this book incorporates some of the conventions found in standard dictionaries and encyclopedias. (Hirsch, Kett, and Trefil 1988: xvii)*

Hirsch's dictionaries immediately explode into impoverished encyclopedias, impoverished because they do not pretend to include the scope or depth of even a very slim encyclopedia, yet they require, like all dictionaries, encyclopedic world knowledge if they are to be adequately interpreted. Both volumes are organized into "encyclopedic" sections such as "The Bible," "Mythology and Folklore," "World History to 1550," and "Life Sciences." The adult version contains twenty-three such sections, the children's version twenty-one. Children are directed to look at sections to determine what they need to learn about a subject and to gain a general picture of what they already know and what they still need to learn. They are told directly that reading a dictionary is not the best way to gain knowledge and are further directed to a bibliography of general interest books at the end of the volume. They are nudged toward mapmaking. Adults are left to their own devices; they are not directed toward any methodology for making use of the book's organization. Adults are not warned away from merely reading the dictionary. Each section in both books includes a short preface that explains the importance of the general subject area to literacy and provides a general introduction to the subject matter.

The paradox of dictionaries and encyclopedias is that they are created by insiders in the know for others who may have great difficulty using them to advantage. Without a map, the list is sometimes worse than useless.

Personally, I find Hirsch's dictionaries—in fact, nearly all reference books—fascinating and fun. One reason for this is that I have developed numerous overlapping maps of local knowledges. But I can vividly remember how baffling dictionaries were when I was a child, and they are sometimes so even today when I find myself reading beyond my areas of expertise and/or familiarity. The process of reading definitions is often fruitless under those circumstances; I must encounter the same word over and over again in context before the dictionary definition comes alive with meaning. There is nothing mysterious or new about this observation, so why is it not accounted for in Hirsch's theory?

Despite Hirsch's claim that his empirical project, his dictionary, is without ideology, it is easy to identify in this project not just his ideology but his misdirection. The semiotics of dictionaries and encyclopedias predict not only that *any* list is trapped in ideology, not the worst thing that ever happened, but that lists in themselves obscure understanding.

Hirsch's claims for his dictionary are overt, but like Disney and the Smithsonian, the plenitude of the dictionary obscures its repressions. Dictionaries create narratives out of de-selection. Plenitude is illusory in such a system. All of these products record the ideologies of their creators. Umberto Eco and Roland Barthes have described how definitions are created by bifurcations created out of a lack. If everything was included in any map, it would, of course, be unreadable.

Definitions must be constructed out of exclusion. For example, things may either move or not move. If they move, they may be dangerous or not. If they are dangerous, they may be human or not, and so on (Eco 1984:80).

All hierarchies proceed on this basis, in terms of something ruled out, in terms of a systematic denial of some attribute. The unconscious of the text is created by this repression and out of these lacks. Hirsch's critics aimed at this unconscious. His dictionary necessarily constructs a map of nation by means of systems of exclusion. It behooves the "philosophers of the encyclopedia" to be aware of this process.

Instead, *The Dictionary of Cultural Literacy* obviates some of its stated goals. For example, cultural illiteracy is synonymous with ignorance of history, yet Hirsch's dictionary emphasizes the recent and the present. Out of twenty-four of its longest entries, ten concern heads of state, eight of those are United States presidents, five of the eight are from the twentieth century. In other words, that portion of U.S. history most likely to be remembered receives the most attention. This emphasis does nothing to foster cultural literacy if it means deciphering texts about Ulysses S. Grant and Robert E. Lee. Neither does emphasizing King Arthur, one of the ten heads of state given extra attention, who is surely one of the most recognized figures of mythological history. In short, this dictionary is short where it should be long and long where it should be short.

The construction of *Einstein,* another of the longer entries, as a genius among geniuses (incidentally, Einstein is represented as an American scientist by Disney and by a statue on the Mall in Washington, D.C.) and the enshrinement of the theory of relativity, to which still another of the longer entries is devoted, deflects our attention away from the integration of science and technology into every aspect of our daily life and parallels the emphasis on heads of state. Einstein becomes a sort of head of science.

The Dictionary of Cultural Literacy's implied plenitude is quickly contradicted by its gaps, many of which are inexplicable. By what logic is the Jerry Falwell entry longer than the one for Jesse Jackson? And both are accorded more space than Jim Crow and the John Birch Society, which are listed in immediate succession without correlation or reference to the Birch Society's racism. The Hank Aaron entry in the history section does not mention his race or the anger that arose after he broke Babe Ruth's record. Jerusalem appears twice but is listed in the index only once—under the world geography section. The cross-references between Jerusalem as religious icon and as modern city are absent, despite their critical relationship and even though both entries contain, in part, identical phrases. Without context, unforgivable gaps appear. Those who rely on the dictionary for literacy will certainly acquire a crippled literacy.

Neither do this dictionary's sections (one easy indication that we are consulting not a dictionary but rather an encyclopedia is the presence of these sections) follow a discernible logic. They are hierarchical, but this hierarchy does not offer the virtue of illumination. The eighteenth-century encyclopedia imagined a synchronic world, but Hirsch's twenty-three sections clank awkwardly through an apparent diachronic progression. Religious- and language-based roots lead to world and national history and geography, to the social sciences, to business and economics, to the physical sciences and technology. Implicit in this progression is a theory of emergent humanism.

Because Hirsch insists that an enormous number of vocabulary items in our popular reading refer to the Bible, Shakespeare, classical mythology, and folklore, the sections "The Bible" and "Mythology and Folklore" appear first, but they account for only 8 of 546 pages. Jerry Falwell et al. could have easily loaned space to Shakespeare, whose entry is not nearly as contextualized as it needs to be. The dictionary inexplicably violates its own stated ideology by devoting less attention to key cultural markers. And in a curious echo of the Jim Crow and John Birch Society entries, Shakespeare is followed immediately by a separate entry discussing "Shall I compare thee to a summer's day?" and half as long as the Shakespeare entry itself. No cross-references to other Shakespeare-related entries are provided. How could any cultural illiterate wade through this series of deflections with any hope of coming out the wiser?

One of the more interesting sequences in the book lists *nonaligned nations, nonalignment, nonperson,* and *nonviolent resistance* in immediate succession. Here we have a series based on an overt lack collected together and banished to an encapsulated corner of the dictionary. The reader is left to decipher the curious relationships between these entries without the aid of the philosopher of the encyclopedia.

Neither does Hirsch's list include the terms *dictionary* or *encyclopedia.* This curious list does not include itself. A little self-referentiality might help illuminate this project for author and reader alike.

Policy is being made as a result of Hirsch's suggestions because they provide ammunition for politically powerful interests represented by individuals like William Bennett, Alan Bloom, Saul Bellow,[15] Diane Ravitch, Lynne Cheney, and others. This group actively writes, speaks, and lobbies against multiculturalism and for monoculturalism. While forcing a monocultural image of literacy on the nation, these same interests are supporting national achievement testing. Such testing will almost certainly be based on some encyclopedic notion of knowledge. Hirsch has demonstrated the power to impose his imaginings of literacy on the nation. In any case, it was already programmed to accept a notion of literacy based on a list. The inertia of developed tests will enforce a static list and a static curriculum. How could it be otherwise?[16]

Lists are implicit in most primary and secondary curricula as second only to skills. Students have already been exposed to many of the entries touched on in Hirsch's lists. They do not engage with these isolated bits. They do not remember the vocabulary. Memorizing isolated bits is what much of school is still about. Forgetting them may be still more intrinsic to schooling. Because curricula do not foster strong mental maps, students cannot make sense out of the nonsense of lists.

OUTSIDER LITERACY

Like Hsiang, those who have limited access to a library are forced to imagine its contents and to imagine what it means to have mastered it. The paradox of the list, the dictionary, the encyclopedia, the library is that while such collections are most useful and helpful for those who are adept, they are sometimes the recourse of those who are not. When outsiders are in unfamiliar territory, they need maps, but when they are without a map they may resort to an address, or a series of addresses, i.e., a list. This list, which is really a series of disconnected addresses, is useful only if a guide (a map) supplies context. Getting from one address to the other is impossible without that guide. Nevertheless, those without maps of broad areas of knowledge sometimes resort to lists until they learn enough to develop an interiorized map. Better crippled literacy than no literacy.

The literature of people of color is filled with descriptions of fascination with dictionaries, encyclopedias, and libraries. Descriptions of obsession with such repositories of knowledge appear in the work of individuals such as Malcolm X and Richard Rodriguez. Their narratives suggest that these fascinations are key moments in their development.

But obsession of this sort is not unambiguously positive. It is a manifestation of the anxiety that afflicts those who feel they are locked out of epistemologies of power. Driven to undo their ignorance, but unclear about what that would mean, they imagine a literacy that can be systematically and logically tracked down and acquired. Jean-Paul Sartre satirizes the folly of such an approach in his novel *Nausea* (1964) by inventing a character known to the reader only as "the Self-Taught Man." "The Self-Taught Man" handles books "like a dog who has found a bone." A pitiable character, he progresses through the library by reading every book alphabetically as it is shelved. After seven years, he has reached the "L"s.

> *Today he has reached "L"—"K" after "J", "L" after "K".*
> *He has passed brutally from the study of coleopterae to the*
> *quantum theory, from a work on Tamerlaine to a Catholic pamphlet against Darwinism, he had never been disconcerted for an*
> *instant. He had read everything; he has stored up in his head*
> *most of what anyone knows about parthenogenesis, and half the*
> *arguments against vivisection. There is a universe behind and*
> *before him. And the day is approaching when closing the last*
> *book on the last shelf on the far left: he will say to himself,*
> *"Now what?" (45)*

"The Self-Taught Man" exemplifies the awkward ignorance of the outsider. At the end of the novel, he demonstrates that his crippled literacy parallels his social ineptitude. A gross error of judgment leads to his disgrace. Clearly, no amount of decontextualized study could have prevented it.

Similarly, Richard Rodriguez describes his own process of alphabetical reading in *The Hunger of Memory* (1982):

> *I was not a good reader. Merely bookish, I lacked a point of*
> *view when I read. Rather, I read to acquire a point of view. I*

WHOSE ENCYCLOPEDIA?

vacuumed books for epigrams, scraps of information, ideas, themes—anything to fill the hollow within me and make me feel educated. (64)

From a list of the hundred most important books of Western civilization, he begins one of a series of reading programs. Although he does not understand many of the books he reads, he dutifully plows through them. Much later, while avoiding completing his dissertation in the reading room of the British Museum, he systematically attacks educational theory. In the process, he reads Richard Hoggart's classic, *The Uses of Literacy,* and finds at last a depiction of his experience. Hoggart's description of "the scholarship boy" describes the agonies of outsiders whose education enables them to pass from one class to another. His systematic and encyclopedic education cannot produce a living map of the territory. Reduced to mimicry because his deficiencies cannot be bridged by dutiful reading alone, the scholarship boy is a "bad thinker."

Despite this crippling methodology, Rodriguez goes on to be the first Chicano to write a book that will reach the *New York Times* best-seller list. In contrast, Malcolm X describes his encounter with the dictionary as pivotal to his intellectual and political development. Unlike Rodriguez, Malcolm X becomes a visionary leader and anything but dutiful.

True to paradigm, Malcolm X was motivated to increase his literacy because of his religious goals. While incarcerated, he begins a letter-writing campaign to Elijah Muhammad because the Nation of Islam has fired his imagination. Malcolm copied his first one-page letter to Muhammad at least twenty-five times. "I was trying to make it both legible and understandable. I practically couldn't read my handwriting myself; it shames even to remember it" (1964:169). Malcolm had decoding skills, but his vocabulary left him without the ability to make sense out of the books he opened up. At this point, he fixates obsessively on the dictionary as the solution to both his handwriting difficulty and his reading problem. He begins copying it page by page, down to the last punctuation mark. The first page took a day, after which he memorized most of the entries. "With every succeeding page, I also learned of people and places and events from history. Actually the dictionary is like a miniature encyclopedia. . . . That was the way I started copying what eventually became the entire dictionary" (172).

He continued to read up to fifteen hours a day, after lights were out at ten P.M., till three or four in the morning by the corridor light outside his cell. This required hiding from the guards every fifty-eight minutes. He entered Norfolk prison with twenty-twenty vision; he left with astigmatism and a very different consciousness: "I still marvel at how swiftly my previous life's thinking pattern slid away from me, like snow off a roof. It is as though someone else I knew of had lived by hustling and crime. I would be startled to catch myself thinking in a remote way of my earlier self as another person" (170).

No ordinary intellect, and with prodigious time and devotion Malcolm X transformed the dictionary into a map. His insight allowed him to see the dictionary for what it was: a disguised encyclopedia. But unlike most, his stakes in opposing the ideology encoded in that dictionary motivated him to study against the grain. Unlike Rodriguez, he is *not* a scholarship boy. He reads with a determined point of view and an intense desire to uncover what was repressed about African and African American history. The first set of books that really impress him supplies an archaeological history of non-European peoples. Malcolm comes to books with a developed standpoint and high stakes in uncovering the hidden ideology in the racist discourses around him. His mapping is extraordinarily successful. He develops what Chéla Sandoval[17] terms "an oppositional consciousness" out of these studies, and he stimulates millions of others to do likewise.[18] He memorizes the dictionary out of necessity, turning it into a virtue. It is extraordinary, but we should not expect to duplicate it via the dictionary as curricula.

MONOCULTURAL VERSUS
MULTICULTURAL LITERACY

Hirsch's prescriptions for cultural literacy open a series of important questions regarding how humans make meaning out of written language and how cultural knowledge limits and advances literacy for people whose backgrounds are not steeped in the monocultural, Western humanist tradition. Such individuals are precisely Hirsch's target population. Illuminating how Hirsch's formula imposes a kind of crippled cultural literacy in the very groups it most seeks to enfranchise is central to understanding imagining literacy.

He insists that the monocultural bias of his earliest lists of what a literate person needs to know were not meant to exclude other cultural knowledges and need not necessarily do so, but the bias of his formula exists in the semiotics of his analysis and his prescription. "Other" cultural items can make up at most 10 percent of his list. If the purpose of cultural literacy is to transmit our common knowledge and there is no enabling literacy outside of this, then uncommon knowledge is a distraction, disabling because it robs us of time that could be used to absorb the essentials of common cultural literacy. Ten percent is all that these other cultural items may reasonably be allowed.

These prescriptions for cultural literacy have entered the larger debates surrounding education, race, and liberal politics in the form of a conservative attack on the term *multiculturalism*. William Bennett appropriated Hirsch's notions as support for his attack on curricular reform and the changing politics of university life, first at Stanford University and later at other colleges and universities around the country. This attack was carefully orchestrated by conservative think tanks that fostered the publication of an unprecedented series of articles in the popular media along with a series of influential books and a broadcast media parade of the individuals responsible for authoring these works. Although Hirsch insists that his concepts do not lead to the exclusion of the knowledges of the disenfranchised, the ease with which Bennett and others appropriated his notions for their political agenda belies that claim. This appropriation can be predicted from the semiotics of Hirsch's discourse.

Worse yet, uncommon knowledge—the knowledges of peoples, traditions, economic classes, and women, which are unrecorded or underrecorded in these great books and their corollaries—represents a structural problem because there is, at the moment, no clear answer to the question of how to collate disparate, often contradictory notions arising from the immense diversity of worldviews represented in these excluded epistemologies.

Cultural diversity and deep contextualization of knowledge are at issue when we discuss Hirsch's examination of the language of *The Black Panther*. Praising it for its "conservatism in literate knowledge and spelling" (Hirsch 1987:23) and citing this as evidence of mainstream cultural literacy, Hirsch points out that this revolutionary newspaper was not only meticulously edited but deployed common cultural terminology such as "free and indivisible," "milk and honey," "law and order," "bourgeois democracy," and the first five hundred words of Jefferson's Declaration of Independence without attribution. What he does not note is the ironic nature of the use of these terms or that they were often bracketed by quotation marks. What Hirsch does not do is include *The Black Panther* in his list of what literate Americans need to know or as an entry in his dictionary. Hirsch is happy for Patterson's support, but he does not take Patterson's description of a dynamic culture in dialectic seriously. If he did, he would have placed his examination of the Black Panther Party's newspaper within context as part of an American cultural revolution. Instead, he treats its product as severed from mainstream culture except insofar as it uses the language of that culture. The Black Panthers remain an accessory after the fact. Cultural literacy is a one-way street for Hirsch. His analysis of *The Black Panther*'s text is superficial and self-serving. Earlier, he admits that "the explicit words [of a text] are just surface pointers to textual meaning in reading and writing," something I have described previously, but when it comes to this instance, he feels free to point to the linguistic conservatism of this revolutionary newspaper without attention to the sophisticated ironies deliberately present in the periodical's use of "conservative" cultural markers. "Free and indivisible" and phrases like it are indeed "just surface pointers to textual meaning." Anyone reading this periodical without cultural and historical context would indeed misread it drastically. By page 18, Hirsch is staking out a territory that marginalizes "multicultural education" and valorizes "American literate culture" without the least critical awareness of a "wider literacy" that is already multicultural.

Another serious problem concerns the denied status of individuals who have not had the "opportunity" of growing up within the canonized cultural tradition. Research in the social class basis of literacy has pointed out that the home is a crucial setting for the acquisition of many skills that are necessarily a part of literacy. These skills are bound up in cultural experience but are not taught by schools and, indeed, may not even be possible to teach in anything resembling a traditional school curriculum. Hirsch claims his list can undo this disadvantage, but Shirley Brice Heath describes the explicit transmission of specific skills in the middle-class home as crucial to the development of certain school behaviors and skills. Working-class families often explicitly teach attitudes and behavior that *contradict* the assumptions of some school methodology. For example, exhortations from parents to "always tell the truth" can be a problem for working-class students who are asked in the school setting to imagine and create out of fantasy.

FROM CULTURAL LITERACY
TO TRICKSTER LITERACY

The discussions that follow emphasize excess as a principle of Disney theme parks and the Smithsonian Institution. Both Disney theme parks and the Smithsonian are manifest encyclopedias covertly delivering a metadiscourse that reinforces our national culture. The excess in these exercises serves to further their credibility. In contrast to the tyranny of the lists produced by encyclopedias, chapter 3 explores the maps contained in the literary texts of a select group of women of color in the United States. These maps cannot be encompassed in a list, which is at best a series of obscure addresses. An address without a mental map leaves you disoriented even after you have arrived. Women of color as a group are usually without the power to produce encyclopedias or the power to dictate curricula, but exploring the interiorized maps of the group of authors selected here can help us understand alternate imaginings of literacy. Not only are these alternate imaginings inclusive of uncommon knowledge, other cultural literacies, but they travel *between* these and the monocultural knowledge canonized by the Western intellectual tradition and reinscribed by Hirsch.

In a diverse culture, the ability to juggle common and uncommon knowledge is a result of a struggle to imagine literacy across the dissonance of clashing meanings. Because of their life circumstances, many individuals cannot maintain the illusion of coherent and unified lists. Many others find themselves similarly situated betwixt and between. What justifies the examination of a certain set of writers as a group, however, is the similarity of the skills and techniques they display, the common themes that surface and the surprisingly similar results. These authors possess common and uncommon knowledge. The results are interesting, complex, and fruitful. The results point toward knowledge organized not like an encyclopedia but like a map.

Three

READING TRICKSTER
WRITING

*Texts are devices for blowing up or narcotizing pieces of
information.*
—UMBERTO ECO, "DICTIONARY VS.
ENCYCLOPEDIA," IN *SEMIOTICS AND
THE PHILOSOPHY OF LANGUAGE*

GINGER ROOT LITERACY

Forty years ago American supermarkets did not generally
carry ginger root. To find it, a shopper had to visit an Asian food market.
Today it would be hard to find a major market that does not offer ginger
root alongside carrots and potatoes. Though many have not come into contact with rhizomes in nature, the iris rhizome being the model I recall from
my childhood, most have seen ginger root, if not eaten it. The appearance
of ginger root as a commonplace is a result of cuisines traveling with im-
migrants to this nation. Ginger is a rhizome. Organic structures without a
definable center or identifiable edges, rhizomes are capable of budding new
growth from any angle, and each bud can repeat that process. Rhizomes can
form intricate webs, webs that can double back on themselves, webs that
can create layer after layer of knotted growth. Rhizomes imply connection
and re-connection, not along a rigid hierarchy of bifurcation downward
or upward, like Bacon's tree of knowledge, but according to a plastic logic.
Indeed, purchasing ginger root often requires an active decision to sever the
root from itself, to make an arbitrary decision to isolate a portion and carry
it away to a kitchen where it will become invisible to the eye but not to the

tongue. Although most produce is countable—"one potato, two potato, three potato, four"—and Bacon's tree is an identifiable whole, a singular entity, ginger root has no beginning and no end. It cannot be viewed as a totality or described as a limited territory. Only portions of it can be isolated and manipulated.

Ginger root, then, can be a powerful image for understanding the structure of knowledge. Remember, Umberto Eco tells us that "the universe of semiosis, that is, the universe of human culture, must be conceived" to be analogous to a labyrinth or net, sometimes taking the form of a vegetative rhizome. A rhizome is an unlimited and infinitely expandable territory. It enables connections between elements and positions. New neighborhoods spring up overnight. Unlike Bacon's tree of knowledge, the rhizome's plastic nature suits our historical period. It is an excellent visual model for an imagining of literacy that is based not on lists and trees of knowledge but on rhizomatic maps, a model for an organic mixed cultural literacy that allows for the concatenation of multiple local knowledges.

Rhizomatic theorizing does not lend itself to listing theses in a rigid hierarchical order. Instead, the multiple theses of this chapter are nested according to a thematic and associative logic. Like traveling on a rhizomatic network, reading this requires patience and the willingness to wait for the next node and the evolution of the next connection. Questioning the ideological bases of literacy definition and its circular and solipsistic tendencies in the earlier chapters has led to an associative model for understanding literacy. Its themes include discussions of reading practices; nets, maps, and rhizomes of knowledge; geographies of literacy; mixed cultures and travel across local knowledges; narrative as an encoding of literacy and the figure of the trickster as a sign of the meaning of language.

READING AND WRITING MAPS, NOT LISTS

Turning from encyclopedias to mapping, from listing to reading, from reading as a technique to reading as a practice, from addresses [1] to traveling, from monocultural literacy to mixed cultural literacy, this chapter places reading and cultural mixing at the center of the literacy discussion. The encyclopedic impulse must be balanced by its counterpoint: the impulse to travel across local knowledges, making a map as you go, weaving a net of connections as you meander and discover. Reading practices are not about creating a canon of knowledge; they are about entering a rhizomatic web of meaning created through association. Reading practices cannot be fixed, texts are not static lumps yielding to invariant decoding. Placing reading at the center of this discussion may seem simpleminded in the extreme, but Hirsch and a multitude of others, not to mention virtually all dominant pedagogies addressing illiteracy, emphasize reading *techniques,* not reading *practices.* They do not emphasize intensive exposure to books or any other texts or sources of information. Instead, they discuss barriers to decoding and prescribe improved methods for inculcating decoding skills. For example, E. D. Hirsch Jr. identifies cultural illiteracy as the cause of disabled reading and bemoans this cultural illiteracy as the logical result of the kind of reading assigned in the early grades, especially textbooks that have been stripped of cultural richness. Who would want to argue against those positions? What he does not do is concretely discuss the necessity of broad and extensive reading as a basis for literacy. He, like most, nods briefly in this direction and then turns his energy to the development of his lists and his dictionaries.

In contrast, literate readers and writers display a fluency that is the result of exposure not to lumpy lists but to webs of information and insights collected as the result of personal experience and exposure to texts. These webs are woven out of wide exposure to a potentially infinite set of texts. These texts are produced out of not just what we understand as "ethnic" cultures but all subsets of knowledge and expertise.

Knowledge of a wide assortment of multicultural texts and all knowledge subsets is critical for literacy in the contemporary world. Fluency in a time of accelerated cultural mixing and dramatic scientific and technological change demands flexibility. Gregory Colomb has observed that students already know that movement between communities of knowledge requires "the skills of an ethnographer and the flexibility of a spy." Studying how fluency is manifested in the writings of individuals forced to inhabit multiple cultures can help us to uncover strategies for literacy that face away from listing and toward more powerful pedagogies.

LITERARY GEOGRAPHIES OF LITERACY

One major stream of literacy theory has taken as its methodology ethnographic description. Researchers such as Shirley Brice Heath and Brian Street have given us methods of study that move away from prescription toward description. If encyclopedists have attempted to collect the universe of knowledge into a prescription (i.e., implicit in the encyclopedia is the exhortation to know it), ethnographers of literacy have attempted to describe individuals and their literacy practices as models for analysis and emulation. For example, writing research has recently studied the practices of skilled writers and extrapolated from those practices suggested pedagogies that are antithetical to traditional assumptions regarding the teaching of writing. In this view, some of students' most unproductive writing strategies are almost certainly the result of primary and secondary school pedagogical errors, e.g., a student's need to create a perfect first draft is obviously reinforced by the requirements of the essay exam and other common pedagogical methods. In contrast, research into writing instruction that describes the professional writing process as including numerous revisions has helped change pedagogy by providing a more realistic and helpful model for teachers and students.

What follows is an attempt to invent an analogous technique, one that centers on the traces of a literacy practice embedded in a text or texts. Traditional notions of what it means to be well educated and a scholar have tended to point to individuals as exemplary models for emulation. Abraham Lincoln studying by candlelight or Malcolm X memorizing the dictionary while incarcerated have become prescriptive archetypes for intellectual development. This theory echoes this notion by using texts as models, shifting the literacy discussion away from simple decoding skills or even individuals as models. If Bakhtin is right in believing that fictions encode heteroglossias, which are, of course, multilayered dictionaries, then they are especially useful texts.

Addressing the encoded literacies of fiction shifts imaginings of literacy away from personality and archetype toward webs of knowledge. Instead of the writer's observable writing process[2] providing clues to literate practices, a literary geography of literacy focuses on the textual product. The text provides clues to the net of knowledge out of which it is made. A text first comes into physical existence as a result of an author's struggle to make a record. That struggle cannot be waged outside of a rhizomatic net of understanding.

Constructed out of portions of that net, the text is woven out of an author's knowledge, an author's literacy. No human has meticulous conscious access to his/her personal encyclopedia of knowledge. The result is that a text is consciously and unconsciously woven out of its author's net of knowledge. A text does not represent that net, but it is rewoven out of portions of the author's particular map of knowledge. Identifying the traces of this net results in a kind of literary geography.

Despite their intent, poststructuralist theories of reading and writing have reproduced dualisms. They have tended to treat the writer/author, text, reader as inert objects. The invention of the text as an object of study has served to repress awareness of the complex relationship between the writer/ author and reader. Focusing on the text as a discursive space that includes the active dynamic between the writer/author and the reader represents one way of invigorating a static object. This can stimulate useful insights.

In this theory, author and reader appear as reciprocal agents in the creation of text. For this reason, the text cannot be fixed, but neither is it entirely elusive. The text is *one* site where meaning is made. Or to put it another way, the text exists as material artifact, an ambiguous record of a wider semiotic process that is constantly in play. That wider process is what Eco has called, rather vaguely, the semiosis of human culture. The author/ writer-text-reader are only one nexus of that semiosis.

The author scratches out a text that records traces of his/her net. Similarly, a reader comes to a text and struggles to decode these scratches, these traces. The author's literacy and the reader's literacy come into contact indirectly at the material site of the text. Reading and writing occur simultaneously from both directions and by both parties. In play are the author's literacy as writer and reader of his/her own scratches and the reader's literacy as reader and active rewriter of the text. Theory seems to be silent on the reading aspect of the author's relation to his/her text. Questions about what is going on during these moments of multiple collision between writer as reader and reader as writer can never be resolved, but ignoring this profound but invisible interior play only serves to further mystify the communicative process. It removes agency from the humans involved, and it places a material artifact, the text, in a position of ascendancy while simultaneously questioning that materiality. This textual nihilism abandons any commitment to communication as a moral exercise.

The erasure of agency produces no payoff; instead, we should reach for a theory that assumes agency produces a system we can analyze. We need to study how individuals are tied together or thrown apart while reading and writing texts. Texts are not produced by God the Father in divine revelation; they are produced, consumed, and contested by human beings. Part of that process is individual: one being struggling with one blank surface at a time. Part of that process is collective: individuals creating texts together as writers and readers. This theory of reading examines texts as sites where authors and readers simultaneously occupy multiple, overlapping dimensions in a hall of mirrors that challenges our notions of a stable reality.

Foucault's claim that the "name of the author" is "produced by the practices whose reproduction it guarantees and that this 'name' turns a collection of discursive practices into a coherent realm" (Pease 1990:113)[3] is friendly to this position. Examining this realm is examining a collection of practices that are a record of literacy practices. Hence the commonplace evaluation "This is a literate text." Mining a text this way is practicing a literary geography of literacy.

Within the text, one can read the methodologies of a particular literacy. Diderot attempted to mediate between the tree of knowledge and the semiosis of the rhizome through the creation of an encyclopedia that would create a list while implying a web, but a text is constructed out of a web. The theoretical encyclopedia (not the actual text of the encyclopedia, which is as semantically rich as any text) represents a narrow and impoverished lens, but a literature can be offered as an alternative.

By approaching a series of texts as alternate representations of multiple universes of knowledge, this notion implicitly redirects literary criticism away from narrow textual interpretation and toward description of the literacy of the author indirectly through the text. This is a kind of historicist impulse. The text becomes a place of meeting, and this theoretical method is an argument for a particular kind of reading. Not the traditional close reading, but rather a reading that searches for the formal elements of the concatenation of knowledges in a text.

It does not propose a Hirschian reading technique rooted in the consultation of a dictionary. Instead, it presupposes that understanding and literacy can be fostered by reading practices consciously rooted in the examination of the text's semiosis. Literary geographies of literacy should provide a series of maps that, when added to one another, define literacy as an open field of possibility, not a closed field of prescription.

Literary geographies of literacy, like Eco's rhizome, have no center and no edges. They implicitly cross boundaries, cross local knowledges. They concatenate. While the encyclopedia is closed and fixed, a succession of texts may be seen as an endlessly open field of possibility. The potential benefits of this theory may extend our understanding of literacy beyond narrow cultural and conceptual boundaries and toward increased awareness of the mixed cultural literacies actually in active play all around us. To practice literary ethnography of literacy means to learn a method of close reading that asks the questions, What are the literacies in operation in the text before us? How does the text challenge our reading skills and literacy? How are the author's practices as a concatenator of local knowledges both visible and invisible? To what extent does the reader's literacy overlap the author's? What happens when chasms open up between these literacies?

What does it mean to possess a map of understanding instead of an encyclopedia? How can it be established that such maps actually exist? How can those maps be identified and described? How do those maps imply connections between local knowledges? How can it be possible to move from one local knowledge to another?

MIXED CULTURAL LITERACY

Because rhizomes have no absolute center, they cannot be described globally. They must be described as "a potential sum of local descriptions." The dragon from Maxine Hong Kingston's *Woman Warrior* can never be described locally because it expresses this potential sum. It is at once local and global.[4] Each node on the rhizome, each scale on the dragon, is a manifestation of a locality that might roughly be linked to a culture with some recognizable integrity: "Every culture has a strongly organized 'center' and a more fuzzy 'periphery,' and in order to change its central concepts, one must expect a radical scientific revolution" (Eco 1984b:85).

Thinking in such a labyrinth "means to *grope one's way.*"

> *A notion of encyclopedia does not deny the existence of structured knowledge; it only suggests that such a knowledge cannot be recognized and organized as a global system; it provides only "local" and transitory systems of knowledge, which can be contradicted by alternative and equally "local" cultural organizations; every attempt to recognize these local organizations as unique and "global"—ignoring their partiality—produces an ideological bias. (84)*

What kinds of mental travel does this imply and what are its costs? What "languages" are necessary for such travel?

Definitions of an idealized monocultural literacy seek to limit knowledge to a finite list that is vigorously bifurcated into discrete disciplines, discrete subcategories, discrete semantic units, and finally collect these units into lists in dictionaries and encyclopedias. The practice of mixed cultural literacy recognizes no such discrete bifurcation. Words mean and things exist simultaneously in many dimensions at once. They have multiple origins. At each moment, a word, a phrase, a concept, an artifact, which is a material manifestation of a concept, represent overlapping, even competing meanings. Making sense of this requires extraordinary skills not even hinted at in the familiar descriptions of literacy.

Millions of Americans use such skills to make it through each day's challenges. They speak one language to their grandmother, another to their teacher. They eat one cuisine at breakfast, another at lunch, and at dinner they mix three or four. They metamorphose through the day. They just do it. Describing their practices can give us an alternate image of literacy.

Toni Morrison's *Nobel Lecture in Literature, 1993* begins with the sentence "Narrative has never been merely entertainment for me. It is, I believe, one of the principal ways in which we absorb knowledge" (7). If Morrison is correct, any literature would serve as an interesting counterpoint to Hirsch's encyclopedic-based imaginings of literacy, but the works of Zora Neale Hurston, Toni Morrison, Leslie Marmon Silko, and Maxine Hong Kingston provide contrast at several levels. Their work illustrates how escape from a monocultural dictionary into a mixed cultural map fundamentally changes the structure of how we imagine what is important and necessary. Obviously, the politics of the exclusion of the alternate knowledges represented in the work of these women of color adds to the usefulness of the comparison.

As Bakhtin has made clear, any literature is a mixed cultural literature. The reading and writing practices of the authors discussed here point toward broad and deep exposure across many local knowledges. This mapping is one heuristic, one method of analysis that serves precise purposes. It should not be literalized. The ways in which these texts do not fall together are not of interest to this text's purpose. Suffice it to say that they are as varied as the cultures they represent and more so. Attempts to break open our vision of the literacies operating in a text will look strange at first. They will almost certainly be misunderstood.

Can the texts that follow point toward concatenated knowledge, one that takes the postmodern movement as just another local knowledge and weaves a still more complex net connecting it with other knowledges? Can these texts provide clues regarding how some individuals concatenate "minority" cultural knowledges, Western canonical knowledge, canonical Western literary knowledge, postmodern realities, the knowledges of speculative fiction and fantasy, and more? If these discourses represent clashing local knowledges, concatenating them is bound to outrage some. Call it one example of trickster literacy.

THE POLITICAL AS LITERATURE

Deleuze and Guattari tell us that, in a minor literature, individual dramas become political rather than oedipal, as in a great literature. What does this mean? These two theorists put their collective finger on an important aspect of minority literature, but Joanna Russ has more to say on this issue:

> *The problem of "outsider" artists is the whole problem of*
> *what to do with unlabeled, disallowed, disavowed, not-even-*
> *consciously-perceived experience, experience which cannot be*
> *spoken about because it has no embodiment in existing art. . . .*
> *Outsiders' writing is always in critical jeopardy. Insiders know*
> *perfectly well that art ought to match their ideas of it. . . . Science*
> *fiction, political fiction, parable, allegory, exemplum—all carry*
> *a heavier intellectual freight (and self-consciously so) than we*
> *are used to. All are didactic. All imply that human problems*
> *are collective, as well as individual, and take these problems to*
> *be spiritual, social, perceptive, or cognitive—not the fictionally*
> *sex-linked problems of success, competition, castration, educa-*
> *tion, love, or even personal identity with which we are all so*
> *familiar. . . . Our current fictional myths leave vast areas of*
> *human experience unexplored: work for one, genuine religious*
> *experience for another, and above all the lives of the traditionally*
> *voiceless, the vast majority of whom are women. . . . I am*
> *talking about . . . fictional myths growing out of their lives*
> *and told by themselves for themselves. (Russ 1978:160−163)*

Indeed, the problem of what to with "outsider" cultural knowledge is intrinsic to definitions of literacy, as we have already seen. As Cornel West has implied, knowledge is for politics' sake when you find yourself with someone's boot on your neck. Awareness of collectivity and community is necessarily a preoccupation of outsider art. And Henry Louis Gates Jr. makes the point that "precisely because successive Western cultures have privileged written art over oral or musical forms, the writing of black people in Western languages has, at all points, remained political, implicitly or explicitly, regardless of its intent or subject" (Gates 1988:132).

In what way do the stories of the traditionally voiceless become political (and, I would counter, therefore great)? The answer: they are political without effort. If your voice is oppositional by virtue of its position in the larger drama, then it is axiomatic that your text will be a kind of sword unless you deliberately disarm yourself.[5] Your literacy is at the service of your politics. You do not have to be a revolutionary for this to be so. Hirsch's literacy is clearly at the service of his politics, as is William Bennett's.

Making language serve revolution requires great strength. It taxes the body to its limits and challenges the spirit. Chapter 2 of *The Woman Warrior,* "White Tigers," is set both in the mountains of China and in Kingston's American home. A multiple-voiced text, "White Tigers" slips seamlessly from Kingston's adult voice into the voice of a female child who is being trained to make revolution in the name of justice. "White Tigers" begins with Kingston's warrior woman waiting to be called by a bird into the mountains. The movement from Kingston's Stockton, California, home to this imagined mystical training ground is signaled by a tense shift from the simple past, "I remembered," to the future conditional, "I would . . ." and "The call would . . ." Kingston wrote drafts in several different tenses. In this text, tense mirrors the simultaneous occupation of multiple locations. This might confuse the reader, or it might pass unnoticed, or both. In any case, it is one signal that inhabiting multiple locations requires special linguistic skills. In this passage, Kingston's voice mingles with the Woman Warrior's. "She" has traveled across knowledges.

> *Instantly I remembered that as a child I had followed my mother about the house, the two of us singing about how Fa Mu Lan fought gloriously. . . . I would have to grow up a warrior woman.*
>
> *The call would come from a bird that flew over our roof. In the brush drawings it looks like the ideograph for "human," two black wings. The bird would cross the sun and lift into the mountains (which look like the ideograph "mountain"). . . . I would be a little girl of seven the day I followed the bird away into the mountains. . . . The clouds would gray the world like an ink wash.*
>
> *Even when I got used to that gray, I would only see peaks as if shaded in pencil, rocks like charcoal rubbings. . . . There would be just two black strokes—the bird. Inside the clouds— inside the dragon's breath—I would not know how many hours or days passed. Suddenly, without noise, I would break clear into a yellow, warm world. New trees would lean toward me at mountain angles, but when I looked for the village, it would have vanished under the clouds. (20)*

Code switching enables this passage to signal border crossing from one system to another. The child who is to become the Woman Warrior has left the village behind. Now she will be trained in another epistemology, one that insists that magic is a manifestation of the power of the earth mixed with the power of a human to know. Form and content are expressing the necessary travel that everyone must undertake to learn alternate knowledges.

The bird and the landscape of China are metonyms for Chinese calligraphy and landscape painting. The Woman Warrior's vengeance and sword inhere in the calligraphic and painted representations suggested by the above description. The landscape is a form of writing that is imagined through the classic representations of Chinese brush painting, itself iconic of a writing system that is also an artistic discipline. The black ideograph and the gray shadings of traditional landscape painting are a subtle commentary and critique of the nature of representation. Kingston's imaginings of China were probably influenced by the Chinese art she had been exposed to in America, since she had not yet visited China when she wrote *The Woman Warrior*. Much like Hsiang's dreams of the territory around his tower, the landscape melts into culture. "The bird, now gold so close to the sun, would come to rest on the thatch of a hut, which, until the bird's two feet touched it, was camouflaged as part of the mountainside" (25).

This tornado of code switching from childhood memory to mythical China to mythical being and back to childhood and then adult American self is accomplished without transition or marking. The absence of marking creates a subtle signal of confusion. This absence is meant to draw attention to itself.

The Woman Warrior knows that the polite answer to the greeting "Have you eaten rice today, little girl?" is always yes. The double-voiced text inserts an aside within parentheses:

> *("No, I haven't," I would have said in real life, mad at the Chinese for lying so much. "I'm starved. Do you have any cookies? I like chocolate chip cookies.") (25)*

Who speaks these lines? Kingston provides no explanation for the juxtaposition of multiple selves, multiple voices, speaking from multiple locations. The local knowledges are just smashed up against one another, creating confusions for readers not steeped in trickster writing.

> *"Have you eaten rice today, little girl?" they greeted me.*
> *"Yes, I have," I said out of politeness. "Thank you."*
> *("No, I haven't," I would have said in real life, mad at the Chinese for lying so much. "I'm starved. Do you have any cookies? I like chocolate chip cookies.") (25)*

Rice or chocolate chip cookies. Why not both? Only those who are not ready to concatenate local knowledges would refuse the combination. Teaching readers to pay attention to these moments in texts can help them understand mixed cultural literacy, can help them acquire it.

After fifteen years of training, the Woman Warrior returns home to her family.

> *In the morning my parents woke me and asked that I come with them to the family hall. "Stay in your nightclothes," my mother said. "Don't change yet." She was holding a basin, a towel, and a kettle of hot water. My father had a bottle of wine, an ink block and pens, and knives of various sizes. "Come with us," he said. They had stopped the tears with which they had greeted me. Forebodingly I caught a smell—metallic, the iron smell of blood, as when a woman gives birth, as at the sacrifice of a large animal, as when I menstruated and dreamed red dreams.*
>
> *My mother put a pillow on the floor before the ancestors. "Kneel here," she said. "Now take off your shirt." I kneeled with my back to my parents so none of us felt embarrassed. My mother washed my back as if I had left for only a day and were her baby yet. "We are going to carve revenge on your back," my father said. "We'll write out oaths and names."*
>
> *"Wherever you go, whatever happens to you, people will know our sacrifice," my mother said. "And you'll never forget either." She meant that even if I got killed, the people could use my dead body for a weapon, but we do not like to talk out loud about dying.*
>
> *My father first brushed the words in ink, and they fluttered down my back row after row. Then he began cutting; to make fine lines and points he used thin blades, for the stems, large blades.*
>
> *My mother caught the blood and wiped the cuts with a cold towel soaked in wine. It hurt terribly—the cuts sharp; the air burning; the alcohol cold, then hot—pain so various. I gripped my knees. I released them. Neither tension nor relaxation helped. I wanted to cry. If not for the fifteen years of training, I would have writhed on the floor; I would have had to be held down. The list of grievances went on and on. If an enemy*

should flay me, the light would shine through my skin like lace.
(34–35)

Even if the Woman Warrior were killed, her dead body could be used as a weapon. In these five paragraphs, language is no abstraction. Words are embodied, although a high price must be paid. The political body is inscribed. Language and bodies intertwined become a tool for revolution. Red, the color of good fortune in Chinese culture, here signals the blood she will soon lose, multiple sacrifices to come, and her ultimate success. Discreetly, the Woman Warrior hides her breasts from her parents. Her now obviously gendered body is tenderly cared for by the body that engendered it. In this key passage, an embodied and enacted literacy serves politics. A serious business, literacy draws blood.

Her skin separates under the ink and knives, and red runs from the gaps opened in her body. Rinsed away by her mother, the blood recalls iron; the wine creates hot and cold pain. Blood and iron, flesh and knife, brush and ink. The words create an absence, opening the surface of her body like a web. "If an enemy should flay me, the light would shine through my skin like lace." The words carved into the Woman Warrior's back are indelible. Her back could be skinned and held up like a scroll. These signs encode historical pain and suffering even as they cause it. More importantly, they are incontestible evidence of injustice, evidence that the body, gendered or not, encased as it is in culture, is made into an agent of power by culture. Naked bodies cannot just be: they are powerful signs. Even the Woman Warrior's inert body could be used as a weapon; it would fairly scream revenge. It must be disintegrated to be silenced, and then even the gap produced by its destruction can be experienced.[6]

Words are carved on our skins by patriarch and matriarch alike. Institutions mark the human body over and over. The carving is a political act, and in this way, language and our bodies are melted together, the politics of their production omnipresent and thereby rendered nearly invisible. In Toni Morrison's *Beloved,* the former slave Sethe wears a "chokecherry tree" on her back, the result of a brutal beating. Sethe knows that it is a powerful inscription, which records a ruling event of her life. Eighteen years after her husband, Halle, disappears without a trace instead of joining her in freedom, Sethe learns that he witnessed not just her beating but the slavemaster's sons suckling milk meant for her infant girl. Like the Woman Warrior's inscriptions, Sethe's chokecherry tree of a back signifies the physical cruelty of enslavement.

The reporting of such acts can be the vengeance; the words can be our swords. So Sethe is aware of her inscribed body as a totem of both her slavery and her defiance. Attaining voice, attaining literacy, can be a revolutionary act because it enables vengeance. Reporting the crimes, reporting the "chink" words, the "gook" words, is an act of deterritorialization. The following passage appears at the end of "White Tigers."

> The swordswoman and I are not so dissimilar. May my people understand the resemblance soon so that I can return to them. What we have in common are the words at our backs. The ideographs for revenge are "report a crime" and "report to five families." The reporting is the vengeance—not the beheading, not the gutting, but the words. And I have so many words— "chink" words and "gook" words too—that they do not fit on my skin. (63)

Is there a more extreme example of the embodied nature of knowledge? This version of literacy does not see words as abstractions on a page. Language has physical manifestation in a world where nature and culture melt into one another. Words and skin are indistinguishable. Colonizing language territorializes the body; deterritorializing language attempts a revolution enacted on and through the body. Indeed, there are too many words to fit on her skin. The job is too big for one back. The racist insults hurled at Kingston's back are burnished into it and extend beyond it. They damage, but words provide other possibilities. Deterritorialized language can provide "a wall at our backs." Literacy can provide a defense.

The red and black of Kingston's "White Tigers" call to mind Gloria Anzaldúa's "Tlilli, Tlapalli, the Path of Red and Black Ink," a chapter in *Borderlands/La Frontera*. For Anzaldúa, writing brings to mind the red and black earth. Writing requires the creation of flesh; bones must be covered. Writing is a girl-child "forced to grow up too quickly, rough, unyielding, with pieces of feather sticking out here and there, fur, twigs, clay. . . . This female being is . . . a flawed thing . . . alive, infused with spirit. I talk to it; it talks to me" (66–67). For Gloria Anzaldúa, words also become a sword reporting crimes and providing a bridge over the war zone. "Shock yourself into new ways of perceiving the world, shock your readers into the same. Stop the chatter inside their heads," she tells other writers (Anzaldúa 1983:172).

For Hurston, the politics are embedded in the particulars of the sexism and racism that one woman's life reveals in *Their Eyes Were Watching God*. For Silko, the politics of war and genocide are written on the body of a mestizo who is curiously more Laguna Pueblo than the full-bloods he grows up among in *Ceremony*. All four of these texts make clear the relation of individuals caught in a symbolic environment of language to embodied political struggles.

THE COLLECTIVE AS A PLACE OF SOLIDARITY: THE BORDER, A HOMELAND FOR *LA MESTIZA*

For all four of these writers, community represents a ground from which to speak. For Kingston, the village, her clansmen and -women, have been transplanted to Stockton, California. She is aware that her inheritance culturally and spiritually cannot be separated from the persons and events in her family's native village in China. Indeed, Kingston's three novels, taken together, identify multiple homelands: her parents' village in southern China; her great-grandfather's virtual slavery in Hawaii, "The Sandalwood Mountains"; her grandfather's sacrifices building the transcontinental railway, "The Grandfather of the Sierra Nevada Mountains"; her pirate uncle and father who came to the United States through Cuba; her black grandmother from Nicaragua; Stockton, Los Angeles, Berkeley, and San Francisco, California, "The Gold Mountain." All these are Kingston's homeland. All these provide one or more local knowledges for her digestion.

Kingston begins her first book by disobeying her mother's instructions not to reveal family secrets from their ancestral village. *The Woman Warrior* breaks this taboo, ending a generation of silence by rewriting her aunt's scandal. Silence can kill. Words can wound. Tricksters play with this double realization. In a "literate" culture, to attain voice is to attain the power to read and write beyond the personal sphere. Kingston's personal attainment of voice is chronicled indirectly in the book's stitched-together stories of her aunts, the Woman Warrior, her mother, other Chinese American girls of her generation, the poet Ts'ai Yen, and herself. Her personal story is grounded not only in those stories of a distant "home" but also in her awareness of the house and laundry in which she spent her childhood. There is a distinct texture to her descriptions of these locations versus the public spaces of the Anglo street and school. She chronicles her movement between these chronotopes. Each shimmers; each is translucent to the others. All of this provides a tropological homeland for Kingston, a place from which she can speak for herself and others. Kingston's *Tripmaster Monkey: His Fake Book* takes multiple homelands to be a given from the first paragraph.

Tropologically claiming these multiple locations, Kingston puts into play a concatenation of knowledges. Her language, her voice, benefits immensely from this. By describing these chronotopes in successive novels, Kingston liberates her language(s), creates a matrix for the inscription of her trickster literacy. In fact, she has stated that it was only in *Tripmaster Monkey* that she was able to put into play all her language(s). Collected together, these languages "cap" on one another, "play the dozens" on each other, revealing that no "language [can] claim to be an authentic, incontestible face." The clash of local knowledges against other local knowledges is recorded throughout Kingston's work.

Multiple languages also express multiple knowledges in Zora Neale Hurston's work. Hurston's recollections of her hometown in Florida, recreated in her fictional town Eatonville, and its vernacular are contrasted with the elegant style of the novel's free indirect discourse. As an anthropologist, Hurston devoted most of her professional life to the recording of Black folk knowledge. In *Their Eyes Were Watching God,* Hurston creates a chronotope and then records its local knowledge in text. She creates a time and space complete with a set of codes, underscoring how language can create a territory from which to speak. Compare these two selections from the beginning and end of the novel:

> *Ships at a distance have every man's wish on board. For some they come in with the tide. For others they sail forever on the horizon, never out of sight, never landing until the Watcher turns his eyes away in resignation, his dreams mocked to death by Time. That is the life of men.*
>
> *Now, women forget all those things they don't want to remember, and remember everything they don't want to forget. The dream is the truth. Then they act and do things accordingly. (1)*

> *"Let 'em consolate theyselves wid talk. 'Course talkin' don't amount tuh uh hill uh beans when yuh can't do nothin' else. And listenin' tuh dat kind uh talk is jus' lak openin' yo' mouth and lettin' de moon shine down yo' throat." (183)*

The contrast between these two registers of language, the double-voicedness of the novel, constitutes a borderland. Oscillating between the standard English of the literary tradition she had absorbed and her childhood vernacular, Hurston identifies a borderland of language. The novel's opening lines, "Ships at a distance," signal a series of gendered preoccupations: "every man's wish," "his eyes," "That is the life of men." Because we have been taught to read *man* and *men* as linguistically inclusive of *woman* and *women*, we may make easy assumptions about the implications of this first paragraph, but the second paragraph prevents us from making this mistake by presenting a clear distinction between male and female dreams. While male dreams are "mocked to death by Time" (with a capital *T*) women can dream the truth, although not necessarily the Truth. At the outset, the novel indicates that it will create a series of divisions and divisions within divisions.

Janie, the novel's central character, can attain voice only after she has come to realize that "she had an inside and an outside now and suddenly she knew how not to mix them up" (68). The road to this realization dictated that she endure years of domination from her husband, years of obedience to his silencing demands. It is only after he kills the love she has for him that she comes to understand her own self-division into an outside and an inside. Barbara Johnson summarizes the importance of self-division within *Their Eyes* in this way:

> If "unification and simplification" is the privilege and province of the male, it is also, in America, the privilege and province of the white. If the woman's voice, to be authentic, must incorporate and articulate division and self-difference, so too, has Afro-American literature always had to assume its double-voicedness. (Johnson 1984:214)[7]

Johnson makes a detailed case for self-division as a necessary founding principle for a woman's voice.

To Johnson's astute observation I would add that from multiply voiced texts we can learn something about the complex negotiations that individuals must make when they switch not just registers of voice but local knowledges. Johnson makes the point that somehow division enables expression. Trickster literacy implies that division between cultures enables a certain kind of expression, a culturally mixed voice. This voice is created out of the matrix of the clash of cultures just as Janie's voice comes out of her realization that she has an inside and an outside and how not to mix them up. It is the awareness of the division and the struggle to somehow bridge that division that enables voice.

> Far from being an expression of Janie's new wholeness or identity as a character, Janie's increasing ability to speak grows out of

> *her ability not to mix inside with outside, not to pretend that*
> *there is no difference, but to assume and articulate the incom-*
> *patible forces involved in her own division. The sign of an*
> *authentic voice is thus not self-identity but self-difference.*
> *(Johnson 1984 : 212)*

The vernacular language of the passage from the end of the novel is Janie's. She is commenting on the local gossip surrounding the final incidents in the book. Regularized by males in the public spaces of the town, gossip can "consolate," but it cannot deliver. This discourse delivers an emptiness equivalent to "lettin' de moon shine down yo' throat." This discourse is represented by cold light, a light that cannot deliver nourishment. Gossip is one discourse Janie has had to learn as just one discourse used for a specific end. Gossip elides into folklore in the community Hurston is describing. But it is Janie's acceptance of the binding and consoling nature of language that allows her to accept her ritual alienation from her community. "Let 'em consolate theyselves wid talk." Let competing representations circulate. Janie does not attempt to counter her community's version of the narrative; in this way, she is able to declare a truce.

Hurston's novel demonstrates a sophisticated awareness of the importance of mastering multiple knowledges, learning to be at home in all of them and learning how to bring each into play at the appropriate time for the appropriate use. Janie understands the discourse of gossip in her town, and she is aware that this discourse cannot represent the specificity of her experience.

> *"It's uh known fact, Pheoby, you got tuh go there tuh know*
> *there. Yo' papa and yo' mama and nobody else can't tell yuh*
> *and show yuh. Two things everybody's got to do fuh theyselves.*
> *They got tuh go tuh God, and they got tuh find out about*
> *livin' fuh theyselves." (183)*

Janie knows she has mastered a number of knowledges outside the experience of this community. She has traveled as a trickster travels, encountering other tricksters, learning her lessons well.

The setting of Hurston's story always presupposes immersion, even encirclement in a particular place. From the home of her grandmother, to her first husband's home, to Eatonville, the town her second husband virtually owns, Janie is limited by a series of chronotopes from which she cannot escape. The moment Barbara Johnson identifies as key, the moment Janie recognizes that she has an inside and an outside, that there are separate systems of knowledge and understanding and that she knows several, lays the foundation for her acceptance of her ritualized banishment. Janie can understand that one system cannot always encapsulate the insights of the other. She has acquired a trickster's perspective.

As Johnson tells us, the movement from metaphor to metonym in the novel is mirrored in Janie's ability to match her image of her marriage to the rooms of her house. Janie's house becomes a metonymic device for her self-division and her ironic ability to articulate. Her love for Jody moves outward from the private space of the bedroom to the public space of the living room. But always this description is based on a conception of Janie's home (211). In other words, Janie's house is still another chronotope echoing Eatonville as chronotope. Out of Janie's increased awareness of both comes her ability to articulate. Janie's language, Hurston's language, claim spaces out of which they can articulate self-division, multiplicity, and paradox. This relation to language is critical to trickster literacy, to the ability to move across a net of clashing local knowledges.

In Hurston's, Kingston's, Anzaldúa's, and Silko's texts, home, language, and voice are inextricable.[8] Literacy cannot be separated from a history. While words are burnished into the Woman Warrior's skin, Kingston's classmate growing up in Stockton has great difficulty speaking in public. Speech becomes possible for Janie because of her identification of self with a physical place, her home, and her body ensconced in that home. "A woman's place is in the home" becomes "a woman's self articulates out of a tropological home." In all these cases, literacy writes itself on the body and thereby remakes the world. Imagining literacy is imagining self and the body, encased *and* liberated.

In her novel *Ceremony,* Leslie Marmon Silko inverts this notion that self is articulated out of home. The novel takes as its subject the alienation of an Anglo and Laguna Pueblo mestizo who has never been allowed to claim his reservation as a home and who cannot survive outside it. Tayo's homelessness almost entirely denies him language in the beginning of the novel. A World War II veteran, he suffers from "battle fatigue" that results in a catatonic silence. As mestizo, Tayo cannot even claim rights to the traditional healing ceremony he so desperately needs. Whenever he tries to articulate what has caused his breakdown, he becomes violently ill. Vomit replaces voice in a man who has no ground on which to stand, no community that will claim him. "He didn't know how to explain what had happened. . . . 'I'm sick,' he said, turning away from the old man to vomit. 'I'm sick, but I never killed any enemy'" (36).

The first extended speech Tayo makes comes some time after the medicine man Ku'oosh performs "the Scalp ceremony." "I'm half-breed. I'll be the first to say it. I'll speak for both sides" (42). This is a major step for Tayo. What tumbles out of his mouth is something his full-blood friends, all veterans, do not want to hear. The war had given them a temporary sense of belonging to the nation-state. As long as they wore a uniform and the war raged, they were respected, white women valued them, military paychecks gave them a false sense of prosperity and inclusion. Now it was all gone, the intensity of the racism they experienced had returned, and with it "that feeling they belonged to America the way they felt during the war" (43).

Tayo, the most displaced of the group, the one whose light-skinned body and hazel eyes express cultural mixing, can see what the others cannot. As a half-breed, he is aware that he speaks out of self-division and for both sides. It gives him the power to say what the others do not see and cannot articulate. "They blamed themselves. . . . They never thought to blame the white people for any of it" (43). Tayo goes on to perform an extended healing ceremony, one that places him at the center of his world.

By the end of the novel, Tayo has claimed a home, carved out a borderland on the reservation, a place that he can claim as his own. His voice not only returns, contextualized against his newly claimed homeland and empowered as never before, but it has serious import for his community. The tribal elders hang on his every word, asking him to repeat his story again and again. Tayo's words are becoming part of tribal myth; he has become the center of his world, a storyteller.

The connection between home and voice makes sense when viewed as a manifestation of the power of local knowledge and the semiotics of making meaning against a web of associations. Words can mean only against a network of similarity and difference; those who are exiled from a tropological homeland cannot make meaning out of context. What individuals have to say and the meanings they make out of bits of information must be contextualized. Perhaps this explains the pedagogical principle around which writing teachers have often structured courses: student writers must begin with autobiographical expressions of self-origin; only then can they develop a stylistically effective voice. Voice and literacy are inextricably tied to one another against a web of meaning.

For Anzaldúa, home is a particular place, the *Tejas*-Mexican border and this topos, this Borderland, becomes a trope for the space inhabited by *la mestiza*. The concept of a Borderland invites occupation by an expanded community. The concept of the new mestiza allows Anzaldúa to express solidarity with a larger community, to do exactly what Deleuze and Guattari suggest may be done:

*If the writer is in the margins or completely outside his or her
fragile community, this situation allows the writer all the more
the possibility to express another possible community and to
forge the means for another consciousness and another sensibility.
(1986:17)*

Compare this passage from *Borderlands:*

*As a mestiza I have no country, my homeland cast me out; yet
all countries are mine because I am every woman's sister or potential lover. (As a lesbian I have no race, my own people dis-
claim me; but I am all races because there is the queer of me in
all races.) I am cultureless because, as a feminist, I challenge
the collective cultural/religious male-derived beliefs of Indo-
Hispanics and Anglos; yet I am cultured because I am participating in the creation of yet another culture, a new story to
explain the world and our participation in it, a new value
system with images and symbols that connect us to each other
and to the planet. (80–81)*

Borderlands is a chant declaring that mixing is both an ancient and a postmodern condition, one that we can no longer afford to forget. Anzaldúa's
notion of mestiza consciousness, a consciousness borne of the need to live
in multiple locations at once, expresses the present moment of confusion
and tension. It explicitly speaks not just to those who are direct descendants
of ethnic mixing but also to anyone who has had to consciously live not in
a monocultural world but rather in a mixed cultural world.

La conciencia de la mestiza is a theoretical expression of Anzaldúa's desire
"to express another possible community." In the crucible of a Borderlands
filled with contradiction, *la mestiza* has no choice but to forge something
else. This new consciousness feeds the growth of a new sensitivity, *la facultad.* It is important to remember that the emergence of "the new mestiza" is
the result of historical forces, that *la mestiza* is a trope for a series of circumstances leading to a different awareness, and that anyone on the planet might
at any time find him/herself caught in these circumstances. Globalization
creates cultural contradiction, intensifies the clashing of local knowledges.

The publication of *Borderlands* in 1987 resulted in a flurry of interest on
campuses across the nation. Part 1 of this book, originally intended as an introduction to the poetry that follows in part 2, grew to an ungainly ninety-
one pages. This is the section taken to be the heart of the book by most

readers. *Borderlands* expresses a moment of confusion, of transmogrification, of metamorphosis. It is not elegant; it is wrong to ask that it be. This is not an elegant moment. This book is valuable for its missteps, for the odd-shaped bits of bone and muscle it displays. It underlies the danger of invention, the problems of expressing that which is still unformed, protean.

> *To live in the Borderlands means knowing*
> *that the* india *in you, betrayed for 500 years*
> *is no longer speaking to you,*
> *that* mexicanas *call you* rajetas,
> *that denying the Anglo inside you*
> *is as bad as having denied the Indian or Black;*
> . . . .
> Cuando vives en la frontera
> *people walk through you, the wind steals your voice,*
> *you're a* burra, buey, *scapegoat,*
> *forerunner of a new race,*
> *half and half—both woman and man, neither—a new gender;*
>
> *To live in the Borderlands means to*
> *put* chile *in the borscht,*
> *eat whole wheat tortillas,*
> *speak Tex-Mex with a Brooklyn accent*
> *be stopped by* la migra *at the border checkpoints;*
> . . . .
> *To survive the Borderlands*
> *you must survive* sin fronteras
> *be a crossroads. (194–195)*

La mestiza makes a virtue out of a necessity. If all local knowledges exile her, she creates her own home, one in which the battle between languages, races, genders, ethnicities, religions, aesthetics, food, architecture, art, folklores is temporarily resolved by imagining and then living in alternate systems that allow radical mixing with *la mestiza* at the center of this mixing.

Like Anzaldúa, the child in *The Woman Warrior,* while confused by the news that the Communists have taken her ancestral lands, is also relieved: "Now the whole planet belongs to us. Wherever we are, that's our land." The tension between a home in Stockton, California, and one in a village in China results in a global awareness of Earth as the only planet we have (for now, at least). Trickster writing is indeed "in the American grain." The exile that *la mestiza* experiences provides an opportunity. This opportunity, the exile's opportunity to travel, to make multiple homelands, echoes the American ethic: be adventurous; go west, young (wo)man; remake the resources of the continent into something else; reinvent yourself in the process.

TERRORIZING AND DETERRORIZING LANGUAGE

Deterritorializing language for Silko is both a problem and a problematic. On the one hand, she is aware of the importance of precise meanings, the importance of grounding a language in its natural context. In *Ceremony*, Tayo's grandmother has brought the medicine man Ku'oosh to the sick mestizo's bedside. He tells Tayo,

> *"This world is fragile."* . . . *The word he chose to express "fragile" was filled with the intricacies of a continuing process, and with a strength inherent in spider webs woven across paths through sand hills where early in the morning the sun becomes entangled in each filament of web. It took a long time to explain the fragility and intricacy because no word exists alone, and the reason for choosing each word had to be explained with a story about why it must be said this certain way. That was the responsibility that went with being human, old Ku'oosh said, the story behind each word must be told so there could be no mistake in the meaning of what had been said; and this demanded great patience and love. (35)*

But Ku'oosh will only be able to partially heal Tayo. Another healer, Betonie, who like Tayo is also a mestizo, becomes the healer of last resort, a kind of unauthentic, dubiously connected medicine man. Tayo's Auntie expresses Betonie's marginal position this way: "What kind of medicine man lives in a place like that, in the foothills north of the Ceremonial Grounds?" Betonie's hogan is placed deliberately above Gallup. Organized by white men who pay tribes from many different reservations to congregate in the summertime for dances, rodeos, horse races, and trading, the Ceremonial Grounds are an affront to serious religious practice. Tourists are sold hotel rooms and restaurant meals; Indians are sold illegal alcohol. Betonie explains his choice of residence to Tayo. From his hogan in the foothills, he can keep track of the Indians who are forced to live on the north side of the railroad tracks, next to the dump, in alleys, and on the riverbed, sleeping in the weeds next to the arroyo. Gallup has defined its borders, and Betonie studies this map, keeping track of the interaction between the cultures below. He watches Gallup as the spider watches its web, paying close attention to the vibrations along its intricate system and watching carefully for entanglements between systems of power and knowledge.

Betonie's explanations to Tayo make it clear that the Native American knowledges have been colonized at the semantic level: "The fifth world had become entangled with European names; the names of the rivers, the hills, the names of the animals and plants—all of creation suddenly had two names: an Indian name and a white name" (68).

The fifth world had become a colonized territory at the level of the sign; deterritorialization must proceed at the level of the sign. It is not only a political process. Or rather, the political process cannot be separated from the semiotic process. For Silko, the language exists to be transformed and to be transformative.

> *"There are some things I have to tell you," Betonie began softly. "The people nowadays have an idea about the ceremonies. They think the ceremonies must be performed exactly as they have always been done. . . . They think if a singer tampers with any part of the ritual, great harm can be done, great power unleashed. . . . But long ago when the people were given the ceremonies, the changing began, if only in the aging of the yellow gourd rattle or the shrinking of the skin around the eagle's claw, if only in the different voices from generation to generation, singing the chants. You see, in many ways, the ceremonies have always been changing . . . after the white people came, elements in this world began to shift; and it became necessary to create new ceremonies. . . . She taught me this above all else: things which don't shift and grow are dead things." (126)*

These passages provide a gloss on Silko's linguistic theories, which are virtually indistinguishable from modern semiotic theories. Signs make meaning through contrast and comparison with other signs; "no word exists alone."

Like Janie's voice in *Their Eyes Were Watching God*, Betonie's ceremonies are a result of his understanding of division. Like Janie's inside and outside, the fifth world and the European world now provide two names for everything, "an Indian name and a white name." Articulation is the result of careful attention to the relationship between these worlds. Language making is culture making and is a human activity and responsibility. Language can be imagined, as Eco has imagined it, to be like an intricate web, one that is always shifting and growing.

Tayo reenters his culture as a result of an extended healing ceremony. While the full-blood veterans are dying slowly of alcohol and violence, Tayo's illness is immediately life-threatening, and the ceremony is his only chance for survival. Initiated and guided by Betonie, Tayo encounters Spiderwoman, a Native American deity of enormous and subtle transformative power. Spiderwoman, like Esu-Elegebara, is "the divine linguist who speaks all languages" (Gates 1988:17). Betonie guides Tayo into contact with Spiderwoman, and she brings this exile back into harmony with his homeland. The connection between Spiderwoman's intervention and Tayo's acquisition of voice cannot be overstated. Spiderwoman incarnates into flesh and gives herself to him sexually, first as a mestiza many years his senior and later as a young woman with ocher eyes.

Spiderwoman's blessing is literally a sign from the gods that this unauthentic mestizo[9] should become his community's new storyteller. Tayo's exile ends because he is able to perceive the value of the borderlands, and he can do this not just because Spiderwoman blesses him by her presence but also because the ceremony she leads him through contains multiple manifestations of mixing. From the old one who takes him to bed to Betonie's grandmother, herself a mestiza, to the cattle that are stolen specifically as stock for interbreeding, Tayo's healing ceremony is a celebration of the border crossing. Tayo is healed because he learns how to straddle local knowledges. He can, as he says, "speak for both sides." Because of Spiderwoman's healing blessing, he becomes the most valued storyteller of his generation.

Naming her novel *Ceremony,* adding no articles or qualifiers, Silko signals an identity between language and healing, between culture and language, between meaning making as religious ritual and storytelling and the narratives people live each day. The novel is not *a* ceremony or *the* ceremony. The novel is Ceremony. Narrative is its own healing act; narrative reinscribes us at the center of our community. *Ceremony*'s healing seems to extend to its readers, who often report a sense that the novel has nourished and centered them.

Silko's *The Storyteller,* an anthology of short stories, poetry, and family history, reinforces this equivalency between narrative and culture. In this book, the central character of the title story becomes a storyteller like Tayo and, in the process, also finds her place at the center of her community. And also, like Tayo, in life-threatening danger, the young Inuit woman tells stories that ensure her future survival. Language remakes the world in an active embodied process. Tayo's ceremony heals him and, it would seem, Silko intends *Ceremony* to be a healing narrative for the planet.

In a poem placed at dead center of this novel strewn with poems (it appears on page 132 of a 262-page work), witchery enters the world. The sick things gain ascendance through a narrative. The poem, clearly meant to signal a revision of history that can lead to a more hopeful future, begins:

> *Long time ago*
> *in the beginning*
> *there were no white people in the world*
> *there was nothing European*

A "long time ago" witch people gathered together from all over the planet for a contest in dark things. The last witch to enter the contest does not display vulgar charms or beads; the last witch, anonymous as to origin or gender,

> *. . . just told them to listen:*
> *"What I have is a story."*

> *At first they all laughed*
> *but this witch said*
> *Okay*
> *go ahead*
> *laugh if you want to*
> *but as I tell the story*
> *it will begin to happen.*

> *Set in motion now*
> *set in motion by our witchery*
> *to work for us. (132–138)*

The story incants Europeans into existence, defines their alienation from the earth, the sun, the planets, the animals, defines and describes their fear, the death they will bring across the ocean with them. Though the poem is a relentless indictment of European culture and attitudes, it restores agency to non-European peoples. Non-European peoples created Europeans (an interesting allusion to anthropological theories suggesting that European peoples spread north from Africa, evolving lighter skins as they moved away from the intense sunlight of the equator). Non-European peoples are responsible for the existence of the European. The evil let loose in the witch contest was a suicidal evil.

> *White people are only tools that the witchery manipulates; and I tell you, we can deal with white people, with their machines and their beliefs. We can because we invented white people; it was Indian witchery that made white people in the first place.*
> *(132)*

This suicidal evil inheres in the *story* the witch is chanting throughout the poem. The story brings Europeans into existence. Narrative itself, language itself, creates the world, creates evil. *Ceremony,* by placing responsibility for history in the hands of all humans, also returns agency to all humans as re-creators of the world. Traveling across local knowledges, Silko acknowledges the exchange of meaning across boundaries. Mixing cultures does not simply destroy meanings, it also creates, concatenating knowledges where no connections have previously existed. This is a human responsibility, Ku'oosh tells Tayo. The connections between the words must be told. There must be no mistake. Language must be used carefully with an awareness of its power to harm and to heal. Mixing cultures requires trickster skills and sensibility, an awareness of the irony, paradox, folly, and fragility of us all. All of this demands great patience and love. Silko makes it clear that deterritorializing language means recognition of the importance of precise signifiers, of the colonization of Native American signifiers and finally of the possibility of a transformation of language that can serve to decolonize and heal.

Hurston's techniques for deterritorializing language rest on the double-voicedness I have discussed earlier and on the power she gives Janie "to play the dozens" on her husband, Jody. "Playing the dozens" is a trickster skill embedded in irony and parody. Jody abuses Janie for more than fifteen years before she finally is able to voice her opposition to him. After he denigrates her body in front of the men who gather at their store daily for conversation, she finally stands up to him. "Talkin' 'bout *me* lookin' old! When you pull down yo' britches, you look lak de change uh life" (123).

The result of Janie's skillful signifying: Jody literally dies of humiliation. And like Tayo's mysterious illness, Jody's disease causes him to waste away without visible reason. Tayo cannot take nourishment, and Jody refuses Janie's food, suggesting that she is poisoning him. Language does indeed terrorize in Hurston's work. Tayo's lack of voice jeopardizes his life. Janie's attainment of voice conveys the power to mortally wound.

For Kingston, as I have discussed, language is a sword with which to terrorize and deterritorialize. Criticism of Anzaldúa's mixing of English, Tex-Mex, Castilian Spanish, Nahuatl, and the Northern Mexican dialect is analogous to the criticism Silko received for her "betrayal" of Native American secret rituals. By translating and modifying them, she both corrupted them and revealed sacred secrets. Kingston has had to endure similar criticism for supposedly intensifying Orientalist attitudes by reinforcing stereotypes. Mestizas who dare to encode mixing have to bear harsh criticism. They are breaking the law of genre. Living in the present would be much easier if those who have an investment in separation and purity would allow those who have an investment in mestiza consciousness a little breathing room. If Barbara Johnson is correct in claiming that the ability to articulate comes out of an awareness of self-division, *la mestiza* must speak out of that awareness or must remain silent. Denying her the right to concatenate knowledges is tantamount to erasure. Anzaldúa's deterritorialization includes:

> *The switching of codes . . . from English to Castillian Spanish to the North Mexican dialect to Tex-Mex to a sprinkling of Nahuatl to a mixture of all of these, reflects my language, a new language—the language of the Borderlands. There, at the juncture of cultures, languages cross-pollinate and are revitalized; they die and are born. Presently this infant language, this bastard language, Chicano Spanish, is not approved by any society. (Anzaldúa 1987: preface)*

This is an apt description of rhizomatic growth, but approval is beside the point when the point is decolonization and breaking the law of genre.

LA MESTIZA, OR BREAKING THE LAW OF GENRE

Genres are not to be mixed.
I will not mix genres.
I repeat: genres are not to be mixed. I will not mix them.
JACQUES DERRIDA

These four texts, *Borderlands/La Frontera, The Woman Warrior, Their Eyes Were Watching God,* and *Ceremony,* all obey Derrida's law of genre. His imperative is to break the imperative, and they do. I read the mixing of genres as a necessity for those who are concatenating knowledges, creating rhizomatic connections. Mixing genres is an anagram of mixing cultures; mixing genres seems to be a formal technique for signaling border crossing. *La mestiza* is a trope for genre mixing.

Their Eyes Were Watching God, in some ways the most traditionally structured of the four works addressed thus far, nevertheless crosses genres. The back cover of this book (texts such as these should not be ignored; they tell us much about the reading and publishing practices attached to a particular work) declares its potential readers to be students of black studies, anthropology, sociology, literature, or women's studies. I suggest that this novel should be read simultaneously as fiction, ethnology, theory, and autobiography. Learning how to read across genres is one of the skills suggested by Anzaldúa's *la facultad*. Breaking the law of genre redefines the border as an epistemological space that can be reconfigured tropologically. Learning how to do this requires formal language skills and, ultimately, a spiritual discipline.

Silko's *Ceremony* is clearly fiction, poetry, myth, and ethnology. Silko, herself a mestiza of mixed Laguna Pueblo, Mexican, and Anglo ancestry, rewrites traditional myths, in the process addressing the position of the Native American, who is diluted by the otherness of Anglo and Mexican blood. She has been criticized for appropriating, revealing, and rewriting secret chants and ceremonies,[10] but what is relevant to this discussion is her persistent willingness to mirror her own mestiza body in the body of her work. Her novel directly challenges the notion of racial and cultural purity through the mixed bloods at the heart of the novel. For her, even the ceremonies must be challenged on the basis of false notions of monocultural purity. Remember, the mestizo Betonie underscores this point in his description of the changes that must be made in the ceremonies:

> *At one time, the ceremonies as they had been performed were enough for the way the world was then. . . . I have made changes in the rituals. The people mistrust this greatly, but only this growth keeps the ceremonies strong.* (126)

The ceremonies in a Borderland shift and shape change just as the mestizas who inhabit it. Silko's work suggests a profound relationship between the text and the ceremony. Ceremonies change and mix; ergo genres must change and mix. These mestizas can be expected to create texts that shape change, that remain in motion.

Because it so thoroughly breaks the law of genre, Kingston's stunning work *The Woman Warrior* has defied categorization. Again, the book jacket deserves attention. It informs us that the story is "a poem turned into a sword" and declares itself unambiguously to be autobiography. (The author submitted it as a novel; her publisher felt it would market better as an autobiography.) As I have suggested previously, however, assign this book to undergraduates and you will be greeted by confused students on the day you begin discussing the book. "Did she really get to be a woman warrior in the mountains?" "How did she wind up with the barbarians at the end?" "I can't tell when this is fantasy and when it isn't," they will query. The book is, of course, not fantasy, myth, autobiography, ethnology, or history, but simultaneously all of those and none of those.

All of these works implicitly mirror mixed cultural knowledge in their formal organization. Deploying multiple techniques, they omnivorously display trickster attributes, no matter how contradictory or heretical. To do this they rely on one mode above all others: paradox.

PARADOX, OR AMBIGUITY AS A HOME

Lyotard suggests that one characteristic of the postmodern is an emphasis on paradox (Schulte-Sasse 1987:6). Anzaldúa and Kingston force paradox into the foreground in explicit terms; Hurston and Silko accept paradox as an agent. Hurston begins her novel, "The dream is the truth," and it is only through the recognition of the paradox of self-identity in division that Janie is able to articulate.

Articulating paradox, articulating the incompatible forces simultaneously in play within the self and outside the self seems to be the ground out of which these writers can give voice to a mixed cultural consciousness. Like Janie, Tayo must struggle with the paradox of self-difference. The victimization of non-European peoples, despite the collective human responsibility for evil and its unmaking, presents another paradox. These paradoxes are the dual fulcrums supporting *Ceremony*. Tayo begins as doubly cursed, exiled from both the reservation and Anglo culture, but the pain of this self-difference, these incompatible forces, enables him to forge another consciousness. Tayo's mestizo self is able to connect with the ancient ceremonies in a way his full-blood contemporaries cannot. The result is so powerful that it stuns the elders into recognizing him as a storyteller of tremendous significance. Tayo travels with difference because he has no choice. It nearly destroys him, but ultimately he is rewarded beyond anyone's imagining.

As Betonie looks down upon the boundaries in Gallup, he gains insight into how he must modify the ceremonies, and he reassures Tayo, "We can deal with white people." Local knowledges need not silence one another. Instead, "culture clash" [11] enables the articulation of differences. Despite the innumerable models all around us suggesting that difference must inevitably lead to disaster, these texts point toward other possibilities. *Ceremony* reminds us of these possibilities.

Even though a witch incanted Europeans into existence and set a new evil into motion, an evil that ultimately threatened native people's survival and brought the earth to the brink of destruction, the "fifth world" was now exerting its own kind of power. European knowledge leads to the creation of nuclear weapons. It is fitting that uranium is "up here in these hills" where the witch contest was held so long ago. Tayo's grandmother tells him she witnessed the blinding light of the first atomic bomb explosion at White Sands as she walked in the middle of the night from the kitchen chamber pot to her bedroom. She asks him,

> *"Now I only wonder why, grandson. Why did they make a thing like that?"*
> *"I don't know, Grandma," he had answered then. But now he knew.*
> *He had been so close to it, caught up in it for so long that its simplicity stuck him deep inside his chest: Trinity Site, where they exploded the first atomic bomb, was only three hundred miles to the southeast, at White Sands. And the top-secret laboratories where the bomb had been created were deep in the Jemez Mountains, on land the Government took from Cochiti Pueblo: Los Alamos, only a hundred miles northeast of him now, still surrounded by high electric fences and the ponderosa pine and tawny sandrock of the Jemez mountain canyon where the shrine of the twin mountain lions had always been. There was no end to it; it knew no boundaries; and he had arrived at the point of convergence where the fate of all living things, and even the earth, had been laid. From the jungles of his dreaming he recognized why the Japanese voices had merged with Laguna voices, with Josiah's voice and Rocky's voice; the lines of cultures and worlds were drawn in flat dark lines on fine light sand, converging in the middle of witchery's final ceremonial sand painting. From that time on, human beings were one clan again, united by the fate the destroyers planned for all of them, for all living things; united by a circle of death that devoured people in cities*

twelve thousand miles away, victims who had never known these
mesas, who had never seen the delicate colors of the rocks which
boiled up their slaughter. (245–246)

In the face of the atom bomb illuminating a chamber pot, Tayo is able to reconcile paradox. What he had not known, he now knew. The simplicity of his realization strikes him deep inside his chest. Paradox is a "point of convergence where the fate of all living things, and even the earth, had been laid." Right there on the land he can finally claim as home, and like the girl whom Kingston describes growing up in Stockton, California, Tayo realizes that the Earth is our collective home; *la mestiza* is all of us. "Human beings were one clan again."

It is paradox that forces this realization on the child in Stockton, and it is paradox that provides the Woman Warrior's most important training, "I learned to make my mind large, as the universe is large, so that there would be room for paradoxes" (35). How does one make room for paradox? How does one learn "to see the world in a grain of sand"? These texts provide no clear answers. Narratives smashed against one another by the historical circumstances of local knowledges made to touch one another at multiple borders provide a fertile ground for paradox, and the ground itself provides the lessons.

It cannot be a coincidence that each of these four works makes claims about learning and paradox. The Woman Warrior *learns* to make her mind large; Janie understands that "she had an inside and an outside now and suddenly she knew how not to mix them up"; Anzaldúa declares that the mestiza "learns to be an Indian in Mexican culture, to be a Mexican from an Anglo point of view. She learns to juggle cultures. She has a plural personality. . . . She can be jarred out of ambivalence. . . . I'm not sure exactly how. . . . It is work that the soul performs. That focal point or fulcrum . . . is where phenomena tend to collide" (79); and Tayo moves suddenly from not knowing to knowing what he had been so close to for so long that "its simplicity struck him deep inside his chest."

Anzaldúa's mestiza learns a tolerance for ambiguity [12] as both a survival skill and a method of keeping ahead of the transformation. *La mestiza* is a shock-wave rider, as John Brunner (1975) puts it, an individual who like "a dolphin rides the bow wave of a ship, out ahead, but always making in the right direction. And having a hell of a good time with it" (53). Shock-wave riders of cultural mixing both anticipate and create original connections. In the process, we all learn new literacy techniques that offer us valuable survival skills.

SIGNIFYING TRICKSTERS

Tricksters inhabit all four of these works at all levels of signification. For Kingston, ghosts are one metaphor for shape-shifters. Hurston's tricksters inhabit the book's plot; just as Janie finally acquires voice and finds her "kissing bees" (25), her beloved Tea Cake transmogrifies into a rabies-ridden madman whom she must kill to save her own life. Silko's Changing Woman[13] comes to heal Tayo and steal his heart, finally leaving him alone again. Anzaldúa's *la mestiza* becomes a shape-shifter:

> *I recognize that the internal tension of oppositions can propel (if it doesn't tear apart) the mestiza writer out of the metate where she is being ground with corn and water, eject her out as nahuatl, an agent of transformation, able to modify and shape primordial energy and therefore able to change herself and others into turkey, coyote, tree, or human. (74–75)*

I repeat. Perhaps a trickster lives in theory.

DIALOGIZED AMERICA: KINGSTON'S TRILOGY— FROM *THE WOMAN WARRIOR* TO *TRIPMASTER MONKEY*

> *Every novel, taken as the totality of all the languages and consciousnesses of language embodied in it, is a hybrid. But we emphasize once again: it is an intentional and conscious hybrid, one artistically organized, and not an opaque mechanistic mixture of language (more precisely, a mixture of languages). The artistic image of a language—such is the aim that novelistic hybridization sets for itself.*
> —M. M. BAKHTIN

Since notions concerning access to a text are at the heart of what is termed cultural literacy, Kingston's work provides an excellent case in point regarding access, literacy, traveling across cultures, and challenges to the reader. Her third work, *Tripmaster Monkey,* has been criticized for being overly dense, too full of obscure literary and nonliterary allusions. All of her texts pose a fundamental problem for a reader who is without what I suggest are trickster reading skills. Kingston's language is polyvocal, hybrid. Her three major works constitute the concatenation of multiple American languages. She has stated that she felt limited by the language(s) in her first two works. Only in her third book did she feel free to use "all her language." While *The Woman Warrior* and *China Men* claimed and reclaimed the languages of her parents, race, culture, class, sex, locality, and childhood, they kept her from traveling as far and wide as she had in adult life. It is only in Kingston's third, most polyvocal, work that she is able to move freely. Under conditions of radical cultural mixing, double-voicedness is no longer adequate. Trickster literates display a complicated mixed voice in their texts. The dualism of double-voiced texts splits into mixed-voiced texts in which multiple local knowledges refract into one another. The seeming cacophony that results can cause disorientation. The self-division expressed in the works of all the authors discussed here is the result of border crossing; multiplicity is its sign. Guillermo Gómez-Peña puts it this way in *Warrior for Gringostroika*:

> One thing I know for sure: my identity, like that of my contemporaries, is not a monolith but a kaleidoscope; and everything I create, including this text, contains a multiplicity of voices, each speaking from a different part of my self. Far from being mere postmodern theory, this multiplicity is a quintessential feature of the Latino experience in the United States. (21)

This multiplicity is a quintessential feature of Kingston's texts as well. They are not stable; they do not lie still within one plane of meaning or one cultural framework. They implicitly declare that one knowledge is insufficient. They refuse to deny multiple knowledges. They refuse to become ideological in this way. In recognizing the semiotic effects of what might be termed "the ideology of signs" within local cultural knowledge (Western European culture can be viewed as a local culture in this sense), they make a revolution.

Kingston's texts defy the injunction not to travel across these "local knowledges," i.e., across the ideology of culture. They defy colonialism by affirming multiple and contradictory ideologies simultaneously. When a text travels across local knowledges, it must (a) contradict itself and (b) outdistance at points *any* hypothetical or actual reader unless the reader's expertise is exactly contiguous with the author's.[14]

In such texts, the maxim "There is no author; there is only the text" becomes "The author's literacy and the text's literacy are one." Or rather, what the author knows becomes the structure for the text and the standard for an "ideal" reading, which can never be attained in practice. The result is a trickster ride into Kingston's mind. It may be that such texts require new reading skills. "We must break reader's block," Kingston tells us. Breaking reader's block might mean learning to travel with the author's literacy, a literacy that itself provides the structure for the text. Such a hidden and secret structure is bound at points to produce frustration and anger on the part of the reader. While it may seem theoretically possible for a reader to come to possess much of the encyclopedic competence[15] of any given author, it does not seem possible in practice. Even a clone raised alongside his/her "parent" could not acquire an identical encyclopedia.

If this is the case, demanding that you as reader command everything in a text is a kind of intellectual colonialism, as if to suggest that you the reader could not bear to let anything remain outside your control. Why should a reader master the whole of any text? Why should this be an imperative? Does anyone actually do this in practice? Denying this sort of intellectual colonialism does not obviate the responsibility an author has to remain reasonably accessible, but it does define the other pole of this issue and it directly challenges the concept of audience as it is often understood. In any case, Eco's theory of an encyclopedic competence assumes that an individual can isolate only *portions* of the net at any moment in order to interpret an actual discourse. But what to do when that discourse travels across local knowledges, knowledges to which you do not have access, that you may not even be aware exist? One suggestion might be that the proper response is a cultivated and deliberate stance of receptivity to the discomfort this creates in you the audience. There is no doubt that it is disrupting; this may ultimately be its main virtue as a revolutionary practice. What is taking place is "a revolution of signs." Words simply refuse to sit still in texts such as Kingston's because everything about the American cultural map is in contention across a dialogized[16] labyrinth of language. Insofar as our realities are based on unitary, colonizing visions of the truth, these visions ought to be contested at every moment in a dialogized America. Kingston's work does this from sentence to sentence, sometimes from word to word.

Another way of expressing this notion might be to suggest that the nature and limits of the reader's encyclopedic competence as played against the author's encyclopedic competence both hold the fabric of any text together *and* threaten to break it apart. The textual fabric may supply much of the meaning; the content of the form may be very real. But the reader's ability to supply much of that form by recognizing certain textual moves may be one key to breaking reader's block. When the textual moves and the universe of semiosis they imply exceed the reader's competence, reader's block takes hold.

Once again, learning to travel becomes the relevant issue. Can the reader both adopt an alternative mode of transportation and adapt the speed, quality, and ground of his/her associations to such travel? The transparent nature of language is at work here, is part of the issue of alternate transportation. The silent and unconscious correlations that readers make between the tacit signifiers and the jumble of associations beneath each of these signifiers and the motion between all of the signifiers belie the complexity of this process. Reader's block is engendered at this level.

We must break reader's block by remaking ourselves into readers who are acquainted with a multitude of local knowledges. The author might be said to "activate" a model reader by traveling through many hot spots on the larger net and asking the reader to follow. Such a ride demands both a suspension of disbelief on the part of the reader and a willingness to be like a child in the wonderland of an alien local knowledge. Like a child, such a reader must be willing to accept that some things remain outside of one's grasp while nevertheless continually reaching toward them. Such an acceptance would represent a profoundly anticolonialist commitment, one that allows for difference and is humble in that realization. A text that demands such a response is not flawed textually or otherwise; neither is its author. Similarly, that the totality of such texts remains outside the grasp of the reader does not suggest a flaw in the reader. We might begin to redefine the virtues of such texts, their authors, and their readers. This is the price that traveling exacts: to know more and less at the same time. We cannot deny travel in dialogized America. We cannot afford not to pay its price.

A text that travels across local knowledges must contradict itself as it encounters paradox. "I learned to make my mind large, as the universe is large, so that there is room for paradoxes (*Woman Warrior* 35)." A text that travels across local knowledges must cast doubt on the real nature of what it is doing at every moment. Hence Kingston names her third work *Tripmaster Monkey: His Fake Book*. It is a fake book. Kingston is alluding to the jazz term *fake book*. A "fake book" contains the initial "riff" a jazz musician lays down. Others improvise over that riff—in other words, add their own literacies. The reader contributes to the structure here, the literacy. The reader must follow Kingston across a net of literacy. This exercise results in a challenge to the reader's encyclopedic competence and an expansion of it. Kingston is hoping to force and guide the reader to an understanding of the necessity to know all these ways in order to survive and enjoy modern life.

If, indeed, it is the play between the reader's and the author's encyclopedic competence that supplies the structure of the text, then we have an explanation for the strange inattention of literary critics to the tremendous structural flaws of some of the most highly regarded canonical texts. Seen this way, the seemingly tight structures of, for example, the realistic novel of the British upper class do not exist. What seems to be a clear, stable discourse is dependent upon the reader's competence in the local net from which the discourse emerges. If indeed the reader is supplying much of the structure of a text, its coherence exists in her mind, or, more accurately, in her mind's encyclopedia. Who is the master of the text, Kingston's title asks. Who is the master of *Tripmaster Monkey?* Who is the author of *His Fake Book?*

Readers must rise to texts with a patience that recognizes the limits of their encyclopedic competence, and they must have the goodwill to expand those limits. We have no justification for our inability to stretch except that we are exhausted and maimed by our imprisonment in certain portions of the net. We should not blame the net or ourselves. We are simply in a certain condition of literacy that is the result of historical conditions. Texts that move beyond double-voicedness to mixed-voicedness require more of the reader. A world that radically mixes cultures in a tornado of technological innovation produces new challenges not dreamt of before. The monocultural perspective cripples us in the face of this reality. The acceptance of our moral responsibility in this regard is crucial to both our own learning and the prospects for multicultural exchange and justice.

TRICKSTERS AND LITERACY

Perhaps pedagogical vision is as crippled as much of the literacy around us. The encyclopedia may be impoverished, but humans are driven by a need to engage the richness of their environment, and the postmodern environment is very rich, even if that richness is filled with horrors. Lush literacies are in constant motion around us. That these literacies often remain invisible is paradoxical. That our impoverished pedagogies cannot learn from these literacies is still more paradoxical.

These individuals and the texts they produce do not exist outside the cultural literacy of our society no matter how intent the majority culture may be on maintaining that illusion. Their texts delight and infuriate, illuminate and confuse, challenge and honor those who are culturally literate within the traditional Western canon. They are transgressive. They transmogrify experience and self. These individuals and their texts were all produced within our culture. America has always already been multicultural.

Studying the mixed cultures expressed in these texts can teach us to balance on the edge of paradox as knowledges clash. They can teach us patience, judgment, how to endure the pain of being torn in multiple directions, how Truth has been transformed into truths, that value is relative to context and that we need not be nervous about this, that we can be open to radically contradictory beliefs and not disintegrate, that to do this we must have courage and we must trust our own confusion as a signal that we are learning, that we are concatenating, that by enduring discomfort we can as a species learn to accept ourselves in our multiple manifestations. Understanding mixed cultural literacy can give us a methodology for acceptance. It provides a needed foundation for a series of baby steps toward cultural maturity.

The knowledge contained in these literatures cannot be encompassed in a list. A list represents a series of addresses that obscures the significance of the locations each address represents. Lists are in league with an unhelpful circular discourse. This discourse, the lists that become narrow encyclopedias and even more narrowly defined tests, represents a violent literacy that seems to repress awareness of the rich literacies necessary for survival in a postmodern, post-print, post-capitalism age. Mixed literacy is the inevitable result of an inventive and courageous response to the violence at the heart of monocultural literacy.

Those without the power to produce canonical encyclopedias or to dictate curricula may produce uncanonical encyclopedias or demand curricular innovations; in any case, the culturally mixed texts that they produce are a reflection of the interiorized maps of knowledge that each possesses. Studying these texts can help us identify a literacy that is inclusive of the monocultural knowledge proselytized by many *and* the multiple cultural knowledges possessed by even more. Studying these texts for the universe(s) of knowledge that they represent can give us an alternate understanding of how movement between local knowledges is not only necessary but already part of the everyday practices of people all around us.

Four	# DISNEY'S LABYRINTH: EPCOT, CAPITAL OF THE TWENTY-FIRST CENTURY

*From this epoch stem the arcades and interiors, the
exhibitions and panoramas. They are residues of a dream
world. The realization of dream elements in waking is the
textbook example of dialectical thinking. For this reason
dialectical thinking is the organ of historical awakening.
Each epoch not only dreams the next, but also in dreaming, strives toward the moment of waking. It bears its
end in itself and unfolds it — as Hegel already saw —
with ruse.*
— WALTER BENJAMIN, "PARIS,"
 IN *REFLECTIONS*

*EPCOT,
despite its ruse,
is a dream world evoking the next epoch.*

A TRAVELOGUE

There is a place where for an admission fee of about
thirty-five dollars (an average cost of two-fifty per hour for up to fourteen
hours a day), the spectator can choke down as much as fourteen miles[1]
of film image projected on screens of unimaginable diversity, employing
every means available for display. The films are rarely delivered in a standard
35 mm or 70 mm format. Instead, the spectator's visual field is filled by 120-,
180-, 360-degree screens, by screens that rotate in complex patterns, by

collections of screens uniquely arranged and constructed, by screens appearing in odd and unexpected places, of all shapes and sizes, in tunnels, in waiting rooms, in the midst of dioramas. In this place, films are delivered via interactive computer networks, videotape, and videodisc; they are displayed in 3-D and embedded in non-film displays of extreme complexity. In this place, the spectator can saturate herself, welcome disorientation, and willingly dissolve into a meticulously constructed environment. This place is EPCOT Center at Walt Disney World, a theme-park-cum-world-exposition, a kind of world's fair that allows for a continual Disneyesque rewriting of history, a Distory, as Stephen Fjellman has called it. Disney World offers its guests multiple pleasures within the context of Disneyesque representations of race and gender. Distory is presented in a framework of disorientation; indeed, its dominant mode is disorientation. Hence this essay's conscious anarchy.

Although WDW is unlike any other topos on the planet, it reflects an image of what we arrogantly call America. Despite Disney's explicit fakery and its implicit message that it is constructing a place apart, Disney World is a distillation of postmodern everyday reality with the horror excised. Disney attempts to create a world where we feel extraordinarily safe. Any fright here is fright for fun. Except for this caveat, Disney and the postmodern American landscape are coextensive. Purposely exporting itself far and wide, its success at this has created a Disney shopping mall reality. Disney "reality" has permeated our cultural aesthetic—or perhaps it is more accurate to say that Disney reflects our aesthetic back to us. Disney's many mutilations of history and body are coextensive with the world outside. EPCOT is a dream of the postmodern, a late-twentieth-century chronotope. EPCOT is a giant library, a mnemonic device, a topos for the memorization of "facts," and a site for a kind of inductive association that threatens to run away with itself.

The terms *Disney, Disneyland, Walt Disney World (WDW), Magic Kingdom,* and *EPCOT (Experimental Prototype Community of Tomorrow)* will often be used interchangeably throughout what follows, despite their reality as separate signifiers with particular referents.

If you have not visited central Florida, it is crucial to realize that this state has ceded forty-three square miles to the Disney Corporation. Within the Disney zone, Florida's Orange County does not have the legal right to challenge land use or to set fees for increased water, sewer, or other services. Disney advertising points out that WDW, which is four miles wide and eleven miles long, is roughly the size of San Francisco and twice the size of Manhattan Island. A more interesting comparison might be seven-mile-wide and ten-mile-long Washington, D.C., which covers sixty-nine square miles. D.C. and Disney are America's major pilgrimage sites. While a remarkable 60 percent of Americans have visited the nation's capital, 70 percent have visited Disneyland or Disney World. The developed portion of WDW covers eight square miles and includes EPCOT (at 232 acres more than twice the size of California's Disneyland), the Magic Kingdom (98 acres), the Disney-MGM Studios (135 acres), numerous resort complexes, including Contemporary Resort, a fifteen-story hotel that admits the monorail into its lobby; Polynesian Village Resort; the Grand Floridian Resort; the postmodern Dolphin and Swan hotels; three golf resorts; a campground resort, Fort Wilderness; six major hotels not owned by Disney; two water games resorts, River Country and Typhoon Lagoon; an endangered species reserve, the 11.5-acre Discovery Island; a 7,500-acre nature preserve; facilities for boating, fishing, and horseback riding; a conference center; six lakes; a shopping center; a nightclub complex, Pleasure Island; and more. Thirty-five square miles of WDW are undeveloped and valued at $650 million.

Shaped like a giant hourglass, EPCOT is divided into Future World and World Showcase. Guests enter through the lower half of the hourglass at a spot coded "Spaceship Earth," EPCOT'S trademark geosphere, named for Buckminster Fuller's concept. Future World comprises seven major pavilions arranged clockwise from its gleaming globe: Spaceship Earth, the Universe of Energy, Horizons, the World of Motion, Journey into Imagination, the Land, and the Living Seas; each is an arcade composed of dozens of dioramas arranged in every conceivable manner. All are underwritten by major corporations like United Technologies and General Motors and dedicated to purveying overlapping corporate-technological origin stories directed toward fostering an acceptance of a bureaucratized, capitalistic utopia. Each of these arcades offers a unique "ride" through a main exhibit. Often the main exhibit is a film, followed by any number of dioramas, organic and inorganic. When one of these "attractions" ends, the "guest" is ejected into a simulated landscape that iconically echoes the main presentation.

The "upper" half of the hourglass, World Showcase, is composed of more-modest arcades arranged around a 40-acre lagoon. Meant to "capture" Mexico, Norway, China, Germany, Italy, "America," Japan, Morocco, France, the United Kingdom, and Canada, these, too, are underwritten by corporations like Telecom Canada, Coca-Cola, and American Express ("The American Adventure"). Each exists as a travelogue and a major corporate advertisement. Significantly, no country south of twenty degrees north latitude is represented.

Disney World, like its parent corporation, is growing constantly, all the while increasing its revenues proportionately. Since I first visited the "park" in 1987, it has made additions totaling at least $1.4 billion. A partial list of the additions includes a new Tomorrowland (1996) in the Magic Kingdom, a new 3-D movie (1994), a Journeys in Space, a Russian and a Switzerland showcase in EPCOT, three new attractions at MGM-Disney Studios, four major new resorts, a Disney Institute, a wedding chapel, and a residential town named "Celebration." Any analysis of Disney World is hampered by the need to describe this immensity at least in outline.

At EPCOT, not only will you be able to purchase Disney character merchandise, EPCOT memorabilia, and traveler's supplies, but you also will be presented with a limitless array of merchandise in shops throughout the park. World Showcase provides the ultimate site for a vast import emporium. You might buy pre-Columbian artifacts; piñatas; embroidered Chinese clothing; Hummel figures; beer steins; traditional German toys; cameo jewelry; Murano crystal; American handicrafts; kimonos; antique toys; Japanese porcelain; Moroccan carpets, brass, and copper; French art, crystal, perfume, wine, and cookware; British tea; Royal Doulton figurines; Scottish wools; or Eskimo crafts. You will certainly consume not just food but carefully marked "foreign" food.

The roots of Disneyland and Disney World lie in Walt's fascination with railroads. After building a steam engine and a half-mile track in his yard and after the Disney Studio property proved too small to accommodate engines from San Francisco's 1915 Pan American Fair, he turned his attention to the creation of Disneyland. Thus, the Disney park connection to expositions begins here at the foundation of his parks and is echoed in his contributions to the 1964 New York World's Fair. The first fully realized Audio-Animatronic figures were produced for four displays at that fair: Ford Motor Company's "Magic Skyway," General Electric's "Progressland," Pepsi-Cola's "It's a Small World," and "Great Moments with Mr. Lincoln" for the Illinois pavilion. Versions of these last three are still on display at Disneyland and Walt Disney World (Finch 1975:145).

Walt Disney's favorite project, EPCOT (Experimental Prototype Community of Tomorrow), was envisioned to be a continually evolving paean to "the ingenuity and imagination of American free enterprise" and was "to take its cue from the new ideas and new technologies that are now emerging from the creative centers of American industry" (Birnbaum 1986:101). Walt fantasized a precisely controlled city filled with carefully selected residents; instead, his heirs created an exposition that fills with approximately sixty thousand "guests" for up to fourteen hours a day, a teaching machine for corporate capitalism. EPCOT is a scientific origin story that ends in a techno-capital utopia at Future World and what Robert Sanchez has come to call a culti-multural[2] collage at World Showcase. In World Showcase, France, China, and Canada's CircleVision-360 travelogues equate countries with landscape while "The American Adventure" presentation constructs an "American history" as metanarrative for the whole of EPCOT.

Although Walt Disney's vision for EPCOT was something far different from its reality, its heart is a Disney heart, seductive, exhilarating, and deeply problematic.

EPCOT delivers a body blow, a somatic experience. Disney's currency at EPCOT is the simulacrum;[3] its integrating medium is film, and its pleasure is sensory.[4] Film is folded into every experience at EPCOT, but the simulacrum is the ground of this experience, and our bodies traverse this ground again and again. EPCOT taxes physical resources as it tugs at associations and remembrances. Simultaneously exhausted by the sheer size of the space and the complexity of the display, her senses disoriented and her intellect massaged, Disney's guest surrenders. The doors of perception are a prime target for Disney. Through these doors, EPCOT pleasures and pains the body.[5] Delivering soma without sex, Disney has created a library that deploys simulacra in the service of a culti-multural, technocratic, utopian landscape.[6] We are all bound in some way to the field of pleasure exploited at Disney World. This is a library that relies on simulacra to create its narratives and soma to capture its audience, while rigorously suppressing race, gender, and class.[7]

Disney World is all that its most vehement critics characterize it as, but it is also a marvelous and energizing landscape and a carefully constructed encoding of American ideologies and knowledges.

This reading of Disney World calls into question the assumption that mass culture and the media stand in strict opposition to any traditional notions of literacy. Ultimately, it will posit that multiple oppositional literacies already exist in tension with traditional European American literacies and that this tension is played out in the arena of mass culture and the media. Part of the pleasure of moving through EPCOT's "library" is the recognition that it is not beyond one's ability to decode, despite its complexity. The seductive qualities of the Disney experience are both a mirror of and mirrored in daily life in America. We are familiar with these seductions whether they emanate from a Disney production or our suburban shopping mall. Disney's familiarity enables a particular kind of exploratory pleasure. Reading this library according to her thirsts and her guerrilla skills is fundamental to a cyborg guerrilla's pleasure. For ambassadors of an alternate epistemology, this means demonstrating their ability to read against the grain of the dominant voices of the culture. Ultimately, this essay asks a series of questions about the varieties of literacy necessary and common to the contemporary scene and makes the claim that literacy is a multidimensional activity, not restricted to the written word or one cultural position.

The questions below might be considered to constitute a preliminary map, a reconnoitering of enemy territory in which the guerrilla is seducer/seduced while remaining partially hidden. Using Walt Disney World as a microcosm of the contemporary media-dominated information age, imagining literacy leads to questions such as, In what ways is EPCOT like library, museum, and world exposition and what does that imply for those visitors who are not located at the center of European American culture? What kinds of literacy must a visitor to EPCOT command in order to "read" Disney World actively rather than passively? In what ways does Disney World exploit and construct the desire to know in a particular way? In what ways does Disney World enforce a particular kind of literacy that excludes the cultural literacies of American minorities and Third World peoples? In what ways does that make such literacies invisible despite the fact that they are active? Is it possible to read Disney World in opposition to some of its most obviously limiting tendencies (for example, its imperialistic and capitalistic versions of world history)? Can we teach individuals the skills they need to "read" landscapes like Disney World? What would instruction in that sort of literacy look like? In what follows, Disney World ultimately becomes a heuristic for thinking about literacy in the contemporary information age, an age whose media images are constantly represented and rerepresented in one technology after another.

In addition, this essay asks questions concerning possible metaphors for literacy implied by Disney World and contemporary culture. The common historical metaphor for literacy, the tree of knowledge of the Enlightenment philosophers, is inadequate to the labyrinthine nature of the contemporary world. Walt Disney World greets one as a labyrinth, a series of exhibitions, which are themselves composed of arcades, which are themselves labyrinths and dioramas and panoramas and labyrinths of dioramas and panoramas. "The labyrinth is the home of the hesitant. The path of someone shy of arrival at a goal easily takes the form of a labyrinth . . . mankind . . . does not wish to know where things are leading to" (Benjamin 1985a:40).

So Disney World is, as the capital of the twenty-first century, a labyrinth into which the population of the planet enters unhesitatingly—for our most fervent wish is to know not where we go but to find what we most desire along the way. Borges's keeper of the books, Hsiang, is lost in his desire to read and protect the books that preserve the emblems, these books that are themselves a literal and figurative labyrinth. Can the labyrinth provide an alternate metaphor to Bacon's tree? Do such metaphors just provide another restriction on our thinking about literacy and our experience of the knowledge transmitted to us or can they be helpful?

A HUNGER IN THE LABYRINTH

I'm not even sure it's a culture anymore. It's like this careening hunger splattering out in all directions.
—MICHAEL VENTURA, "A REPORT FROM EL DORADO"

Like the America that Michael Ventura is trying to describe, Disney's labyrinth is a field of desire. Like all labyrinths, Disney promises that our desire will be fulfilled around the corner. But those who enjoy the challenge of a labyrinth may constantly search for an alternate reading or exit even while they take pleasure in their disorientation. It is the potential for exit combined with the immediate knowledge of entrapment that makes mazes attractive. Oppositional figures have powerful oppositional desires. These desires give them some of the tools needed to reread the canon that Disney has collected. The trickster's hunger is for knowledge of the world. And reading and desire and the desire to read are at the heart of literacy.

An alternate conception of literacy might posit an individual who moves from one cultural position to another with deliberate attention. Such a person would be highly skilled in a different way. The models for such an individual already exist. This individual's primary interest might be to remain in motion between often contradictory topos, doing this with a great deal of awareness of the costs of such traveling and the difficulty of developing and maintaining such skills. Such a person might be drawn to "hot spots" in a library of the world's knowledges. Such places might be particularly interesting, either because they are sites of much activity or because some local element is potentially relevant (has meaning for some other epistemology). This alternate conception of literacy emphasizes travel, flexibility, the ability to tolerate contradictory inferences. Its advantage is that it both tracks and makes the connections along the labyrinth of epistemologies on the planet.

Traveling is a serious issue when applied to epistemology. Steven Rugare (1989) points out that Future World frames the entire EPCOT experience, since one is obliged to traverse it twice, and that World Showcase offers little option to determine one's own travel plans, since the lagoon forces a serial exploration of the pavilions.

> In its basic functioning, the World Showcase reproduces many of the characteristics of the suburban environment that is proliferating through central Florida somewhere beyond the boundaries of the Disney domain. It is an outdoor space in which a surprising array of styles, forms and symbols are juxtaposed in such a way that difference is represented so as to presence identity. . . .
> Looking into the little streets of the various "countries," one sees the effort to break up walls and surfaces, to allow the boundaries of the street to expand and contract, so as to give the effect of an interrelated, accidental, unplanned, organic, humane urban space. This kind of false streetscape was developed by the Disney architects and has since become a prime tenet of shopping mall design, as well as a favorite technique of postmodern architects. . . . The function of these mall like spaces is, in fact, almost exactly that of the shopping mall, to get people to slow down and browse, to get them to narrativize the process of consumption. (67–72)

This correspondence between the now everyday experience of mall shopping in America and the spaces at Disney World is not to be passed over lightly. Rugare cites William Severini Kowinski's *The Malling of America* (1985). In a chapter titled "Mousekatecture on Main Street," Kowinski astutely points out that malls in America are meant to "embody a dream, . . . an idealization of [a main street] with just the right touch of obvious artificiality to make it permanently extraordinary" (Kowinski 68).

In writing about the world exhibitions of the second half of the nineteenth century, Tim Mitchell (1989) observed that the Middle Eastern visitors whose responses to these exhibits he chronicles discovered that

> there was much about the "real worlds" outside (in the streets of Paris and beyond) that resembled the world exhibition; just as there was more about the exhibition that resembled the world outside. Despite the determined efforts to isolate the exhibition

as merely the perfect representation of a reality outside, the real world beyond the gates turned out to be rather like an extension of the exhibition. This extended exhibition continued to present itself as a series of mere representations, representing a reality beyond. We should think of it, therefore, less as an exhibition, than as a kind of labyrinth, a labyrinth that, as Derrida says, includes itself in its own exits. (224)

And like the "real worlds" outside in the 1990's, EPCOT is unified by computer control. Located inside Earth Station, which itself serves as the pier to which Spaceship Earth is tied, WorldKey Information Service provides a computerized introduction to EPCOT. These computers are arranged in a semicircle within Earth Station, a general information center. An integrated system, WorldKey Information connects laser disk pictures of EPCOT with a full index of the park and live operators. All computers in EPCOT are minus keyboards. Touch-sensitive screens enable anyone to access the available programs. The alphabet is passé at EPCOT. Instead, a kind of technological orality or touchality reigns. If the computer cannot answer your question, a multilingual live operator who can see and speak with you will appear on your computer screen in response to your summons. WorldKey Information will tell you most of what you need to know about EPCOT, from where to buy "authentic" deerskin moccasins to the contents of each pavilion, complete with full-color pictures of the highlights.

DE'TOURNING DISNEY

While Disney ideology permeates everything it produces and is especially obvious at its parks, making money at Disney is predicated on delivering pleasure, not ideology. And while pleasure and ideology cannot be centrifuged apart at present, the Disney corporation would dump its cultural ideology tomorrow if it thought that ideology was reducing profit. Both its simulacra and its guests are configured and re-configured accordingly, but it is a mistake to assume that Disney's ideology represents a radical departure from the American norm. Its appeal is based on careful attention to centrist values.[8]

WDW does not just suppress people of color and women, as does the larger world; it has a tendency to suppress anything problematic, no matter how central to European American history. This suppression is part of its pleasure contract. People spend a lot of money in Disney parks in order to forget everyday unpleasantness and participate in a certain set of remembrances. EPCOT, produced as it was after many social changes (it opened in 1982), is more likely to acknowledge problems because history had already undergone tremendous revision in the sixties and seventies. Instead of obliterating all things negative, "The American Adventure" depicts the Great Depression as a healthy obstacle and World War II as a positively charged transformation (Fjellman 1992:99–107).

The standard philosophical critiques of Disney, his representations on the screen and in his theme parks, his political and philosophical position vis-à-vis American capitalism and colonialism, while valid, interesting, and important, miss a key point. Yes, Disney *is* the apotheosis of consumerism. The world becomes a commodity at Walt Disney World, and America is the ultimate consumer of that commodity. WDW reproduces and inculcates colonialism. What in these United States does not do so? Certainly little or nothing in the mass purview. We could visit Disney World through the eyes of a Louis Marin or a Jean Baudrillard or a Teodor Adorno, but we are not taking that sort of trip. I resist such puritanism. The same instinct that causes me to distrust Disney causes me to distrust such analyses: for anyone who cannot have *some* fun at and with Disney is frighteningly out of touch with the field of pleasure that most are bound to in some way. And this is precisely the point: how to enter this problematic world, be seduced and resist simultaneously; how to feel the pleasure and pain of such a seduction; how, as a wounded subject, to enter WDW aware that it enforces a certain kind of contact with itself and its representation of the world and live through it without being destroyed; indeed, how to reread that world so that Disney's map does not remain in control. This is the task at hand in the larger world because Disney *is* the larger world, or to put it another way, contemporary life on the North American continent has become one endless vacation coextensive with Disney's images. I want to say yes to Michael Ventura's observation that to "vacation" is

> *an idea only about one hundred years old. To "vacation" is to enter an image. . . . What thrills tourists is the sense of being surrounded in "real life" by the same images that they see on TV. . . . Our recreation is a re-creation of America into one big Disneyland. (179)*

But I want to offer a promise and a hope that we can learn to walk through Disney without losing ourselves, that we can acquire a skill, an oppositional literacy[9] that might give us power analogous to Disney's but be able to serve our goals, and perhaps even be able to seduce others. We must enter Disney with a confidence that we can move through this world despite its difficulties because we already live there and have no other ground from which to save ourselves.

> *Disneyland is there to conceal the fact that it is the "real" country, all of "real" America, which is Disneyland (just as prisons are there to conceal the fact that it is the social in its entirety, in its banal omnipresence, which is carceral). Disneyland is presented as imaginary in order to make us believe that the rest is real, when in fact all of Los Angeles and the America surrounding it are no longer real, but of the order of the hyperreal and of simulation. (Baudrillard 1988:172)*

Disney has both mirrored the commodification of the contemporary scene and intensified it. Despite ourselves, we desire these landscapes. Despite ourselves, we spend weekends at the mall.

We all enter the world with desire. We are all manipulated by that desire. We would do well to learn some of Uncle Walt's skills, dubbed "The Magic of Disney" by the advertising executives of his empire, for they represent the power to reach our imaginations. It is still my hope that this faculty can be turned in many directions, not just to the ideological right.

In this essay, Disney World ultimately becomes a heuristic for thinking about literacy in the contemporary information age, an age whose media images are re-technologized constantly. Its working hypothesis is that EPCOT does not so much enhance your literacy as challenge it. Precisely because much of public space is structured á la Disney, WDW becomes a "test" space, where much of the pleasure of the experience rests in recognizing that you already know how to read it.

Literacy testing at Disney World, like literacy testing outside this world, has to do with skills embedded in general knowledge. It probably does not have to do with consciously remembering "information" or absorbing new concepts. In fact, there is so much information/image overload at WDW that it is almost impossible to hold on to a coherent sense of what you have seen. Writing about Disney reminds one that the questions regarding the relationship between memory and literacy are not trivial. Asking anyone to demonstrate his/her literacy by answering questions such as "What did you learn today?" "What can you tell me about?" will often result in a confused silence. Humans simply do not access the ineffable fund of "what they know" through such questions.

At WDW, much of what you see is either irrelevant to the stated topic or falsified, and what you do not see is at least as important as what you do. Disney World can be seen as a test of one's ability to move through a library catalog that possesses much ideology but little depth. What does one learn from such an exercise? Perhaps only to make or unmake connections. Much of Disney World may make sense only if you already recognize the symbols before you; for those who do not, the entertainment factor compensates for the gaps.

There is some evidence that WDW visitors are already adept at making their way through the maze that it presents to them. They are probably more literate than average. A high percentage of Disney World's visitors have home computers (*Compute* 1988:86). This may correlate with the general affluence of its visitors, but EPCOT in design and operation assumes that its visitors will at least be willing to play with its computers, will take them as an accepted part of the scene. The computers are simply there, spread throughout the park. There is no particular inducement to use them.

Here are two anecdotes about failed literacy at Disney World. Alexander Moore (1980) describes the Haunted Mansion in the Magic Kingdom as a rite of passage that is meant to simulate real terror while simultaneously signifying to its visitors that we all know this is just in fun, that such horrors do not exist. But some visitors have not bought into the scientific narrative subtext at the heart of this pavilion.

> *A working-class black woman of my acquaintance . . . was so terrified by [the Haunted Mansion] that she fled to the chartered bus and remained there the rest of the day, refusing to see any other attractions. The message is for middle-class Americans acquainted with science. (217–235)*

Moore's interpretation of this reaction is self-serving, even mildly racist in its undertones. He might have said: "The message is for white middle-class Americans acquainted with science." Perhaps he would be right in making such a statement.

Still another visitor spent an entire day in Tomorrowland, thinking it was the complete park (Birnbaum 1986:71). Tomorrowland is part of the Magic Kingdom (roughly equivalent to Anaheim's Disneyland), but the Magic Kingdom in total is less than half the size of EPCOT, and Disney World contains far more than either of those two major attractions. This visitor failed utterly to grasp the extent of the place.

All of this implies a complex set of relationships between a Disney World visitor's expectations, skills, knowledge, and desires. While the place may assume a level of literacy and participation in a set of cultural assumptions and keys, the sheer number of emblems results in a cascade that the visitor is ultimately free to order as s/he wishes. It may be that once you enter WDW with a level of literacy that is equal to the assumed common denominator, you are free to use an alternate literacy, a literacy that can both tolerate the manipulation and laugh in its face.

In "A Theory of Expositions," an essay written before his visit to Disney World but after visiting Expo '67, Umberto Eco imagined that expositions of the future might become collections of symbolic objects and necessarily ambiguous; they would allow for many possible interpretations. "We know that when this form of communication takes place it can have good results and increase the freedom and creativity of the recipient of the message" (1986:303). Another possibility for expositions is that they will become "educational instrument[s], teaching device[s]." Eco was sanguine about the possibilities of such places. He called for an "avant-garde didactics, a developing pedagogy, a revolutionary way of teaching" leading to expositions that would

> *utilize systems of popularized communication, valid for any visitor, which other means of communication, from TV to newspapers, cannot employ with equal intensity. . . . The Canadians, masters of experimental and documentary moviemaking, used different systems of projection on many screens or on panoramic screens of unusual sizes and format . . . the simultaneous projection of many movies, the sense of rhythm, the contradictory or complementary play of competing images, the suggestion of new spatial effects, were superior to any known Cinerama techniques. Here the visitors, to whom humanity's history on earth was told with beautiful images, received a clear, informative message. They felt aesthetic emotion from communication that gave them ideas and data to think about, decisions to make, conclusions to draw. In this case, we talk about the pedagogy of the avant-garde, because the communication was directed to educated and naive visitors alike, in such a way that both could get what they understood and were struck by. (305)*

Clearly, Disney modeled much of EPCOT on the principles employed at Expo '67. Eco ends his essay with an observation that is relevant to the basic purposes of this study:

> *Even if an exposition could be a perfect teaching device, as we have suggested, is it worth the expense and effort? To organize an exposition means to organize a teaching machine dedicated to all the peoples of the world. But, as we know very well, the visitors to Expo (with the possible exception of the Canadians) were well-to-do people, and these people generally can obtain ideas from innumerable cultural sources. They are the ones who least need these universal teaching devices. The world is able to produce splendid expositions but cannot allow all its children to move freely (politically and economically) to attend the Expo school. An exposition anywhere inevitably becomes a sort of mass communication for elites. In a pessimistic moment we might thus become convinced of the uselessness of expositions (though still recognizing their experimental and stimulating value). But we can draw other conclusions and make other hypotheses. For example: Isn't it absurd that in our century we still build stationary expositions? Shouldn't the designers of future expositions confront again the problem of Mohammed and the Mountain? (306–307)*

Indeed, the problem is not just how to enter WDW but how to get there. For many of those who cannot afford the trip are members of the same cultural and racial groups that are invisible at Disney World.

MARCO POLO AND KUBLA KHAN: DESIRING THE CANON, CANONIZING THE EMPIRE

Italo Calvino's *Invisible Cities* (1974) begins with a Marco Polo newly arrived at the court of the Khan and ignorant of the Levantine languages. He is required to report on the Khan's vast provinces, but he

> *could express himself only with gestures, leaps, cries of wonder and of horror, animal barkings or hooting, or with objects he took from his knapsacks—ostrich plumes, pea-shooters, quartzes. . . . One city was depicted by the leap of a fish escap-*

*ing the cormorant's beak to fall into a net; another city by a
naked man running through fire unscorched; a third by a skull,
its teeth green with mold, clenching a round, white pearl. The
Great Khan deciphered the signs, but the connection between
them and the places visited remained uncertain. . . . But, obscure or obvious as it might be, everything Marco displayed
had the power of emblems, which, once seen, cannot be forgotten
or confused. In the Khan's mind the empire was reflected in
a desert of labile and interchangeable data, like grains of
sand. . . .*

   *. . . "On the day when I know all the emblems," he asked
Marco, "shall I be able to possess my empire, at last?"*

   *And the Venetian answered: "Sire, do not believe it. On
that day you will be an emblem among emblems." (21–23)*

In *Invisible Cities,* the Great Khan's empire represents the illusion of totalizing knowledge. For Khan, knowledge is abstract; it resides in the emblems that are his only access to a world too vast for him to experience directly. For Marco Polo, knowledge is concrete: it resides in the objects he
pulls out of his knapsacks and in his own practical ability to negotiate the
world. Both desire knowledge. Polo is Khan's lieutenant in this project of
canonizing the empire. For Khan, knowledge of his empire represents total
power over it. He cannot accept what Polo probably knows but cannot articulate: knowledge is local, embedded in the concrete signifiers of a particular place and its cultural codes. But Khan cannot control his desire to know
the unknowable. His appetite is voracious, and it feeds on his fear of how
the unknown threatens his political empire.

WDW *can* be read as Uncle Walt's identical desire to possess the American empire and everything beyond it as his own, simultaneously masking
what Walt could not and would not know of himself. Walt found a way to
do this without leaving home, without leaving dead center. Like *Invisible
Cities,* WDW as a whole represents an illusion of totalizing knowledge. But
as I write this with full awareness of the murderous results that such impulses
lead to, I cannot repress an affection for Walt, who brought me real pleasure
as a child and even as an adult. Neither can I repress an affection for Khan,
for his hunger to know is too similar to my own to dismiss as simply the will
to power.

Walt's collection of emblems is as potent as the Khan's. Once seen, they
cannot be forgotten. Backlit ice sculptures on the village square in the dark
of a winter night in Northern China, Banff in the Canadian Rockies, a bal-

loon ride along a lazy river in the French countryside, all press deep into the memory. His emblems take their place in the mind as markers for the world.

We can follow Disney's and the Khan's lead and reach for a kind of power over the whole, or we can move through it like Marco, with a mute fascination, a delicate touch, and a reverence for the emblems themselves because the objects produced by a people are not trivial; they are the material encodings of their lives, and the physical landscapes against which those objects can be seen are part of the lives of the people and the production of the objects. And although EPCOT is chock-full of Disney-manufactured simulacra, it is also chock-full of originals, "real" museum pieces: a 150-year-old Wells Fargo stagecoach, telephone wire from 1920, restored automobiles, eighteenth-century Chinese clocks, antique Japanese kites. Many of these items are displayed in dioramas that are otherwise full of replicas, a practice that has the effect of further confusing the visitor as to the importance of the distinction between original and reproduction.

How to travel like Marco Polo on this "net" of literacy that has no center and no edges? Remember Eco: "The main feature of a net is that every point can be connected with every other point, and where the connections are not yet designed, they are, however, conceivable and designable" (1984b:81). Such knowledge is partial, just as the local knowledge is partial, but it can—because it passes through many local knowledges—(a) be highly adaptive, changing, ready for change, and precipitating change and (b) be creative, able to engender new local knowledges through cross-fertilization. Labyrinthine literacy would enable its possessor to make multiple hypotheses, would *require* such a series of acts. From this mode can come enormous understanding and tolerance, creativity and product. Codes that cross cultures, multicultural codes, open the field of meaning to constantly shifting possibility in the midst of paradox. They syncretize the field of meaning.

Gloria Anzaldúa's *Borderlands* is one example of the kind of travel I postulate. Like Marco Polo, Anzaldúa is traveling through a "net" of knowledges. Her "*la conciencia de la mestiza*," "consciousness of the Borderlands," is the result of what is in America a forced travel between cultures, races, classes, genders, sexualities, and all manner of positions. *La mestiza*'s self, her body, the result of the rape of Native American women by the conquistadors, is a physical representation of what it means to cross over. The material conditions she experiences (e.g., inhabiting geographical borders like the Southwest or a complex urban borderland, and/or Mexican, Native American, and Anglo cultures, and/or multiple classes at once as when she is born into one class and educated into another, and/or multiple sexualities, and on and on and on) force her into a new consciousness.

This consciousness of the borderlands results in a tolerance for contradictions, a tolerance for ambiguity. *La mestiza* "learns to be an Indian in Mexican culture, to be a Mexican from an Anglo point of view. She learns to juggle cultures. She has a plural personality" (Anzaldúa 1987:79).[10]

For Anzaldúa, "*me zumba la cabeza con lo contradictorio,*" her head buzzes with contradictions that are the result of inhabiting multiple positions simultaneously. The new mestiza is in possession of a skill, a labyrinthine literacy that enables her to travel through local knowledges and engender new local knowledges through cross-fertilization.

ECO'S LABYRINTH: DISNEY'S ENCYCLOPEDIA

Remember that Eco tells us that "the universe of semiosis, that is, the universe of human culture, must be conceived" to be structured like a labyrinth and that every attempt to codify local knowledges as "unique and 'global'—ignoring their partiality—produces an *ideological bias*" (1984b:83–84). Such local knowledges have the potential to "be contradicted by alternative and equally 'local' cultural organizations" (84). In other words, paradox becomes a familiar part of such a net. I cannot imagine a better description of Disney's labyrinth. Its ideological bias can be understood in part to be the result of its attempt to globalize (canonize) one local knowledge, American capitalism. But even more interestingly, its richness can be understood to be a manifestation of the power it conveys to travel between local knowledges. It makes explicit the possibility of exchanging information between all points.

DISNEY'S CLOSED TEXTS

Another of Umberto Eco's notions may be helpful when addressing the issue of alternative readings of Disney and may explain his own interest in expositions. In *The Role of the Reader* (1984a), Eco defines *closed* and *open* texts.[11]

> *In the process of communication, a text is frequently interpreted against the background of codes different from those intended by the author. Some authors do not take into account such a possibility. . . . Those texts that obsessively aim at arousing a precise response on the part of more or less precise empirical readers . . .*

> *are in fact open to any possible "aberrant" decoding. A text so
> immoderately "open" to every possible interpretation will be
> called a closed one. . . . My ideological reading [of Superman]
> was only one among the possible: the most feasible for a smart
> semiotician who knows very well the "codes" of the heavy
> industry of dreams in a capitalistic society. But why not read
> Superman stories only as a new form of romance that is free
> from any pedagogical intention? Doing so would not betray the
> nature of the saga. Superman comic strips are also this. And
> much more. They can be read in various ways, each way being
> independent from the others. (8–9)*

Closed texts are formulaic, familiar. Disney's texts are closed; therefore an individual can read them as s/he wishes, according to her desire. One moment s/he may undermine the ideological effect, the other s/he may be swept up by it.

Closed texts are also what Eco terms "iterative," narratives that are highly redundant in structure. They hammer away at the same meaning we acquired earlier in another text of the same genre or series. Detective novels, serials, situation comedies, soap operas are all iterative. Iterative texts exploit the human hunger for repetition. The hunger for entertaining narrative based on these mechanisms is a *hunger for redundance.* From this viewpoint, the greater part of popular narrative is a narrative of redundance (120).

Eco goes on to observe that the continually unsettled nature of contemporary life feeds the need for redundancy in entertainment and this provides a brief respite and "invitation to repose, the only occasion of true relaxation offered to the consumer" (121). The typical intellectual moralism regarding escapist entertainments fails to note that in fact, such activity may be innocuous, even beneficial, at times.

If closed texts are seen in this way, as open to every possible interpretation, and we can identify Disney's texts as closed and iterative, we have a key to both their seductive power and their weakness on the ideological level. There is nothing exotic at Disney that is not surrounded by an iterative structure. The pavilions are textually similar, often identical: a "ride" moves the individual through the central "narrative" of the pavilion,[12] whether that be Disney's history of communication or agriculture or transportation; this "main attraction," as it is termed, is supplemented by more-traditional museum-type displays, whether they be hands-on or static; the crowd-control spaces of the pavilions often contain warm-up entertainments.

All of these texts do precisely what Eco suggests: they aim at arousing a precise response in an average reader. In doing so, the closed text opens itself to variant interpretations while at the same time providing a space for relaxed reverie. But it is not just the major pavilions that work this way at Disney. Virtually every sign on the scene is closed and iterative. Disney's characters themselves all remain within tightly constructed definitional bounds. Mickey is echoed by Minnie, Donald, Goofy, Dumbo, and all the rest. The transportation system incorporates every conceivable trope for movement,[13] but in a curious way all these conveyances, from steam trains to monorails to conveyers to submarines to paddle wheelers to moving auditoriums, feel the same. The ratio of scale by which everything from mailboxes and lampposts to the Eiffel Tower and Mexican pyramids is reduced not only marks the surroundings in a particular way as "other," it also wraps every emblem in an aura of familiarity. This is one way to encase the exotic, but it also creates a closed text.

Disney's closed and iterative texts ultimately work against themselves, giving us choices if we enter WDW with a different set of desires and providing redundance that enables us to relax in the face of what seems like an endless stream of emblems. As it is, this structure gives us freedom to organize the labyrinth as we wish. As we wander through WDW with our desires, they help us alight where we will. Closed texts have their uses.

CONJECTURING RE: BENJAMIN AND DISNEY

The pastiche that follows began with the author's fascination for Walter Benjamin's ability to think and write cultural theory through the agency of imaginative figures. The Paris of the 1840's produced a genre of mass literature known as the *physiologies,* illustrated volumes that caricatured dubiously identified social types of the period. Walter Benjamin takes the image of the flaneur, one of the types on the scene at the time, as a central metaphor for his unfinished surrealist historiography, *Das Passagen-Werk* (Sieburth). The Parisian arcades of the nineteenth century were the setting for the flaneur, a dandified creature who strolled through these arcades with a cultivated attitude of detachment, who sometimes walked turtles while he perused the crowd and the shops. The flaneur, Benjamin tells us, liked to let the turtles set the pace. Susan Buck-Morss (1986) explains Benjamin's fascination with the arcades:

> *The arcades, interior streets lined with luxury shops and open*
> *through iron and glass roofs to the stars, were a wish-image,*

expressing the bourgeois individual's desire to escape through the symbolic medium of objects from the isolation of his/her subjectivity. On the boulevards, the flaneur, now jostled by crowds and in full view of the urban poverty which inhabited public streets, could maintain a rhapsodic view of modern existence only with the aid of illusion, which is just what the literature of flanerie—physiognomies, novels of the crowd—was produced to provide. (103)

Benjamin's Angel of History, rag-picker, sandwichman, and flaneur were all "figurative" constructs that he used to face and unpack history, past and present. The sandwichman became the last incarnation of Benjamin's flaneur, a dandified "window-shopper" who habitually "walked" turtles through the glass-enclosed arcades of Paris. Recalling at once the notion of the sandwiches of the working class and the walking signboards used to advertise (Buck-Morss 1986:107), the sandwichman's incarnation in the second half of the twentieth century might be the T-shirt wearer who advertises everything from Coke to Jaguars. The Angel of History gave Benjamin an image that expressed his despair that no power could halt the horrible catastrophe that history piles at the Angel's feet (Benjamin 1985b:257).

So the flaneur came to serve as a powerful image around which Benjamin could organize his analysis of modernism. Like all of Benjamin's images, the flaneur needs to be apprehended ambivalently. The flaneur's mode of attention cultivated both a slow and distanced reverie and a quick and distracted glance; he is a spectator who sometimes scans the surface (and that only for an instant), sometimes stares carefully through the scene as if he could see it and erase it simultaneously. Adorno pointed to the station-switching behavior of the radio listener as a kind of aural *flanerie* (Buck-Morss 1986:105). This scanning behavior is typical in contemporary America. The flaneur either slows to a fourth dimension or speeds up to a fifth; he is nowhere and everywhere at once. This perceptual strategy functions as a kind of psychological strobe that catches images otherwise flattened by the frames of normal time. This strategy sometimes captures those surface features that hint at what lies below, or at least the flaneur thinks this is so. In the late twentieth century, the electronic flaneur "grazes" through the cable networks with a remote and fast-forwards through a video.

Benjamin lived on the edge of the Disney age—by the 1930's, Disney's first features were already a success in Paris (Buck-Morss 1986:100)—and Disney World is a direct descendant of the expositions and arcades that fascinated Benjamin. Hence it is not surprising to learn that Benjamin's reflections on film and mass culture consistently touched on Disney (Hansen 1993:27).

The flaneur at Disney World is at home in the world of technology, art, and mechanical reproduction. He moves from diorama to diorama as much at home among Disney's facades of the past, present, future as he is in his hometown arcade, his hometown mall. EPCOT's computers are his libraries, its 360-degree theaters his cafes. "The arcades are a cross between a street and an interieur." EPCOT is a cross between a botanized arcade and space travel.

The flaneur strolls through the maze of arcades that is Disney. Aware of the riches, the impossibility of connecting, the will to commodify, he oscillates between this aimless sauntering and a driven will to absorb all. "He catches things in flight; this enables him to dream that he is like an artist" (Benjamin 1983:41). The flaneur believes he can catch and then create. The endless juxtaposition of simulacra, of tropes, stimulates intense original visions. The flaneur rearranges the simulacra, creates private dioramas from new combinations. But it is a truism that Disney *is* surface, so everything *must be* sucked from the surface, and the dialectic of the saunter/frenzy somehow makes this possible. The reproduction *is* the authentic. The world is all there at EPCOT; the past is all present at the Magic Kingdom. Historicity and geography jell in every object.

> *The world exhibitions glorify the exchange value of commodities. They create a framework in which commodities' intrinsic value is eclipsed. They open up a phantasmagoria that people enter to be amused. The entertainment industry facilitates this by elevating people to the level of commodities. They submit to being manipulated while enjoying their alienation from themselves and others. (Benjamin 1978:152)*

"The flaneur . . . goes botanizing on the asphalt" (Benjamin 1983:36). The natural world is carefully controlled by the architecture of the arcade; the "live" is allowed its privileged place. There is no discernible line between the organic and the inorganic. Disney's arcade is well planted and populated by animal species that are carefully orchestrated into the whole. A small flock of flamingos makes the EPCOT lagoon its home. Still living in colonies of some twenty thousand in the nineteenth century when John Audubon visited, the nearly extinct Florida flamingo no longer lives in the wild. Disney's flamingos, a hardier species that tolerates asphalt, are imports from the Caribbean.

THE FLANEUR MEETS EL PACHUCO
AT DISNEY WORLD

The spectator at Disney World alternates between a distanced assessment and a druglike, hallucinatory state that is a kind of engagement, the deep engagement of a chemically induced meditation.

The flaneur at Disneyland walks a turtle among thousands of screens, each frantically/limitlessly/furiously flashing superficial images of history that paradoxically reveal history's inner reality. The crowd at Disney is purposefully purposeless.

> It is to him, aimlessly strolling through the crowds in the big
> cities in studied contrast to their hurried, purposeful activity,
> that things reveal themselves in their secret meaning: "The true
> picture of the past flits by" ("Philosophy of History"), and
> only the flaneur who idly strolls by receives the message.
> (Arendt 1985:12)

The image of the flaneur at Disney World is the image of a wanderer who is attempting to control the space/time around her by choosing a unique path through a labyrinth designed by Disney. The flaneur at Disneyland is assaulted from all corners, so that distance from the commodity cannot be maintained. Disney happens to you. His simulacra hit you and lodge in you. "The work of art of the Dadaists became an instrument of ballistics. It hit the spectator like a bullet, it happened to him" (Benjamin 1985b:238). In the same way, the commodity at Disney World invades the flaneur's cool and then retreats around the bend of the endless panorama. The power of the flaneur to apprehend, to connect with everything, is fostered by the endless parade, which suggests infinite possibility. But the flaneur at Disneyland is powerless to control the parade of panoramas. The images and constructs collide with the flaneur.

There is a remarkable resemblance between the attitude and style of the flaneur and the American pachuco. The pachuco was a distinctly American "type," most famous for the zoot-suit riots of 1943 in Los Angeles, which were triggered by U.S. military personnel who engaged in pachuco-bashing. Contrary to racist memory, the riots were remarkably nonviolent; no one was killed and property damage was slight (Mazón 1984:5). For many Mexicans, the pachuco represented the crystallization of the *pocho,* i.e., a Mexican born in the United States, alien to both cultures, fluent in neither Spanish nor English (Mazón 1984:1).

The pachuco adopted a dandified and exaggerated style of dress that centered around the zoot suit. The origin of the style is uncertain, but it may have been invented at the close of the nineteenth century. Some believe it derived from Clark Gable's dress in *Gone with the Wind* (Mazón 1984:7). As a distinctly American type, it has been portrayed in Luis Valdez's *Zoot Suit* and Edward James Olmos's *American Me* and surfaces again in Spike Lee's *Malcolm X*. It may have been copied back and forth between African American and Latino communities. In any case, the pachuco was clearly caught between cultures and invented both the style of dress and behavior as a defense against his entrapment.

Octavio Paz notes that the young men and women of France in 1945, descendants of Benjamin's flaneur, wore clothing not unlike the American pachucos. Amazed at the similarity, he inquired as to its roots. Virtually everyone he questioned insisted that it was a strictly French phenomenon that arose at the end of the Occupation. More important, Paz was convinced that the pachuco's

> hybrid language and behavior reflect[ed] a[n] oscillation between two irreducible worlds—the North American and the Mexican—which he vainly hopes to reconcile and conquer . . . his clothing spotlights and isolates him, but at the same time it pays homage to the society he is attempting to deny.
> (Paz 1961:16, 18)

The pachuco, like the flaneur, is a creature of ambivalence. A wounded subject on the scene,

> the pachuco tries to enter North American society in secret and daring ways, but he impedes his own efforts. Having been cut off from his traditional culture, he asserts himself for a moment as a solitary and challenging figure. He denies both the society from which he originated and that of North America. . . . The pachuco does not affirm or defend anything except his exasperated will-not-to-be. He is not divulging his most intimate feelings: he is revealing an ulcer, exhibiting a wound.
> (Paz 1961:17)

The zoot-suiters were attacked by servicemen and civilians, absorbing much displaced war anxiety. Mauricio Mazón speculates on the motives for the attack: zoot-suiters appeared nonsensical because, among other things, they took pride in their ambiguity. The narcissistic self-absorption of the zoot-suiter in a world of illusory omnipotentiality was in opposition to the modesty of individual selflessness attributed to the defense worker and the soldier (Mazón 1984:9).

Our pachuco is a cyborg guerrilla. He forces the question of how to replace a male European American image and imagining with an oppositional image and imagining, a trickster who understands the simulacrum's game because s/he has been out and about playing that game for a very long time.

PACHUCO MICKEY

Clowns are good because they show the image is not the fact. They say, "I am not the ultimate image. I am transparent to something." The Trickster points out that no matter what system of knowledge you have, it is partial.
—JOSEPH CAMPBELL, *THE POWER OF MYTH*

The library of the future will take on a profoundly different materiality, appearing more and more like EPCOT.[14] The shelf as a method of storage is passé. Film becomes potent in an electronic archive in a way it could not have been earlier. Individuals enter a virtual network of film in an electronic mediation of experience; EPCOT provides a literalization of this process. Film and body are caught together in this electronic archive.

Disney's narratives, like all, are ideological constructs, and the live bodies traversing EPCOT are narrativized and constructed into the scene. Surely this is part of the exhilaration. Ironically, while the human body is absent from most of EPCOT's didactic films—natural force, landscape, and edifice standing in for human agents, simulacra for human actors—the spectator's body is engaged as often as possible. The bodies presented here (usually as part of numerous overlapping origin stories) are beautifully crafted fictions. If the body is intrinsic to semiosis, EPCOT is a sophisticated engine for furthering a complex set of messages aimed at pleasuring the guest's senses while representing a configured and idealized male body. The bodies of people of color and women, and therefore the narratives surrounding them, are largely absent in EPCOT's displays.[15] They are deleted even when the narrative positively demands their participation. When they are included as tokens, their agency is bleached away. Disney, as the master trickster on the scene, has taken control of bodies, mutated and mutilated them without mercy in the service of his narrative.

Three of EPCOT's presentations are particularly interesting in this regard: the CircleVision-360 *Wonders of China* film, the multimedia presentation "The American Adventure,"[16] and Michael's 3-D film *Captain E/O*. WDW's film cannot be described with traditional vocabulary. Part of its somatic contract is to appeal to more than the visual; movement and smell are especially important. While the parks are giant technologies for the re-inscription of multiple ideological agendas, they are also sensory training grounds where millions, eventually billions, of humans are being trained in an environment of sensory overload to adjust to new technologies of representation. Theme parks à la Disney may find a place alongside virtual-reality technologies in a continuum of replicated experience in postmodern life.

WDW's intense sensory overload is preparing us for virtual-reality entertainments that are already in existence but are not yet commercially available for mass consumption. These new entertainments will offer increasingly addictive bodily pleasures and will surely be turned into teaching machines of one sort or another. Virtual-reality literacy will become another literacy challenge.

WDW's 180- and 360-degree travelogues are sensory delights during which flight over a mountain, a valley, a castle, a river, or some other geographical feature or built structure in France, Canada, China, or the United States is replicated with enough visual cues to stimulate the sexy illusion of free flight. Disney's 360-degree, 3-D, and multiple-screen theaters combined with sensarama and smellarama go beyond the average person's everyday film experience to which the postmodern audience has become somewhat immune. The split-second timing of multiple images and sensations in many analogous mediums is intoxicating.

This mode of representation calls upon reading skills that extend beyond the visual. How is reading done at the somatic level? Disney has found the answer. It involves sound, motion, touch, and smell. Disney's outdoor sound systems are probably the best in the world; the air is filled with alternately soothing and stimulating music.

Disney uses multiple screens and multiple visual media to create displays of enormous complexity, integrating film seamlessly into other displays. Newer exhibits use off-screen space even more effectively than earlier ones. By definition, 3-D film breaks the frame, but *Captain E/O* does so before the film begins by sprinkling the borders of the screen with stars that enhance the illusion of depth as the film progresses; the Muppets 3-D film is preceded by a multiple video pre-show, which suggests that the Muppets are moving into an offstage, "real" space. Inside the 3-D theater,

Audio-Animatronic[17] Muppets in box seats to the right side of the screen banter with the film's stars. All of this helps to wrap the spectator's body in a carefully constructed envelope of experience. This body becomes part of the narrative and is redrawn according to its dictates. The spectator must interpolate her body into Disney's narrative.

Other symbolic methodologies for breaking the frame result in complicated inclusions of the viewer/voyeur at Disney parks. At points, the spectator's body and/or representation is included in the scene, presented as part of the show, recruited as an actor, or even referenced by the show—for example, when the Muppets (in the MGM-Disney Studios park) ironically point to each audience member in 3-D and say, "All these other people think I'm talking to them, but I'm really just talking to you."[18] Who is synopticoning whom at Disney?

While the "guest" gazes, s/he is under surveillance. At EPCOT, the Worldwide Information Service attendants can be summoned via a touch screen computer; while they speak directly to you, at first you do not realize that they can see you. These confusions add to the disorientation and serve to further envelop the spectator.

Another methodology for enveloping the body is CircleVision-360. These 360-degree travelogues become a sensory trope for freedom and pleasure that is echoed in Disney's use of water throughout the parks. Water is visual stimulus in the form of lakes, fountains, canals, pools, ponds, and even at the extraordinary water displays at "Journey to the Imagination." But water also stimulates through movement, as guests are conveyed over it in any number of vehicles; through smell, as aromas are pumped into displays; and through touch, as it contacts your skin. The sensation triggered by floating on water is a distinct pleasure that Disney has not forgotten, and water scenes are key to many park films, especially the CircleVision-360. Thus, liquid simulacra in the form of artificial lagoons, ponds, lakes, rivers, and so on, are echoes of the representations of water inside the theaters, working together to envelop the spectator.

The visitor to WDW encounters water directly. Damp air is created to enhance presentations like the "Universe of Energy"'s primeval dinosaur forest and "The Land"'s boat ride through a hot, damp rain forest; conversely, it is withdrawn during "The Land"'s desert diorama. The Muppets' 3-D film sprinkles you lightly; the Backstage Studio Tour at MGM-Disney Studios includes an earthquake that causes a broken dam carefully to dampen those seated on the left side of the tram. There is so much water-based simulation at WDW that an employee was heard to announce to visitors who were being pelted by an all-too-frequent Florida rainstorm, "This isn't real rain. It's Disney rain" (Fjellman 1992:217).

From the center of EPCOT's hourglass, at the spot where Future World meets World Showcase, China is a quarter-mile walk[19] past Mexico and Norway. China's attractions are arranged in a rough circle. Passing under an ornate ceremonial gate, the pedestrian is attracted by a small footbridge just ahead and slightly to the right. It showcases a pond to the left and right of it and leads to the entrance to China's main attraction, one of two Circle-Vision-360 theaters at EPCOT. Housed in a building based on a section of Beijing's Temple of Heaven, the anteroom to this theater is one of the few at EPCOT that provide seating. While guests wait for the film to begin, they can visit the museum to the left, the House of Whispering Willows. In 1993, it was filled with a beautiful display of dragon iconography. Titled "Dragon: Ruler of the Wind and Waves," the display's figures are contextualized within a stereotypical Disney narrative. An Orientalist paragraph on the center wall presents dragons as fairy tale with no hint that the dragon calls upon a spiritual tradition as subtle as the Christian Trinity.

Inside, the nineteen-minute travelogue, *Wonders of China: Land of Beauty, Land of Time,* is one of Disney's finest. Made in partnership with the China Film Co-Production Company (a subsidiary of the PRC's Ministry of Culture) and filmed in 1981–1982 during Deng Xaioping's "opening to the West," some of its aerial scenes were shot by Chinese crews, while the Disney people were kept on the ground (Fjellman 1992:238).

Uncharacteristically narrated by a guide, eighth-century Tang Dynasty poet Li Bai, played by actor Shich Kuan, it is much less Orientalist than it might have been. And it is stunningly beautiful. The audience is told to lean, not sit, on the supportive railings and is assured that the theater does not move despite the distinct somatic feedback cued by the visual images. CircleVision-360 provides one of the most intense somatic effects at WDW, delivering its wallop during aerial scenes, summoning autonomic physical sensations. In this film, Chinese landscape painting is effectively juxtaposed with filmed footage of "actual" landscape. China's art and geography are one, we are told. Geographical touring via body sensation is a major methodology in CircleVision-360 and its close technological cousins.

Water is figured in this presentation not just as a soothing and exciting entertainment but as a historical actor. Li Bai intones:

> *It may be said that the history of the Chinese people is not written in ink but with water. Water, at times too much and*

sometimes not enough—it has been China's sorrow for ages. Along the 3,000 miles of the Yangtze River live and work one-tenth of the population of the world; they are no longer the servants of water, but its master.

The Yangtze becomes a stand-in for thousands of years of exploitation and oppression by unnamed political actors. Dangerous water can bring us more than sensual delight, but we can contain it. This message is intrinsic to the rest of EPCOT; humans are willfully mastering the environment with the help of science and technology. It is interesting to note that water is a central trope in Chinese culture and is configured as an immense force. For once, Disney's methodology dovetails nicely with key elements in a cultural narrative, except that water does not simply pleasure and nourish. The Chinese narrative overwhelms Disney's formula. Nowhere else in Disney World does water threaten danger.

Ordinarily, Disney grossly distorts culture differences, homogenizing them into a happy culti-multural mix from which every alien element emerges Mickey-clean and ready for shopping mall consumption. It has at its disposal a vast array of techniques that neatly reinscribe difference, writing over bland diversity. From the Gobi Desert, to Tibet, to Inner Mongolia, to the Forbidden City of Beijing, to Suzhou, Shanghai, Harbin, Guilin, the Yangtze, it is no accident that China's culti-multural travelogue reinscribes the East/West vocabulary of North America on the Asian continent. On the eastern coast, "Shanghai, the city of cosmopolitan delight," is presented as European and sophisticated. On the other hand, even in modern times western China is represented as filled with "traditional" Mongolian horsemen. And "the world's most inland city," Urumqi, is located in the "wilderness" of Xinjiang Province despite the wraparound view filled with the smoke of industrialism. Disney has managed to inscribe onto the vast Asian topos a classic North American dualism: the East signifies culture, the West, primitive nature. This must slide down smoothly for American and Americanized visitors who are all too familiar with our master narrative. Their literacy within this universe of knowledge helps to organize the cascade of difference that is China. This beautiful film delights our senses and is more informative than the average, all the while containing China's powerful dragon, white tiger, and monkey spirits in mythological discourse and understated visuals. It suggests that China's human bodies have never suffered, and though we are told the continent has a long history, we are never introduced to it.

This is definitely not the case at EPCOT's centerpiece, "The American

Adventure." A long walk from China past Germany and Italy, "The American Adventure" is unlike any other presentation in the park—or anywhere else, for that matter. It combines film with Audio-Animatronic figures in one of the few traditionally styled theaters in the park, signifying stability to its audience even in its architecture and theatrical modes. Most major attractions include a "ride-through" presentation, but in this centerpiece pavilion, the audience remains stationary, as it would outside Disney World, while the figures and stage move. This is a somatic cue to swallow the ideology, to "sit still" and imbibe it. Housed in a Georgian colonial edifice built with handmade pink clay bricks, it combines thirty-five Audio-Animatronic figures with the world's largest rear-projection screen (seventy-two feet wide) and ten sets that rise and rotate from below (Birnbaum 1986:93, 150–151). The "live" pre-show is delivered inside the rotunda by the vocal group the Voices of Liberty. What follows this no-tech presentation is fifties Disney technology taken to its apotheosis.

The engine that drives Disney lives underground, a skillful appropriation of the sea-level Florida swamp. Lang's *Metropolis* could not have got it more right. Like NORAD, the power that counts is underground. Even the food emerges endlessly from the lower depths. One vast room is occupied by the computers, which direct everything above. Belowground are stored the world's largest working wardrobe, a photo library and darkrooms, and the wig department. Benjamin noted the underground nature of the modern metropolis: "The Paris of his [Baudelaire's] poems is a submerged city, more submarine than subterranean" (1978:157).

These underground engines drive Disney's most audacious simulacra, his Audio-Animatronic figures. Since 70 percent of Americans have visited Disneyland or Disney World and more have watched televised film of these "robots," virtually all of us are prepared to "read" these mechanical figures as both representations of the famous people they often depict and conjurings of the associations surrounding them. The thirty-five figures that "animate" "The American Adventure" pavilion include representations of Benjamin Franklin, Mark Twain, Frederick Douglass, Chief Joseph, Susan B. Anthony, Alexander Graham Bell, Andrew Carnegie, John Muir, Teddy Roosevelt, Charles Lindbergh, and Rosie the Riveter. The voices of many of the figures in "The American Adventure" were reproduced with painstaking attention to detail. For example, Will Rogers's actual recorded voice was used, his words edited and reedited from published quotations. Bell's voice was "created" from comments about his clarity, expressiveness, and articulation and the fact that his father taught elocution (Birnbaum 124). Jackie Robinson, Marilyn Monroe, Dwight and Mamie Eisenhower, Elvis Presley, Walt

Disney, John Wayne, Lucille Ball, Margaret Mead, John F. Kennedy, Martin Luther King Jr., Muhammed Ali, Billie Jean King, and others are represented in a film montage.

Presented by Coca-Cola and American Express, this twenty-nine-minute pageant begins with John Steinbeck's words delivered by Benjamin Franklin to Thomas Jefferson: "America did not exist. . . . We built America and the process made us Americans." America the topos, the chronotope, did not exist, but America the continent most certainly did. "The American Adventure" spans four centuries and begins with this erasure of Native American peoples and culture.

Disney takes great pains to advertise the authenticity of its simulations. Nevertheless, it has no qualms about writing an entire speech for Chief Joseph, the only Native American represented in this program; his lines are pure Disney except for the unforgettable surrender, "I will fight no more, forever!" (Fjellman 1992:104). This Distory includes only three African American men and three women, all Anglo, in its Audio-Animatronic narrative. No other people of color are represented during this expensive segment. Chief Joseph's sequence segues into Susan B. Anthony delivering a bland speech. She is held in check by simulacra of Alexander Graham Bell and Andrew Carnegie at the 1876 Pennsylvania Centennial Exposition. Similarly, Frederick Douglass is depicted poling through a Mississippi swamp instead of delivering speeches and meeting with political leaders in Washington. Locating him in a wilderness setting strips him of his intellectual and political persona. Later, two Audio-Animatronic African Americans share a Depression-era rural gas station porch and an unrealistically relaxed and equal dialogue with the only anonymous European American Audio-Animatronic figures in this sequence. The final segment in the main portion of the show features two Rosie the Riveters bemoaning the absence of men during World War II, after which the penultimate "Golden Dream" sequence begins. Thus two of the three African American men are anonymous, exactly paralleling the anonymous Rosies and European American men. This is equal opportunity simulation. Its mechanistic notion of balance only underscores the narrative's shortcomings.

For less than five minutes out of the twenty-nine, the series of images presented in "The Golden Dream" forgoes the expensive Audio-Animatronic simulacrum for still photos and film portraits from the twentieth century. Iconic figures and symbols fill the screen at dizzying speed while a sentimental and stirring melody reinforces the illusion of flying and freedom since the audience is not treated to the somatic thrill of movement or water. The song's lyrics supply the only dialogue for this sequence of images.

"Flying high . . ." The audience is all too familiar with the narrative: America equals freedom.

"The American Adventure" provides some evidence that Disney is sometimes forced to respond to the increasing sophistication and diversity of its audience while remaining within the enforced limits of that same audience's literacy and cultural exposure. The revised "Golden Dream" sequence, which now includes European American women and men of color, clearly tries to undo some of the objectionable omissions and distortions of the earlier Audio-Animatronic segment, which could not have been reconfigured without great expense. But because Disney's research revealed that Will Rogers was not recognized by today's high school students, plans to make him the central narrator were canceled (Fjellman 1992:105).

Unfortunately, it reinscribes some of its earlier sins. The Vietnam War is represented by six photos that disappear so quickly they are barely registered. Forty-six individuals appear in "The Golden Dream," including six African Americans, twelve women, and the only two Latinos and the single Asian American to appear in the entire program. Of the twelve women, only two can be said to have had any agency, Eleanor Roosevelt and Gloria Steinem.

Because the male gaze dominates at Disney, with these two exceptions, the women represented in "The American Adventure" have been influential because their bodies have entertained. Even the female athletes portrayed here are representatives of sports that lend themselves to the male gaze: tennis, gymnastics, and figure skating are represented by Billie Jean King, Mary Lou Retton, and Kristi Yamaguchi. Except for Yamaguchi and the Spirit of Heritage statue (an iconic "Indian Maiden") at the right side of the stage, women of color are entirely absent from "The American Adventure" presentation. In this aspect, Distory is no different from canonized history.

Other problematic bodies are also represented so as to repress their potential political force. The heterosexuals Ryan White and Magic Johnson iconically recall AIDS, while Rock Hudson's homosexuality is diffused by Elizabeth Taylor's presence in the same frame. The juxtaposition of Walt Disney, Tinker Bell, and Albert Einstein forms a fascinating triptych of creator, invisible body, and brain.[20]

This impressive and entertaining production ends with EPCOT's theme song. An omnipresent sensual pleasure at Disney World, song envelops the body and the library. Song is precisely the point.

Music "authenticates" much of the experience at EPCOT. If African American intellectualism cannot be represented here, the black minstrel can. Michael Jackson is the only African American ever accorded prominence in this park. Another long walk around the lagoon and past Japan, Morocco,

France, the United Kingdom, and Canada returns us to Future Showcase and the Journey into Imagination pavilion. Inside its Magic Eye Theater, the fifteen-minute 3-D production *Captain E/O,* which has been removed from the Journey into Imagination pavilion but is still shown in Anaheim's Disneyland, is distinctive for several reasons. This science fiction short is the only film at WDW not produced by Disney. Created by Jackson, George Lucas, and Francis Ford Coppola, its entirely fictional nature contrasts with the didactic narrative that is standard everywhere else at EPCOT; *Captain E/O*'s purpose is ostensibly pure entertainment.[21] Jackson's affinity for Disney and his parallel ability to layer childhood onto his own adult body make him particularly suited to this scene.[22] That Jackson tropes his body constantly only adds to the complexity of his art and the thesis of this essay. In this film, Jackson is both Mickey[23] and a postmodern Peter Pan accompanied by bodies created by Lucas.

When Disney decided to incorporate rival popular contemporary entertainment icons, it admitted into its domain competition for Walt's alter-ego trickster figure, Mickey (Brockway 1989:24–34). These alien figures present interesting challenges to the Disney ideology. It is no accident that the Muppets show at MGM-Disney Studios is one of the few that parodies Disney and comments on the viewer as mutual participant in a negotiation of meaning. Similarly, *Captain E/O* presents explicit challenges to the Disney monolith. While it is one thing for Disney to encase Frederick Douglass in a simulacrum in the service of Distory, it is another to admit a figure of Jackson's considerable cultural capital into its empire. This capital trails into EPCOT with his 3-D image.

While Jackson's public persona deconstructs age, gender, and race, the preshow for *Captain E/O,* a filmed slide presentation, is an extended advertisement for heterosexual reproduction. Produced by Kodak, it manages to trace a male child from infancy through marriage and fatherhood without picturing a single female who has or is about to reproduce.[24] Females are babies, children, teenagers, and brides, but apparently they are not photogenic after that, despite the fact that female guests roam EPCOT in enormous numbers. Perhaps this does not so much contrast Jackson's androgyny as prepare us for it. If Michael can be so pretty, women are entirely unnecessary.

Any review of Michael Jackson's public self over more than twenty years confirms that he was always a beautiful and compelling being. Despite this, Jackson's confessed dissatisfaction with his appearance mirrors modern preoccupations with the body as perfect commodity and obviously reflects the damage heaped upon him as an abused child in a racist society.

To his ambiguously coded gender, plastic surgery and his bleached skin have now added ambiguous race. As one African American television commentator remarked, "It is almost as if racism has caused Michael Jackson to want to jump out of his skin." His transmuting body enacts and reenacts the multiple problematics of race, generation, and gender. This multiply coded and unstable identity presents a problem for some of his audience. In a vigorously racist and sexist society, a shifting identity on those two axes presents dangers because it is an explicit challenge to those ideologies and the ideology of identity construction. Of course, since Jackson's disgrace, his identity has become anathema. This probably gives Disney execs palpitations when they consider including other living icons in the parks.

While Jackson's skin disease is a genetic accident, his manipulation of gender is entirely deliberate, clearly a part of his long-term artistic agenda. In his videos, Jackson has taken his own body and many other bodies through successive transmogrifications with costume and computer. Many of these mutations systematically blur boundaries between human and other species and between animal and machine. He has remade himself into Cleopatra and panther, ghoul and superhero. A psychologist might point to this as evidence of disease, but this boundary confusion is well within a long tradition of African American and Disney trickserism. Undoubtedly a conscious methodology, the cover art for his *Dangerous* album places the well-recognized trickster figure, a monkey king, over Jackson's portrait. Enacting the trickster role is a dangerous but powerful option that threatens whoever takes up the challenge. Michael Jackson is body and being, persona and construct. These multiple selves and conjoined aspects can be and are caught in a complex web of semiosis that disturbs some in his audience and rebounds on his material and psychic self.

Despite appearances, Jackson's metamorphosis from child to adolescent to adult was not produced by Disney or computer. A physical presence, his material body can be beaten and burned, remade under the surgeon's knife; it can succumb to disease. And at the end of 1993, it can be shamed by scandal and photographed nude under the auspices of legal inquiry.[25]

But Jackson's body is also a virtual body turned into commodity and corporation. Jackson's video *Black and White* uses advanced computer techniques[26] to seamlessly mutate a series of human faces into one another, producing a visual deconstruction of the physiognomy of race and gender, echoing the transformations of his "real" body. The earlier *Moonwalker* is an explicit biographical record of Jackson's public transmogrifications. Submitting numerous simulacra to increasingly extreme transmutation in this video, he becomes child again, animated cartoon, fantasmic supermobile, pachuco dance man, robot, and spaceship. These cyborg selves strike back at evil and defend Jackson against rational and irrational fans.[27] All this is strong stuff, too strong for Disney.

Nevertheless, the theme of *Captain E/O* is precisely this: transmutation. A classic David and Goliath story, it attempts magical mutation of the face of evil. *Captain E/O* does not take Jackson's methodology as far as his other productions do, but it does contain identical key elements. Greek for light, E/O, in his white spacesuit with traditional Jackson military flourishes, cape, and white gloves, appropriates Mickey's persona in the "Sorcerer's Apprentice" segment of *Fantasia* and, by extension, appropriates the persona of Walt himself. In *Fantasia,* Mickey makes music and magic from the ends of his wand, and current depictions of Mickey in Disneyland's "Fantasmic" show depict his white-gloved hands emitting magical light. Similarly, Captain E/O possesses the sorcererlike ability to make magic from the ends of his gloved fingers, which emit laserlike energy.[28]

Jackson and Mickey intersect on other unexpected axes, which help to create other iconic similarities. Jackson has paid subtle homage to famous film dancers Fred Astaire and Gene Kelly and to the pachuco style in his videos. His white suit, hat, and spats in numerous scenes in *Moonwalker* are clearly influenced by this forties Chicano style, which itself represents a complex mixed cultural interplay of African American, Hollywood, and perhaps even global fashions of the period. The white zoot suit of Jackson's *Moonwalker* video becomes a white space suit in *Captain E/O*. The "Smooth Criminal" segment of *Moonwalker* is the centerpiece of this video, clearly drawing much of its referential power from Jackson's sexual presence wrapped in an envelope of contained violence. The pachuco's sometimes feminine flourishes in a macho context, a particular sensibility, neatly describe Jackson's eclectic costumes and persona.[29]

Although Mickey's sexuality is normally repressed, one of Mickey's costumes in the late forties and the fifties was also reminiscent of the pachuco costume. He wore spats and donned an overly large straw hat. Rather than evoking a traditional turn-of-the-century gentleman, the style is cartoonishly extreme. Disney was producing Mickey in the Los Angeles area from 1928 on. The exaggerated pachuco style had to be familiar to him. Although the 1928 sound cartoon *Steamboat Willie* is acknowledged to be Mickey's first public appearance, two earlier silent films, later remade with sound, had been previously rejected by distributors (Brockway 1989:26). One of these, *The Gallopin' Gaucho,* appropriated a Latino style. And in the nineties, Mickey donned oversized clothing associated with juvenile gangs, a nineties style that itself echoes the pachuco. Mickey's persona reverberates in *Captain E/O*. Even Jackson's high-pitched voice recalls the mouse.

Captain E/O's crew is composed of an Ewok-like Tinkerbell named Fuzzball; a creature called Hooter appropriating Dumbo's persona in the chronotope of outer space; a two-headed furry creature named Geex whose heads are called Idy and Ody; an animated robot called Major Domo who turns into a drummer; and a Minor Domo who becomes an electronic synthesizer. Fuzzball plays the string bass while Hooter plays the synthesizer, and Captain E/O turns into a song-and-dance man. The pleasure of this presentation largely rests on the titillation of 3-D and the enjoyable confusion of ambiguously coded bodies. These creatures and machines are "humanoids" who blur the boundaries between animal and machine. They represent intertextual references to Disney, Lucas, and Jackson productions. The "signifyin' monkey" is alive and well within Jackson's work, and Jackson is completely within the tradition that Henry Louis Gates has documented.

Mapping is central to our experience at Disney World, so it is consistent that Sensaround travelogues provide a set of geographic maps. When our maps are very tentative, as in "The Wonders of China," Disney has thoughtfully provided a guide. "The American Adventure" and its Audio-Animatronic figures provide another set of maps of American history carefully calculated to remain within recognizable ideological outlines. But Michael Jackson in *Captain E/O* provides us with an alternate map, one that makes the semiotics of the body explicit while simultaneously deconstructing and pleasuring through transmogrification.

Is it coincidence that as the film begins Hooter has eaten the map provided by Central Command? Like the map provided to Captain E/O by Central Command, Disney enforces a map, but both are myopically unaware that a trickster like Michael can do without one in a pinch. Indeed, Captain E/O arrives at his destination sans the ingested map. Tricksters have the ability to chart their own trajectory. One of the pleasures at Disney is precisely this: the spectator's ability to make an original map. Experienced negotiators can enjoy Disney while they subvert its meanings for themselves.

Those who are excluded from master narratives must regularly draw alternative maps, rewrite narratives to move from a place of invisibility to one of imaginative inclusion. This is precisely what they do every day: live lives of complex negotiation within a simulated and distorted landscape. All of us have the potential to make an alternate and fruitful map. Disney cannot stop this. The ability to read critically is hardwired into the human organism. Jackson, as an alternate trickster on the scene, has created a countertext to Disney's master narrative. In *Captain E/O* and his other productions, Michael Jackson's musical talents are equated with his magic and are key to his alternate readings and writings. The film portrays E/O as possessing the power to transform the dystopian, Dark Star genre planet into a colorful, sylvan landscape through music and dance. E/O's mission is to find the Supreme Leader and present her with a gift that turns out to be music and dance. These talents amount to the magical ability to transform her and her minions from colorless cyborgs into a racially mixed cadre. It is certainly no accident that Michael Jackson as Captain E/O sings, "We are here to change the world" in a presentation in the techno-capitalist utopian heart of Disney World. Neither is it an accident that the viewer, who is largely white and middle class, hears as one of the few intelligible, oft repeated and last lines of this earsplitting film, "You are just another part of me."

Jackson is singing to the Supreme Leader, played by Angelica Huston, who is costumed as a white-faced, Medusan postmodern cyborg, a machine encased in a body, one of the few female figures of prominence in the entire park. The transformation of her guards and soldiers from "Borg"-like minions[30] into dancers, many of whom are regulars in Jackson's videos, precedes the Supreme Leader's unexpected mutation into a darkly tanned woman in a rainbow-colored gown. The figures before us become people of color wrapped in rainbows. Even Jackson's costume and the background color scheme recall Jesse Jackson's rainbow coalition. Whatever the liberal tendencies of Michael Jackson's ideology, these depictions represent a radical departure from the rest of the narrative in the park. And whatever the problematics of his inclusion as a "pure" entertainer at didactic EPCOT, his interventions were not unconscious. Whether they amount to an effective counterpoint is another question.

It might be argued that the "age of mechanical reproduction" has produced powerful images precisely because humans have long been prepared to accept representations as pleasurable and useful. Disney delights us for ancient reasons while its ideology and corporate structure propagandize our social selves, educate our imaginations, and appropriate our bodies. May Pachuco Mickey strike back soon.

CYBORG READING

A cyborg is a cybernetic organism, a hybrid of machine and organism, a creature of social reality as well as a creature of fiction. . . . The cyborg is a matter of fiction and lived experience that changes what counts as women's experience in the late twentieth century. This is a struggle over life and death, but the

boundary between science fiction and social reality is an optical
illusion. . . . I am making an argument for the cyborg as a
fiction mapping our social and bodily reality and as an imagi-
native resource suggesting some very fruitful couplings. . . . By
the late twentieth century, our time, a mythic time, we are all
chimeras, theorized and fabricated hybrids of machine and
organism; in short, we are cyborgs.
— DONNA HARAWAY, "A MANIFESTO
    FOR CYBORGS"

How does a cyborg read? Trickster readings ought to make one chuckle.
Disney reduces the problem of creating a library of the world to an anagram
of cyborg coding. As Donna Haraway has suggested, cyborgs imply

> *the translation of the world into a problem of coding, a search*
> *for a common language in which all resistance to instrumental*
> *control disappears and all heterogeneity can be submitted to dis-*
> *assembly, reassembly, investment, and exchange. (1985:83)*

What can cyborgs teach us about reading a colonialist language? What can
they teach us about guerrilla tactics at Disney World? Donna Haraway's cyborg notions suggest a different sort of reading:

> *"Women of color" might be understood as a cyborg identity, a*
> *potent subjectivity synthesized from fusions to outsider identi-*
> *ties. . . . Contrary to orientalist stereotypes of the "oral primi-*
> *tive," literacy is a special mark of women of color, acquired by*
> *U.S. black women as well as men through a history of risking*
> *death to learn and to teach reading and writing. Writing has a*
> *special significance for all colonized groups.*
> *. . . Releasing the play of writing is deadly serious. The po-*
> *etry and stories of U.S. women of color are repeatedly about*
> *writing, about access to the power to signify; but this time the*
> *power must be neither phallic nor innocent. . . . Cyborg writing*
> *is about the power to survive, not on the basis of original inno-*
> *cence, but on the basis of seizing the tools to mark the world*
> *that marked them as other. . . . Cyborg politics is the struggle*
> *for language and the struggle against perfect communication,*
> *against the one code that translates all meaning perfectly.*
> *(1985:93–95)*

Hungry as always, Trickster slips into EPCOT wearing Mickey's skin. Trickster has wandered here, attracted by the eighteen-story "geosphere," the golf ball visible from the skies along both of Florida's coasts. The pavilions ahead are an aphrodisiac that Trickster doesn't need. She tastes China on the air, Italy, France, and more. Trickster's other selves are here. None of them is a polite guide. You will need to stay close as they travel in violation of Disney's crowd control.

These cyborg simulacra appear here at Disney World. Benjamin's flaneur is stuck in Disney's Paris. His turtle would like to swim, but he is not ambitious or amphibian enough. The flaneur's desire to remain detached has crippled his literacy. His cynicism and limited courage will be the death of his tribe. In contrast, our pachuco and his flamingo have as their resources at least two modes of travel, a tranquil walk through a reflecting pool and a flight across the Caribbean. Our pachuco only pretends detachment. He hangs around the mariachis in front of the Mexico pyramid, but it is only out of habit. The World of Motion seduces him away for a quick trip. El Pachuco loves the slow rides through Disney but hates the fast pace of the dioramas presented there. He holds himself separate from the other simulacra. For him, connection carries the added risk of annihilation, even though he is "hybrid," a creature of the "new world." Even for Disney World, El Pachuco is too flamboyant. Worse, his body threatens violence at any moment. El Pachuco knows that the library collected here was not meant for him. His eyes seem distant, but underneath is a glint of hunger for the knowledge and power represented here. The conquistadors' armor displayed in the Mexico pavilion reminds him that his metal-encased, proto-cyborg ancestors had both power and a different sort of knowledge. The conquistadors destroyed the immense Aztec libraries, destroyed half of El Pachuco's epistemological heritage, and set in motion forces that would continue to deny him the epistemologies of the other half. El Pachuco's resentment and hunger are centuries old. Like our keeper of the books, his access is limited to fantasy. Unlike our keeper of the books, his reverence is not unambiguous.

La Curandera is hungry, like all "good" tricksters. She knows that knowledge leads to healing. She knows that the mutilation that she heals regularly in herself and others responds to the cures she has collected in her bag of herbs, herbs that wed nature and science into a potent medicine. They come not from her grandfathers but from her grandmothers, not from Iberia but from the ancient wisdom of the "new" world. She appears and disappears regularly throughout Disney World. She can be found botanizing on the asphalt late into the night, after the park has closed. She has no intention of breaking short her search for Disney's healing secrets. They are unlike her own, but she believes they are vulnerable to guerrilla appropriation. The dolphin who listens to her songs from the lagoon is both her teacher and her student. Together they plot the release of the dolphins captured in the Living Seas pavilion. Healing is their mutual project. La Curandera's hunger is a matter of life and death. Is not all hunger a matter of life and death? There are those who would name her evil because she dares to possess forbidden knowledge. She challenges those who would forbid her to know.

The Woman Warrior would avenge her brother and sister. She desires the power that knowledge can offer and the justice that such power can win. Her tiger is impatient and wild. Disney likes him even less than El Pachuco. The Woman Warrior restrains herself on her first trip through Disney. She would like to tear much of it down and rebuild. She would like to reveal the curses written on her back and frighten the flamingos and the flaneur. She would like to negotiate with Walt, but her training keeps her in check. A direct descendant from Kingston's Woman Warrior, she has learned how to be quiet. She remembers her teacher's lessons: "'You have to infer the whole dragon from the parts you can see and touch.' . . . Unlike tigers, dragons are so immense, [she] would never see one in its entirety" (Kingston 1977:34).

Disney's labyrinth is like the mythical tiger that rides on the dragon's back. The tiger sometimes deludes itself that it knows the whole dragon, but this is impossible. He is an inversion of the totalizing knowledge that Disney attempts here. By definition, the dragon cannot be collected or represented. By definition, the dragon is the net that has no center and no edges and is only partly visible. By definition, only woman warriors can sense the dragon and the tiger, and even they get burned and bitten.

Like all "good" tricksters, these simulacra desire freedom and joy, the pleasure of pleasure in reading, in the text. Pleasure can be necessary to survival and "survival is at stake in this play of readings" (Haraway 1985:96). And because the stakes are this high, these cyborg guerrillas appear here only briefly. Wink at us. Tease us. Make us wait. My cyborg simulacra "dream not of a common language, but of a powerful infidel heteroglossia" (101). Like all good guerrillas, they have their secret glossary. Like all good guerrillas, they are not likely to give it up until they trust you. Like all good guerrillas, they reconnoiter and withdraw so they might fight again.

Five

THE SMITHSONIAN'S ENCYCLOPEDIA: MUSEUM AS CANON

The Museum is a visual technology. It works through desire for communion, not separation, and one of its products is gender.

—DONNA HARAWAY, "TEDDY BEAR PATRIARCHY," IN *PRIMATE VISIONS*

FIRST LIBRARIES, FIRST MUSEUMS

Three thousand miles from the Smithsonian Institution, California's first library is preserved in its original location at Carmel Mission, which is both a museum and a working parish. By 1778, Father Junipero Serra had accumulated 30 books, and at the time of his death in 1784 the library had grown to 50 volumes. By 1834 it comprised 179 titles. That same year, William Hartnell founded California's first college, called Patrocino de Señor San Jose, near Salinas. Its original library collection is also preserved at the mission. Hartnell's corpus included Stockdale's Shakespeare; *The Elements of Euclid,* by Robert Simon, M.D.; a seventeen-volume set of *Obras del V. F. DeGranda;* a nine-volume Bible; and a Spanish translation of the history of Cicero. California was always already manifesting mixed cultural literacy.

Public museums reach back only a little more than a century. The development of this public institution cannot be separated from a series of interlocking trends: the expansion of Western empires spreading colonialist ideology and racism, the growth of Western science and industry, the acquisition of enormous wealth by capitalist exploitation of the first two trends, and a need to address the cultural dislocation created by industrialism, urbanization, secularization, democratic revolution, massive migration, and radical transformation in systems of representation (see Harris 1986; Hein 1993; Karp, Kreamer, and Lavine 1992; Karp and Lavine 1991; MacDonald 1987a, 1987b, 1992; and most especially Donna Haraway's "Teddy Bear Patriarchy," in Haraway 1989, which in large part inspired this project).[1]

Museums present spaces where culture can be imagined actively or imbibed passively, where identity can be reinforced or erased, and where multiple literacies can be enacted, tested, and/or reinforced. The process of identity formation is crucial to audience experience and response in museums, expositions, and theme parks and is tied to cultural literacy.

> *What is at stake in struggles for control over objects and the modes of exhibiting them, finally, is the articulation of identity. Exhibitions represent identity, either directly, through assertion, or indirectly, by implication. When cultural "others" are implicated, exhibitions tell us who we are and, perhaps most significant, who we are not. . . . Still, the audience has ways of escaping control, from refusing to follow the exhibition plan to seeing their assumptions about identity confirmed in the design and arrangement of objects. (Karp and Lavine 1991:15)*

Reading, in a museum, represents an oscillation between imagination-of-self and imagination-of-culture. How do those whose identities are marginally represented navigate "reader's block" at the museum? These issues are part of the contemporary discussions regarding the museum.

THE SI AS NATIONAL MAP

The SI is an unlimited territory, a vast net of signs, an imperialist collector's dream, a material library, and a site for memorizing nationality and self-identity within nation. In the face of its immense array of choices, its "cabinet of curiosities" gone wild,[2] the SI, like any text, requires its readers to find points of entry. Reading the SI requires individuals to negotiate constructions of race and gender, class placement and identification. This is complicated by a modern exhibition rhetoric that relies on the intricate nesting of what Umberto Eco has called open and closed texts. Decoding these open and closed texts calls upon many skills not named as part of the museum experience or as intrinsic to literacy. Individuals must call on different literacies at the appropriate moment and in the appropriate context. Some of these literacies are easily identifiable: knowledge of science, math, and constantly mutating technologies, the ability to interpret the electronic media and visual arts. Others are barely recognized or articulated as intrinsic to cultural literacy: the use of the senses to organize and process experience into webs of knowledge, webs constructed in a culturally mixed matrix, information transformed into narrative and recirculated by readers to other readers who are present and are also weaving their own narratives.

In 1846, twelve years after Hartnell founded California's first college, the Smithsonian Institution was born as the result of James Smithson's more than half-a-million-dollar bequest "to the United States of America, to found at Washington, under the name of the Smithsonian Institution, an establishment for the increase and diffusion of knowledge among men."[3] This means that the Smithsonian came into being just as the museum *qua* museum was constituting itself as cultural artifact. Smithson, the illegitimate son of the Duke of Northumberland, was a recognized chemist and mineralogist. François-Suplice Beudant, a noted French geologist, conferred the name "smithsonite" on carbonate of zinc after Smithson read his second Royal Society paper, "A Chemical Analysis of Some Calamines," in 1802. Smithson, a resolute bachelor, was convinced that

> *it is in his knowledge that man has found his greatness and his happiness, the high superiority which he holds over the other animals who inhabit the earth with him, and consequently that no ignorance is probably without loss to him, no error without evil. (Hellman 1967: 26–55)[4]*

Smithson died in 1829, but the bequest first went to his nephew, who would have kept it in the family had he not died childless just six years after Smithson. In July 1836 Congress appropriated thirteen thousand dollars to send Richard Rush to England to collect the money. Richard Rush was the son of Dr. Benjamin Rush, one of the leading figures of the American Enlightenment and a signatory to the Declaration of Independence, whose medical theories about race and mental illness were to have a lasting effect on the American culture.[5]

Before Rush could return to Washington with the British gold, Levi Woodbury, the secretary of the Treasury, advertised that he would have approximately half a million dollars to invest. On September 1, 1838, the gold was deposited into the United States Mint in Philadelphia, melted down, and recoined as $508,318.46. In the eight years that followed, Congress argued about the potential uses of the fund and even suggested that it be returned to England. Meanwhile, virtually all of the half million was invested and lost in Arkansas bonds. In August 1846, after former president John Quincy Adams championed the Smithsonian's cause, Congress appropriated $757,298 for the creation of the Smithsonian Institution. This action replaced the principal with interest and guaranteed the Smithsonian an additional 6 percent interest per annum in perpetuity. Even so, Andrew Johnson, who later became an ex officio Smithsonian regent as vice president and president, argued for the abolishment of the institution (Hellman 1967:46).

The Smithsonian Institution is the result of happenstance, dubious political and financial dealings, and James Smithson's imaginings about the nature and importance of knowledge.

The institution's first secretary, Joseph Henry, was committed to building a research establishment devoted to science; his lieutenant and successor, Spencer Baird, at only twenty-four, became the Smithsonian's curator during its first months. Over time, Baird managed effectively to counterpoint Henry's research interests by making the SI—originally meant to include a library, a museum, and a gallery of art—a repository for objects. Henry succeeded in ejecting the library function and transferred forty thousand volumes to the Library of Congress in 1866, forming the basis of what is known as the Smithsonian Deposit. Baird attempted to trump Henry's research interests by stimulating international acceptance of the SI as an archive. Between 1846 and 1877, the SI sent eleven thousand "knowledge diffusing packages" around the world and received more than a hundred thousand submissions from other countries. Henry's interest in research was effectively compromised in these early years. Today, the SI includes 137 million objects housed in sixteen museums and numerous research facilities. But by 1876 Henry was already complaining not just about the number of objects continually sent to the SI but about the perception of the SI as a museum rather than a research facility,

> It is the design of the museum to continually increase its collection of material objects; of the Institution, to extend the boundaries of human knowledge . . . every civilized government of the world has its museums . . . while there is one Smithsonian Institution. (Hellman 1967:85)

Henry's claim and his tug-of-war with Baird neatly outline two key elements in the SI's knowledge and debates about itself. It both collects and researches, displays and invents, and it is unique, filling a global niche of its own creation.

In 1900, fifty-four years after the SI's birth, Franklin W. Smith, a Boston businessman, proposed the creation of a series of museums from the Potomac to the Capitol along the north side of the Mall. Smith imagined that Washington and these museums would become a major destination for scholars and students, citizens and foreigners, all invested in a pilgrimage to the cultural sanctuary of democracy and American nationalism. Although Smith did not envision the Smithsonian as part of this march of museums, Washington is now a major tourist destination, and the Smithsonian is part of exactly this sort of pilgrimage journey to the icons of American democracy and culture (Doering and Bickford 1994: 1, MacDonald 1987b, 1992). These pilgrims come knowing very little about the Smithsonian but intent on imagining their place within the metanarrative of democracy in this nation.

Today, the SI is the world's largest museum and research complex. As a result of Baird's early public relations, the SI is imagined to be a repository of everything "fit to save." Curator and visitor make a narrative out of things. Its main buildings are arrayed in parallel lines along the east side of the two-mile-long rectangular Mall that forms the center of our nation's capital. And like EPCOT Center at Walt Disney World, which is itself modeled after world expositions and which, along with WDW as a whole and Disneyland in Anaheim, competes with D.C. as North America's top tourist destination,[6] this rectangular mall, consciously planned as part of D.C.'s overall design, can also be imagined to *hide* an hourglass or figure eight (Disney's literature describes EPCOT as hourglass-shaped). At the top of this imagined figure eight, the United States Capitol building mounted on Capitol Hill looks down the Mall toward the Lincoln Memorial at its far western limit. The Washington Monument punctuates this expanse at the center of the imaginary figure eight and is reflected in a rectangular pool that stretches to Lincoln's monument. Similarly, EPCOT's trademark geosphere punctuates that chronotope and serves as its iconic representation, although it appears at the entrance to EPCOT, at what would be the bottom of Disney's metaphorical figure eight. At the bottom left-hand corner of the Mall's hidden figure eight, or along the northwestern end of the rectangle, the Vietnam memorial has been half buried in the earth. Thus, Lincoln, while commenting on our Civil War of the North and South, surveys that other civil war of the north and south, a war that may be serving to reshape our nation as powerfully as the one fought on our soil.

If you face east at the Washington Monument, the Capitol building dominates the horizon, but tucked along the Mall to your right stands first the

National Air and Space Museum, followed by the Hirshhorn Museum and Sculpture Garden, the Arts and Industries Building, the Smithsonian Institution Building (recognized and known as "the Castle"), the National Museum of African Art, the Arthur M. Sackler Gallery (of Asian Art), and the Freer Gallery of Art. To your left along the Mall and a little to the northwest, the National Museum of American History, the National Museum of Natural History/National Museum of Man, and the National Gallery of Art march in a line toward the Capitol. (It is a common misconception fostered by the SI's own official guidebook and brochures that the National Gallery, the Kennedy Center for the Performing Arts, and the Woodrow Wilson International Center for Scholars are under the aegis of the SI; however, their institutional connection to the SI is largely a function of the federal budget process. They are separately administered by their own boards of trustees, although they are listed in the SI internal directories.) The National Museum of the American Indian will soon be built on the last remaining Mall site, just to the east of Air and Space. The National Portrait Gallery, the National Museum of American Art, the Renwick Gallery, and the new National Postal Museum are located just to the north of the Mall. The National Zoological Park is located three miles further north. The Paul Garber facility is located in Suitland, Maryland, the Anacostia Museum in southeastern D.C., and the Cooper-Hewitt National Museum of Design in New York City.

Although this essay concentrates on the SI's exhibition function, the institution must juggle its research, educational, acquisitions, and preservation functions. According to many, it does not do so gracefully. In the process, it provides information regarding everything from the historical importance of an object to crime scene identification, and it presents or fosters the performing arts, festivals, and traveling exhibits. The SI is, of course, now a node on the Internet, further institutionalizing its presence around the globe.

Entering between two and three separate museums a day, the average SI visitor probably traverses the mall at least once in order to cross the thresholds of the three most popular museums: the National Air and Space Museum, the National Museum of Natural History, and the National Museum of American History. These visitors come by the millions; the SI's exhibit halls are crowded nearly year-round. Like Disney's theme parks, it is a ritualized space (itself encapsulated within the ritualized space of the nation's capital), which draws ten million visitors a year.[7]

In Italo Calvino's *Invisible Cities,* Marco Polo is charged with reporting to Kublai Khan about the emperor's vast kingdom. Since Marco has not yet learned the Levantine languages, he is forced to express himself with "gestures, leaps, cries of wonder and of horror, animal barkings or hooting" while removing from his knapsacks objects collected during his travels. These trophies could be recognized, but "the connection between them and the places visited remained uncertain" (Calvino 1974:21). In this rendering of Polo's history, it is clear that Khan desires to possess his territories through a totalizing knowledge of its emblems. And

> everything Marco displayed had the power of emblems, which, once seen, can never be forgotten or confused. In the Khan's mind the empire was reflected in a desert of labile and inter-changeable data, like grains of sand, from which there appeared, for each city and province, the figures evoked by the Venetian's logogriphs. (22)

Like Borges's keeper of the books, whose experience of the library is that "the shelves / stand very high, beyond the reach of my years," Kublai is frustrated because the totality of his empire remains beyond reach. For the Venetian trader, knowledge is concrete, residing in the objects he pulls from his sacks, but the Khan dreams of an abstract knowledge that can reify his possession of an empire so vast he will never see all of it.

The Smithsonian presents just this problem—the totality of what is shelved here remains outside our reach, not just to its guests but also to its guardians, who often express wistfully that they will never experience the complete Smithsonian. It tantalizes, just as Khan's empire and Borges's library tantalize.

All of us have our favorites. Out of these favorites, we construct what James Boon (1991) has called "aphorisms of coincidence." Paloma Picasso's pearl necklace, Beatien Yazz's black-and-white engraving,[8] Jacqueline Kennedy's mini skirt, the Wright Brothers' Flyer, spiderwebs, Dali's *Last Supper.* These are one set. Make your own. You surely will.

At the outset, the Smithsonian contained too much. Its sign is therefore excess. From the beginning, its power to accumulate exceeded its power to store and display. Even James Smithson's personal belongings, manuscripts, and rich collection of minerals and precious stones, which had been willed to the institution along with his British gold, presented a storage problem. These, like the gold, were lost (Hellman 1967:41).

An enormous engine for canonizing cultural knowledge, the SI has the power to stimulate our imaginations into producing and restructuring personal maps of what we know and what we want to know, who we are and who we might become. Identity construction at this site requires cognitive mapping of self and others in relation to the museum as a canonizer of both its exhibits and its audience. This is part of our reading technology for the museum. But making a map requires an entry point, a "you are here." It is these points of entry, or the lack thereof, that trouble some visitors more than others. Both the content and the rhetoric of museum exhibits challenge visitors whose history, self, and experience are underrepresented at the SI.

If exhibits are a nested collection of what Umberto Eco has called "open" and "closed" texts, the educated European American middle class that flocks to the SI finds itself represented in the Smithsonian's content and able, because of its training, to decode both its open and closed texts so as to reinforce that representation. However, those who lack representation, whose histories are excluded, are not just affectively alienated, they are challenged to somehow make a cognitive map without first finding a point of entry, a "you are here." Reading technologies not ordinarily recognized as operative might help all visitors find multiple entry points. Spatial recognition and synesthetic stimulation may be powerful aids to the breaking of "reader's block" and may provide unrecognized aids to cognitive mapping.

Because the SI has the status of a ritualizing authority, cognitive maps constructed here acquire the aura of the institution and the objects it collects, an aura conveying the status of the "real" and the "important" in the context of the "nation." Museums create a synthetic experience out of a set of authentic objects, artifacts, or specimens surrounded by simulated settings. Thus the narrative they create acquires the aura[9] of the real and the objective. Museums are just beginning to acknowledge this, even as the majority of visitors continue to react unconsciously to this rhetorical strategy.

Mentally mapping the fragments of exhibits into a personal system is probably central to our experience of any museum. The cognitive map that this produces may be the major educational function of the museum. Mapping may be one of the earliest symbolic activities of the human brain. Indeed, it may be an early cognitive strategy that stimulated the evolution of human intellect, forming the basis for the development of language.

Roger Peters and others believe there is evidence that the ability to create cognitive maps may have been an intellectual adaptation favoring hunting. In Peters's essay, "Communication, Cognitive Mapping, and Strategy in Wolves and Hominids" (1978), theories concerning the parallel evolution of wolves and hominids as predators of large to intermediate-size game have led to insights regarding cognition.

Humans regularly encountered objects over large hunting ranges and needed to remember the locations of those objects relative to the terrain and prey. They needed to find alternate routes when pursuing prey, and they needed to convey this information to others. This necessitated cognitive mapping and the invention of symbolic information systems (Peters 1978: 95–107). Nancy Tanner, Adrienne Zihlman, and Donna Haraway have taken pains to argue against the hunter hypothesis as a dominating factor in hominid development. Peters and others emphasize the role of hunting large prey in the stimulation of this intellectual innovation. There is abundant evidence that females were innovators in gathering. An approach that simply adds "gathering to hunting to get a mixed economy" (Haraway 1989:345) does not produce a scientifically cogent theory. The primary adaptive behavior that stimulated evolutionary divergence from the apes was probably the bipedal gathering of vegetation and small prey. Gathering required the ability to travel long distances (an ability that does not differ by sex) while carrying food, digging sticks and stones, objects for defense, and offspring. Containers for offspring and food were necessarily developed for gathering (Zihlman and Tanner 1978:176). The australopithecines were

> a cooperative kin group where both sexes engaged in gathering, butchering and defense and where food was shared among close kin. . . .
>
> Natural selection would have enhanced those processes adaptive for the gathering way of life: greater intelligence for cognitive mapping of food sources, for communicating this information to others, and for participating in complex social relations. (181)

Zihlman and Tanner believe that pursuing large prey with sophisticated tools became common only after gathering was fully developed and that tool-aided gathering provided the technological base for hunting. The fact that large prey move over wide ranges may have provided just one more challenge to cognitive mapping, but it may equally be said that gatherers would have needed to anticipate the most likely locations for food based on the geography of vast areas. Indeed, it may have soon become obvious that tracking small animals could lead to vegetative food sources.

If all this is so, it is no surprise that cognitive maps are intrinsic to the museum experience. This experience echoes down a hominid history of the quest for prey. Although the modern experience seems filled with intellectual and spiritual purpose, it calls on cognitive modes rooted at least in part in hunting. No wonder museums are haunting reminders of death and destruction![10]

Perhaps equally important is the relation between the construction of cognitive maps and the three senses usually ignored by our intellectual tradition—smell, touch, and taste. Peters's discussion of the similarities between hominid and wolf cognition describes in detail how wolves rely on olfactory investigation and marking to construct their cognitive maps. Science has barely begun to study the relationship of sensual information to cognition; however, synesthesia provides one model for understanding.

Synesthesia has been accepted as a documented neurological anomaly for about two hundred years. Ostensibly "a union of the senses," its most well-known form involves the visualization of a color in relation to a sound. The wolf uses smell to create a cognitive map of spatial terrain. This cross between smell and sight constitutes an example of synesthesia in mammals.

In the process of researching the relationship between cognition and maps, I discovered that certain visual modes by which I organize information are regarded as "number form" synesthesia (Cytowic 1989:190−237). This may have significant implications concerning the modes of analysis of this study. My synesthesia may have partially prompted my fascination with the Smithsonian and may be driving my quest for a description of reading the museum that includes the body and the senses as implicated in reading physical environments.[11] In short, reading terrains such as museums may involve creating cognitive maps out of a collation of sensual cues, a process rooted in our pre-hominid intellect.[12] Museums can learn from theme parks how to structure exhibits consciously so as to appeal not just to visual and auditory senses but also to other sensory modes. "After all, synesthesia is what we all do without knowing that we do it, whereas synesthetes do and know that they do it" (Ommaya, foreword to Cytowic 1989:viii).

If these other sensory modes are alternate and/or supplementary routes to the construction of cognitive maps, appealing to and pleasuring all the senses is one key to increasing comprehension and memory of museum exhibits. In fact, it is hard to deny that the museum pleasures in ways that we rarely articulate but tacitly acknowledge. Making a map of any terrain may involve the stimulation of not just the visual and the auditory. It may involve sensory experiences not consciously appealed to by traditional museum design. Taste, touch, and smell are in operation in the museum as much as anywhere else, and these senses may be affecting the audience more than anyone realizes.

So maps, be they constructed of visual or other sensual cues, may be our primary method for aligning ourselves with what the Smithsonian offers us because maps are hardwired into our cognitive strategies and make it

possible to take isolated incidents, experiences, and so on, and arrange them intellectually so that there is some coherence, some total relation, instead of individual isolation . . . mapping is considered to be the most fundamental way of converting personal knowledge to transmittable knowledge. . . .

Everything is somewhere, and no matter what other characteristics objects do not share, they always *share relative location, that is, spatiality; hence the desirability of equating knowledge with space, an intellectual space. (Robinson and Petchenik 1976:4)*

Cognitive maps help us to arrange the museum's cornucopia into a recognizable set and help us to "see" ourselves in physical relation to that set. And the mapmaking that can go on at a museum or any other site where objects are collected seems to be fundamental to semiosis.

The quality of utilitarian permutations that are possible with words, numbers or map marks is unlimited, for all practical purposes. In the map, then we seem to be dealing with something clearly fundamental, something which has nearly unrestricted potential utility. (Robinson and Petchenik 1976:14−15)

"How things mean" cannot be separated from how they are arranged in space or in the mind's eye.

The considerable analytical work in what is called "cognitive mapping" makes it clear that humans and some other creatures appear to process some forms of sensory input such that information obtained from the milieu is arranged or converted so that they can operate as if there were an internal space like a map. In our view, whatever it is that actually occurs, this is the phenomenon that makes one a mapper. Creatures that have an elevated eye level and the mental capacity to arrange what they see into some sort of spatial framework are all potential mappers. Such an assertion covers a wide range from the high flying eagle to the darting dragonfly to no longer earthbound man. The eyes may range from the binocular equipment of the whole man to the "vision" of the fingertips of the blind, but the essential sine qua non of the mapper is the ability to operate in a spatial mode. At the minimum this is two-dimensional (x,y) and at the maximum it is three-dimensional (x,y,z), with the possibility of

some sort of integration of time as a fourth dimension, but the
spatial framework must exist as part of the cognitive endowment
of the mapper. Nothing else is really essential. (Robinson and
Petchenik 1976:17)

Robinson and Petchenik interestingly describe the importance of spatial reasoning to cognition. This essay suggests that other senses may be equally important. Spatial reasoning and synesthetic cues may help us determine the relation between the myriad "elements" encountered during our Smithsonian travel. In other words, there may be a relation between our ability to absorb information and our capacity for spatial recognition and all the senses, not just the visual.

The relation between spatial reasoning, mapmaking, and learning may be expressed in our desire to travel, on earth and in outer space, in our fictional constructions of other worlds and other dimensions, in dreams of an afterlife. It makes sense that religious understanding during the Middle Ages was tied to conceptual maps of heaven, earth, and an underworld and that systems of knowledge had to conform to these maps or be branded heretical. These maps helped Europeans "know" where they were and gave them the courage of conviction that enabled the launching of the Age of Exploration. Another example of religious mapping and spiritual echo location might be Navajo sacred paintings. Written in sand, these paintings are symbolic maps of the location of points of spiritual power overlying the four directions of the compass; they implicitly narrate a story about our place in this world.

The maps of the Middle Ages gave Europeans a context, a pretext, and a rationale for reconstructing the globe around a set of cultural and economic assumptions supported by religious beliefs. Perhaps the Western world's amused fascination with Marco Polo's travels is due in no small part to Kublai Khan's inversion of Western dreams of dominance. He believed himself to be at the center of the universe, but the European narrative unravels his belief because Marco eventually returns to Venice, *his* center, and the map constructed from his travels only reinforces Europe as master over all that could be discovered and reported about, including Khan's ignorance of the limits of his dominion. Europeans did indeed know where they were.

Maps sedulously reinforce and protect our sense of where we
are. . . . They are our main means of aligning ourselves with
something bigger than us, and so may be thought of as semi-
religious in nature. (Harbison 1977:124)

Europeans believed in their divine connection to God's plan for everyone. And like Polo's European audience, Kublai Khan's fascination with his lieutenant's travels only deepens as time goes on. The emperor desires to align himself with the heavens. He has created a mental map of his kingdom out of the objects and pantomimes that Marco presents. Each new piece of information finds a place on that map. But this only feeds his hunger.

> As the seasons passed and his missions continued, Marco mastered the Tartar language and the national idioms and tribal dialects. Now his accounts were the most precise and detailed that the Great Khan could wish and there was no question or curiosity which they did not satisfy. And yet each piece of information about a place recalled to the emperor's mind that first gesture or object with which Marco had designated the place. The new fact received a meaning from that emblem and also added to the emblem a new meaning. Perhaps, Kublai thought, the empire is nothing but a zodiac of the mind's phantasms.
>
> "On the day when I know all the emblems," he asked Marco, "shall I be able to possess my empire, at last."
>
> And the Venetian answered: "Sire, do not believe it. On that day you will be an emblem among emblems." (Calvino 1974:22–23)

Because the SI is vast and because it is not possible to mentally construct a global view of it, Calvino's delicate descriptions of the relationships between emblem and possession, between map and territory, are relevant and helpful. The SI mimics Eco's notions regarding the universe of human knowledge. No one can ever know it. It is only possible to isolate portions of it and make connections between locations on a net of interconnected knowledges. To do this, one must know who and where one is, using any and all faculties at one's disposal. Self-identity and orientation in space are intrinsic to anyone's grasp of what Eco and others call a local knowledge situated within a larger web of knowledges. Only partial solutions are possible. The whole can only be inferred from those parts. On the day any one individual knows all of the Smithsonian, on that day, s/he will join the Smithsonian as an artifact, just another emblem recording the human desire for knowledge among an infinite set of objects making the same statement.

Institutional studies have repeatedly identified the SI's audience. Like "shoppers in a mall, travelers in airports or railroad stations or users of public libraries," museum visitors are mobile populations (Doering and Bickford 1994:4). Add to this list theme park guests and tricksters of all sorts. The SI's guests are travelers (76 percent live outside of D.C.). They are male slightly more often than female, overwhelmingly European American (86 percent), in their childbearing years and accompanied by their children, and they are college graduates. Indeed, educational level seems to be their most distinguishing characteristic. While only 20 percent of the U.S. population has graduated college, 61 percent of the SI's visitors have. While only 7 percent have earned an advanced degree, 28 percent of the SI's visitors have earned a master's or other professional degree (Doering and Bickford 1994:5).

Their visits are social events with family and friends. Only 8 percent come alone. Half of them are repeat visitors who are not searching out any particular exhibit; rather, they are on a more generalized quest (Doering and Bickford 1994:15). One individual often interprets for the others in a group. This person is often the male; sometimes it is a child when the child has some expertise (as with computers) that the adults do not. Females defer here, as elsewhere.

Very often the narrator of the group steps forward to explain a specific artifact, object, or mechanism. He may have a history connected to the iconic significance of that object, special knowledge, or relevant skills. He may simply "recognize" "it." Curiously, or maybe predictably, this recognition factor stimulates an affective response that often obscures the exhibit's message. For example, the authenticity of the first ladies' gowns interferes with the curatorial message (Doering, in conversation). In this case, it is likely that a series of affective associations is the result of not just fascination with fashion but the recognition factor that comes along with the first lady's fame.

That one person often interprets what he has recognized for the others in a group provides the basis for socialization and the reinforcement of hierarchy among family and friends, a means of determining identity (e.g., "I am the individual who knows this, has experienced that, has been there"). This phenomenon also stimulates wider storytelling between visitors in a lyrical response to the narratives presented by the exhibits. Storytelling among visitors needs to be observed carefully. It may reveal much.

My experiences at the SI confirm many of the conclusions of visitor studies and my own theories. During one tour, a friend and I took turns narrating the sights to one another. His expertise was aeronautics and jet engines, mine was cultural criticism and the specifics of postmodern representation, but both of us blundered our narratives. Specifically, I mistook the ceiling of the Castle's refectory as authentic stone (after all, it is a red sandstone building); he correctly identified it as a Disney-like painted simulation. Conversely, he carefully explained the workings of a jet engine in Air and Space while I pointed out that we were looking at the wrong end. The museum *is* disorienting, but a more likely explanation for this irony is the notion that we were both focusing on the narratives we already knew and the occasion the SI gave us for sharing those narratives, for finding an entry point, a "you are here." Answering the questions "How do I and what I know fit into the larger scheme of things" and "How can I make this fit into your system" may be an implicit challenge presented by the museum to its audience. Some studies suggest that visitors pay attention to that which is familiar and which calls upon current knowledge (Koran, Foster, and Koran 1989:242). This is reminiscent of E. D. Hirsch's lists of cultural literacy, themselves implicit tests of knowledge. The museum is also a kind of test. Clearly, whole groups of people refuse to submit to the examination.

On another visit to the SI, my companions, all trained biologists and all people of color, were able to respond to the Museum of Natural History as experts reviewing familiar and beloved territory. Though they searched hard for points of entry to the SI based on their family and cultural backgrounds, their high levels of education and their scientific expertise afforded them easy access to it at other points. Even for this group of scientists, the personal narrative concerning where and when they first encountered this species or that concept dominated their interaction with the museum and their companions. By recognizing the already familiar and narrating to the others in their group, they echoed earlier observations about reading and the museum.[13]

Jim Volkert of the National Museum of the American Indian describes two peak museum experiences that bring together the "you are here" awareness and synesthesia. The first involves touching the bats of three baseball icons—Brooks Robinson, Jackie Robinson, and Babe Ruth. His memories include the weight of Ruth's bat and the realization that he was touching the very same molecules that the Babe had touched. Similarly, his younger brother was able to play a Stradivarius as a result of a private visit to the SI's archives. My own memories of the Enola Gay include not only witnessing the plane scattered in pieces around the Garber facility as it was being prepared for exhibit but also touching it. Because of this, I have had two physical contacts with the Hiroshima bomb: this one and a melted and resolidified tile from ground zero that is in my possession. Both contacts taught me that my inclusion in the stream of twentieth-century history is more than abstract.

So institutions like the Garber facility, which allows visitors to witness the making of knowledge and thereby allows them to enter an exhibit, are models for more-accessible rhetorics of display. Ironically, the finish of a polished exhibit can reduce the quality of the experience.

Visitor studies tell us less than we want to know; they raise questions faster than they answer them. They appear primitive because our thinking about visual literacy and synesthetic modes of learning is primitive. Although schools and colleges are expected to document that people are learning inside them, museums are neither expected to prove this nor can they. Indeed, it is amusing to imagine a public discourse questioning the validity of the museum experience that is parallel in content and tone to the common controversies surrounding schools. These facilities are sacred entombments of cultural canons, and as such, they justify themselves apart from their educational function, no matter how disputed that function may become on financial or political grounds. Clearly, the museum controversies that interest the citizenry are questions of the politics of canonicity, as the SI's *Enola Gay* debacle painfully illustrates.[14] When asked if museums were educational institutions, William Bennett replied that he thought of them as experiences (Kitty Smith conversation, July 1994). No doubt his experiences in these institutions only served to round out his already well-reinforced sense of identity as an influential culture maker.

THE PRINCIPLE OF CONNECTIVITY,
OR "YOU ARE HERE"

In Leslie Marmon Silko's *Almanac of the Dead* (1991), a group of Lagunas visit a Santa Fe museum after receiving a message from "the Pueblos up north." The message told them to look for their stolen "little grandparents" in Santa Fe.

> *The theft of the stone figures years ago had caused great anguish. Dark gray basalt the size and shape of an ear of corn, the stone figures had been given to the people by the kachina spirits at the beginning of the Fifth World, present time. (31)*

Eighty years have passed by the time the delegation visits the museum. When an old cacique recognizes the "lithics," he begins to weep,

> *his whole body quivering from old age and the cold. He seemed to forget the barrier glass forms and tried to reach out to the small stone figures lying dreadfully unwrapped. The old man kept bumping his fingers against the glass case until the assistant curator became alarmed. . . .*
> *For these were not merely carved stones, these were* beings *formed by the hands of the kachina spirits. (33)*

Sacred objects, even human remains, are commonly ensconced in museums. Recognizing your personal connection to the objects collected in museum halls is inextricable from weaving a map of understanding. The "little grandparents" had been stolen and violated. The entire delegation's relationship to this and the other objects in the Santa Fe museum is connected to their personal and tribal histories as genocidal targets. The violations are ongoing. Finding a point of entry into the narrative that this museum constructed was all too easy and all too tragic for these Lagunas. The map these visitors see is unique to their relationship to these objects. What they learn here has everything to do with reinforcing a series of lessons about genocide.

As individuals construct personal maps of knowledge, each learns a semiotics of the body and its enmeshment within vast webs of meaning constructed by the unlimited semiosis of this chronotope, the SI. For each visitor, understanding his/her enmeshment is central to understanding his/her place in the narrative of nation presented here. Visitors are fascinated by the SI; they are motivated to "get it"; they want to know what to do there. If the individual is gendered female, if s/he is ethnically or racially "other," less educated, economically less enfranchised, constructing this map, learning this semiotics, is more difficult.

Such individuals are already constructed as lacking, and they will have to work hard to find a point of inclusion within an institution that partakes of nothing so much as addition and excess. To lack representation in such a space is to be doubly negated.

If creating a personal map of knowledge at the SI allows us to align ourselves within its system of knowledge, its active definition of nation and culture, and nature versus culture, finding an entry point can become a second- or third-level problem that must be solved before any personal map can have a point of origination.

The content and the form of the exhibits before the visitor serve to include and exclude. Both the content and the rhetoric of the exhibits weave an intricate narrative. This narrative must be entered imaginatively at a point of identification inseparable from experience. Finding this point of entry is a quest that each visitor implicitly accepts upon entry. At the SI, the sheer panoply of choices implies a guarantee that this quest will be successful, but some visitors must struggle longer and harder. The difficulty of their quest is itself a lesson to the visitor: your place in this metanarrative of nation is small, is insignificant.

For example, because the National Portrait Gallery is charged by an 1962 Act of Congress with displaying "the portraits of men and women who contributed substantially to the political, intellectual, social and cultural history of the U.S.," it implicitly highlights categories of people whom the institution believes mattered most—and "identifies groups who didn't matter enough to be included" (Smithsonian Institution 1994:27). Faced with this ontological and epistemological problem, our nation's minorities visit the SI in relatively small numbers, but no "minority" is more excluded from this metanarrative than the U.S. Latino. A special SI task force has produced a strongly worded report, *Willful Neglect: The Smithsonian Institution and U.S. Latinos* (1994), detailing the exclusion of Latinos from nearly every aspect of the institution's operations. U.S. Hispanics are the only major contributors to American civilization still uncelebrated by any specific, systematic, permanent effort in this country's major cultural institution (47).

Because of this "willful neglect," U.S. Latinos visiting the SI will find few points of entry from which to construct a cognitive map. This double negation, the lack of a "you are here" representation, in an institution implicitly all-inclusive and excessive in that inclusion, is consistent with a national narrative that has yet to produce a mythology for the Latino experience that parallels the narrative of slavery, or Native American genocide, or even the Chinese American contribution to the transcontinental railway.

This absence of a central narrative that includes Latinos as national culture makers cannot be accidental. As *Willful Neglect* points out, the Quincentenary Commemoration offered a model for understanding *Mestizaje* and multiculturalism particularly appropriate to the Latino experience. The quincentenary programs were

> *unique in being truly multicultural. Their message of* Mestizaje *reflected the Spanish, African, Asian and indigenous roots of the Americas, a model of multiculturalism which accurately reflects the American heritage and population—and is important to all residents of this multicultural society. (47)*

But this is perhaps our nation's most consistent nightmare: that "racial" mixing produced us, that our identities are already multicultural. Our national mapping of self has systematically suppressed this awareness. The SI perpetuates this not just through the exclusion of Latino representation but also by reinforcing a metanarrative in which African Americans are the ultimate other pole by which Americans define identity, Native Americans are innocent children through whom we can mourn the loss of the wilderness for the higher purposes of industry, science, war, and space travel,[15] and Asian Americans are our link to a sophisticated but ancient artistic tradition, i.e., one that is no longer viable.

To include an integrated examination of U.S. Latinos in this narrative would destabilize its semiotic symmetry. U.S. Latinos *must* remain invisible, lest they force a remapping of the terrain to include a fundamental acceptance of *Mestizaje* as expressed in the bodies of our nation's people. That the quincentenary exhibits were "truly multicultural" guaranteed that Latinos would be squeezed out of the current canon of everything "fit to save." Even though these

> programs came with an institutional promise of being transformed into a permanent and sustained Latino presence at the Institution. . . . resources which had been specifically appropriated for the Quincentenary were redirected, and the nascent programs allowed to wither and die. No permanent, effective Hispanic programming emerged. (47)

THE POLITICS OF PREREADING

If cognitive maps at the SI are constructed by means of an entry point equaling "you are here," it is no surprise that World War II veterans and others reacted powerfully to Air and Space's plans for an exhibit of the *Enola Gay*. When they obtained a rough draft of the proposed exhibit, they read themselves into its narrative as the villains of the piece. The specifics of the exhibit's proposed content are not nearly as important to this reader/response theory as the process through which this audience rejected any representation of the Hiroshima bomb narrative, which violated its collective sense of identity. The exhibit's curators were invested in narrating a multilevel, multiperspective history. The veterans and their allies see the SI as validating a unitary version of history, one in which World War II veterans remain unquestioned heroes and our nation, therefore, purely heroic. Including the *Enola Gay* in the SI's displays was indeed opening up a rhizomatic web of understanding that threatened to take us all into a scary underworld.

The Pleasure of Scale

While Disney parks[16] are famous for reducing the scale of their simulated landscapes, Washington's scale is deliberately monumental. Inclusion or exclusion is written on the body's experience of its travel across this landscape. Reduced scale at Disney produces a sense of intimacy—"you are there," "you are important." Reduced scale involves the body in a series of kinesthetically enveloping experiences. In Washington, monumental scale produces the opposite effect. The visitor's body is overwhelmed and excluded.[17] Paradoxically antidemocratic in ethos, D.C.'s architecture reduces the visitor's sense of him/herself as an important participant. Monumental scale is an antidemocratic trope. Perhaps, D.C. architects found the celebration of democracy more difficult than has been suggested. Even the Lincoln and Jefferson Memorials represent these men in enormous scale.

Although theme parks can be exhausting, they provide numerous opportunities to sit or even to relax while eating and watching the scenery. This is not the case in D.C. or at the SI. There are few places to rest within SI buildings; they are generally crowded and there is no transportation between them. Theme parks can well afford these luxuries because of their admission fees; the SI is free and presumably has not thought of its visitors in these terms.

Indeed, the SI largely ignores pleasuring the body, whereas Disney parks deliberately evoke the senses to excited response. The SI is visually pleasurable, but Disney's liberal use of bodies of water at WDW to soothe its guests, and its use of innumerable modes of transportation, pleasure our kinesthetic sense. The SI has few fountains or pools, and the pools at the east and west ends of the Mall are not within sight of the major SI buildings. Neither is the Mall landscaped down its two-mile-long expanse. As a relatively barren expanse of grass, it provides an intriguing blank canvas for festivals and political demonstrations, but it offers few spots for repose, and traversing it on foot can be exhausting. In contrast, a primary appeal of Disney parks is "the ride," troped within the parks as a seemingly endless series of alternate methods of transport. These "rides" give theme park visitors time to rest and stimulate the pleasure response of movement without effort. The luxury of transport contrasts with what must be hominid memories of the quest as a physical trial. Despite these luxuries, however, theme parks are at least as exhausting as the Smithsonian.

Rest is just what you can get in the SI's beautiful underground museums. The National Museum of African Art and the Arthur M. Sackler Gallery (of Asian Art) are located behind the Castle. Relatively lightly attended, African Art hosts about four hundred thousand visitors a year, but because the Sackler Gallery links African Art to the Freer, this figure is distorted by the back-and-forth movement between buildings. Before they were built, there was some consternation that the choice of this location represented just another exclusion. No one seems to have noticed that the map of the Mall in the SI's official guidebook does not include African Art and the Sackler, although it does include the National Gallery, which is not technically part of the SI's operation but is certainly part of its iconic identification. Whatever the justification, these museums are beautiful in tone and atmosphere largely because they are underground. A welcome respite from the crowds and the heat of a summer's day on the Mall, they invite repose and even meditation, and because of beautifully integrated skylights reaching down three stories, they do not feel confining. Anything but monumental in scale, they implicitly affirm the human body. Visiting them reminds one of burrowing for knowledge along our rhizomatic web rather than of stretching toward unreachable shelves. As art museums, they attract a much smaller population. Neither do they, because of their subject matter, reinforce a Middle American sense of identity. They present a marked contrast to the larger and more populated aboveground museums. The placement of the SI's museums results in a hierarchy of emphasis, greatly influencing the maps that each visitor can create. Cognitive mapping is also influenced by the disciplinary sorting enacted by museum genres. Though these museums are conveniently located, it is easy for visitors to ignore them in favor of the march between the triangle points of the three most popular aboveground monuments. They represent "other" knowledges, and it is significant that they remain invisible even on some official SI maps.

Those familiar with the traditional rhetoric of the natural history museum know full well where to look for the "other." The inclusion of the "other" as artifact and curiosity in museums of natural history is now recognized as a fundamental ethical problem in museum practice. Nevertheless, change is slow, and disciplinary sorting at the SI is maintained by the difficulties of bureaucratic organization as much as anything else. For example, Native American art is still exhibited in Natural History, where it gets more exposure but where it must inevitably be mapped by the European American visitor as "other," as curiosity along with the bones, the dinosaurs, the rocks, and as qualitatively not equal to the Hirshhorn's standards. The creation of the Museum of the American Indian is not likely to change this equation, and its directors are well aware that it will likely be "a postcard stop on the way to Air and Space." Spatial arrangement has everything to do with our cognitive mapping, not to mention our physical routes through the SI. Rethinking how the visitor's path (which is ultimately translated into a cognitive map) could be redirected ought to be part of the Institution's larger plan.

THE RHETORIC OF EXHIBITS:
OPEN AND CLOSED TEXTS

Reader/response criticism has made it clear that reading is the result of a complicated negotiation of authorial intent, encoded text, and audience response. Ivan Karp has noted that this is as much the case at the museum as anywhere else. Umberto Eco's theory of open and closed texts provides one method for unpacking this process. Authors often have in mind an ideal reader whose familiarity with a certain context is a given. In *The Role of the Reader* (1984a), Eco points out that "a well-organized text presupposes a model of competence coming, so to speak, from outside the text, but on the other hand works to build up, by merely textual means, such a competence" (8). Museum texts are no exception. Clearly, they presuppose a model of competence. The fact that they attract a well-educated set of visitors in itself suggests this; however, they also seek to build up competence. Putting aside whether they succeed or not, it is possible to use the notion of open and closed texts to theorize about the reading strategies stimulated by a museum exhibit.

Eco's notions of open and closed texts are counterintuitively named. Closed texts "obsessively aim at arousing a precise response on the part of more or less precise empirical readers" and, in the process, leave themselves open to "any possible 'aberrant' decoding" (8). Such texts are rhetorically predictable because they are composed out of a limited set of recognizable structures. Eco's examples include Superman and Ian Fleming's James Bond novels. The SI's texts certainly seem to be constructed so as to appeal to the "average" educated Middle American with a series of very recognizable exhibition styles and rhetorics. This ideal reader certainly fills its exhibit halls. Because of the predictability of closed texts, however, they are open to alternate, even subversive, readings, and each reading can remain independent of the others. Such texts are closed because of their form, but "open" because the familiarity of their structure frees readers to subvert authorial intention.

In contrast, open texts require that each interpretation be "reechoed by the others" (9). Open texts address not an average ideal reader but an "ideal reader" who is able to

> master different codes and eager to deal with the text as with a maze of many issues. But in the last analysis what matters is not the various issues in themselves but the maze-like structure of the text. [An open text dictates that you] cannot use the text as you want, but only as the text wants you to use it. An open text, however "open" it be, cannot afford whatever interpretation. An open text outlines a "closed" project of its Model Reader as a component of its structural strategy. (9)

Using these models, it is possible to interpret museum exhibits as a series of nested open and closed texts. Virtually always mazelike in their physical structure, they present their readers with a series of problems to be solved. Sometimes the rhetoric is familiar; sometimes it requires attention to the violations of recognizable rhetoric. This asks the reader to work hard to unpack meanings. Open texts threaten to create "reader's block."

In exhibits, cognitive maps must be constructed in response to the physical disorientation of the maze and the unconscious reading techniques that this stimulates. The physical maze of the museum exhibit is an anagram of the theoretical maze that Eco is describing. This maze is a powerful kinesthetic lesson to the reader; it may even call upon synesthetic modes of cognition. It asks the reader to call on literacy skills that have been developed over long exposure to intertextual layerings of knowledge. While traveling through an exhibit, the reader may be confronted with a closed and therefore predictable text or with an open and therefore unpredictable text. The exhibit as a whole may be more or less structured according to recognizable rhetorical forms creating a closed text, or its dominant mode may be implicitly "open." More likely, it will be a mixture of both, unless it is very dated or very avant-garde.

A good semiotician, trained in the visual arts, could probably unpack a traditionally structured exhibit of, let us say, Impressionist painting. This unpacking would reveal a series of significations not consciously observed but nevertheless subtly embedded in the exhibit's design and arrangement. In the unpacking process, the semiotician would call on many different well-developed modes of literacy. But any visitor without similar training could interpret the same exhibit by drawing on another set of literacies. Pre-dictably closed texts give the reader this freedom. Despite the reality—that curators construct art museums for those already trained to read art—even the most naive audience would be able to squeeze signification out of a typ-ical exhibit. After all, the notion of "quality" or "masterpiece" would be well understood by virtually anyone. Putting aside individual disagreements with the curatorial decisions regarding worth, visitors still make meaning out of their affective reactions and personal preferences. The predictable form of the art exhibit may make the rejection of its content all the more possible. As a closed text, it may immoderately open itself to any "aberrant decoding."

Conversely, it is possible to imagine open museum texts that present a different set of challenges to interpretation. Innovative museum exhibits break the traditional rhetoric of display, relying on everything from hands-on exhibits, to computer simulations, to live actors interacting with visitors. They include film and video, special theater formats such as IMAX, and soon probably, virtual-reality displays. Alternate exhibition design is begin-ning to reflect non-Western and minority cultural values. Exhibits arranged according to family ownership or non-Western aesthetic concepts based on emotional response and synesthesia, deliberately evoking a sensual experi-ence of taste, touch, or odor, might be structured according to a different rhetoric.[18] These rhetorics create a multilayered text.

In contrast, the NMNH's "Spiders" exhibit, while ostensibly a collection of innovative and open texts, was overwhelmed by the closed nature of its medium: technologically based hands-on demonstrations. Constructed to appeal to children, it was immensely successful at drawing huge crowds of excited young people. Watching them, however, while myself trying to learn from these exhibits, was enough to convince this semiotician that the familiar technology of this exhibit overwhelmed the content that its design-ers sought to transmit. The "content" of this "form" seems to have been "technology is fun." Its subtext, "the SI offers you technological toys," pos-sibly overran its overt content. This exhibit, which meant, I am sure, to be a multilevel open text, ended up as a closed text with this insistent message. As such, visitors were free to make what they wanted out of it.

Museum display that breaks the traditional rhetorical frame calls on an-other set of literacy skills. Eco's theory implies that innovative display directs the addressee to attend closely to a series of embedded significations, them-selves built out of a series of violations of expectations (for those trained to decode a more traditional display). Open texts make emphatic their pur-poses. Visitors cannot immoderately make any meaning they choose out of open texts, and they must usually possess the ability to read meaning into the violations of the traditional rhetoric. This requires that the reader have extensive experience with traditional rhetorical forms and the modes by which these styles can be violated, i.e., signified upon or troped.

Modern museum display cuts both ways: as it tries to improve communication and the transmission of complex information,[19] it calls for different literacies. In doing so, it usually privileges the more highly educated. If this is even partially true, those who are not very interested in museums already—that is, the less educated, the less wealthy, and people of color—will continue to have difficulty squeezing pleasure out of reading museums. Open texts ask the reader to work hard, but perhaps there are ways to make them less difficult. Certainly the inclusion of "you are here" cues for "minority" visitors will help, but synesthetic forms of display might also help, for they cue skills not explicitly taught in the school setting. Lack of formal education should be less of a barrier when synesthetic cues are built into exhibitions, and alternate cultural codes could be more easily included via alternate rhetorical designs. Perhaps this is one method through which non-Western cultural codes can find powerful expression in museums that are historically constructed out of colonized cloth.

Officials at the National Museum of the American Indian seem to be moving in this direction as they redefine the rhetoric of display. However, the "average" American reader is likely to experience "reader's block" when faced with exhibits organized according to non-Western cultural codes. Making the museum an explicit lesson regarding the ideology of cognitive maps could mitigate this.

THE POWER OF MAPS—THE EXHIBIT

One especially interesting SI exhibit might be used to thread together a number of propositions this chapter has made. "The Power of Maps," curated by Lucy Fellowes and Denis Wood at the Cooper-Hewitt, was by all accounts highly successful in transmitting its central abstractions. It is significant that this exhibit caused its visitors to think critically about maps as systems of knowledge constructed out of ideology. It seems to have been explicitly about learning as mapmaking and mapmaking as an encoding of knowledge. As such, it directed the museum visitor to become aware of a key process in the museum experience, the process that this study is trying to tease apart.[20]

A detailed visitor study of "The Power of Maps" demonstrated that it, unlike many exhibits, was able to convince visitors of its thesis (Doering, Kindlon, and Bickford 1993). Even more highly educated than the average SI visitor, individuals who saw this exhibit were able to absorb its abstractions. Visitor studies strongly suggest that people remember the objects, displays, and architectural spaces of museums far more than the concepts that curators embed in exhibits.

Although "The Power of Maps" was dismantled before this study began, the curatorial notes were published in an illustrated booklet, and it was possible to review the archival material out of which the exhibit was structured.[21] Because visitor responses were so clearly reflective of the explicit meanings embedded by the curators, it is a good bet that this exhibit was a well-structured "open" text, deliberately leading its audience along a predetermined path. Its curators likely understood the power of well-structured maps. In contrast, "Spiders" had the potential to create a powerful example of this sort of museum text. Since maps, webs, and tricksters are an interest of mine, I was invested in its success. However, its reliance on the notion that "technology is fun" may be the most powerful closed text of all time.

Discussions that the NMAI planning staff are having include designing its exhibits with a similar awareness of the ideology of narrative. Key questions include: How can exhibits collect multiple truths about objects? How can contradictory histories be represented as simultaneously true? Can new rhetorics of display be invented to represent these paradoxes? The curatorial role is being redefined in institutions like the NMAI. When American Indians make choices about display, instead of academics or American Indians in collaboration with academics, the canonizer function shifts radically. But innovations like this are only a first step. Rethinking display has led to suggestions for installations that include the opportunity for the guest to commune with the objects, to make something in response, and for another party to record the first (Volkert conversation, 1994). Possible points of entry can be multiplied exponentially in such designs. The "you are here" effect can be stimulated by synesthetic cues.

RE-IMAGINING LITERACY AT THE SI

The national map constructed by the SI is indeed an unlimited territory that requires its visitors to call on many skills, many different literacies at the appropriate moment and in the appropriate context. By concentrating on a narrow definition of literacy, we have crippled our understanding of the multiple challenges that museums present to their readers. By suppressing the importance of the "you are here" effect, we have willfully denied the obstacles that metanarrative erects for many. Race, gender, and class placement are just some of the identity negotiations that visitors must perform in silence and without assistance. If the educated are able to resolve these issues in such a way so as to derive pleasure from their visits, are able to weave themselves into an exhibit, answers to questions about how they can do this are important not just for museum studies. These answers can tell us a great deal about the construction of epistemologies and how epistemologies can magnify human differences. New rhetorics of exhibition design that consciously take into account the use of the senses and sentiment, or *raza*, as Goswamny has described it, can help visitors weave themselves into exhibits and reweave their own webs of knowledge in response to narratives that they encounter.

MIXED CULTURAL MAPS

Multicultural inclusion requires that the museum structure itself so as to increase the ability of its audience to cognitively map its terrain, to imagine itself as audience and participant in a system of knowledge. Adding to its collections in such a way as to build a more inclusive canon will increase not just affective interest but reading and retention. This is particularly important for its minority visitors. Permanent, self-reflexive exhibits like "The Power of Maps" (a temporary installation) have the power to redirect audience expectations about the ideology of systems of knowledge. Radically restructured permanent exhibits addressed to race, ethnicity, gender, and national definition should be the result of rethinking museum theory and are the ethical responsibility of institutions that were invented to celebrate global exploitation. Such exhibitions must be multicultural and multidisciplinary. They must include the physical sciences in a continuum with not just physical and cultural anthropology but also history and art, and the sacred not as covert ritual but as overt, albeit questioned, practice. The knowledge that race has no scientific basis and that ethnicity has been constructed around a chimera created by racism needs a prominent place in the SI's canon. Unmasking the ideology of these canons will take as much energy as creating them. Finding the resources is an urgent matter. Such exhibits need to be decentralized and sprinkled throughout the museum, both as a means of hooking visitors into their narratives (especially at the major SI destinations, namely Air and Space, Natural History, and American History) and as a means of integrating and educating museum personnel across the divides of its relatively autonomous units regarding the important issues of exclusion, multiculturalism, and especially *Mestizaje*. Although race is a chimera, racial and cultural identification are concrete realities expressed in physical bodies. A decentralized but permanent "exhibition" (which in fact would be a series of exhibitions) would have the potential to tie together many of the disconnected narratives of the SI. It would be one way for the institution to read itself against itself. This is one possible cognitive map. It mirrors this author's personal cognitive map of knowledge by theorizing a method of inclusion. The sign for "you are here" must be integrated across the institution. Exhibition design and content must consciously work to include the bodies of people of color, women, and others who cannot find a point of recognition and thereby a point of entry. The SI's exhibit design should make explicit that all knowledge is partial and that all of us are narrating our version of a larger story at the museum. The SI needs to recognize that we are testing ourselves *and* the museum at every moment.

Conclusion # IMAGINING LITERACY IN A MIXED CULTURE

This thesis weaves together a series of delicately related strands. Like the rhizomes of knowledge it discusses, it knots over itself again and again. In so doing, it fails to follow many leads to their ultimate conclusion, often coming to a stop, swerving, and beginning again in another direction. This is what rhizomes do. This text mirrors the tropes it suggests we should use to imagine literacy. Like the tricksters it names as intrinsic to our confusions about the nature of knowledge, it transmogrifies itself. This is no more perverse than tricksters are perverse. The methodology bred itself out of itself. It taught its author lessons even as it caught her in multiple frustrations, dead ends, and embarrassments. Musing about literacy is painful. The potential rewards must be imagined before they can be experienced, just as literacy must be imagined before it can be acquired.

The goal of this study is to redirect these imaginings, to remind us again and again that all knowledges are partial. It attempts to draw a preliminary map of the travels we might take through a radically revised epistemology, one that enables rather than disenables. Along the way, we should find that we cannot choose between mixed cultures and mono-cultures, between print literacy and visual literacies, between knowledge of the "mind" and the "body," between pre-electronic, electronic, and soon-to-be organic technologies, between one genre and another, between rhetorics. All these choices are configured from within a dialectical order emphasizing a subject/object dichotomy intrinsic to the modern era.

If we are to undo the violence of literacy, we will need to break the hold of dualisms like literacy/illiteracy, literacy/orality, reading/writing, reading/misreading, even speaking/silence. They do nothing but reinforce a damaging semiosis. If we are to undo the ideology of the list, the dictionary and the encyclopedia, we must learn to travel along a rhizomatic web of knowledge, one based not on dualistic bifurcations but on multidimensional alternatives.

Why do many reject the "old" literacies? As Elspeth Stuckey has asked, "Why would so many people choose to disqualify themselves from the possibilities of labor?" (1991:17). Or, to put it another way: why would so many choose to remain vulnerable in the face of an increasingly complex and dangerous global system? Perhaps they are overwhelmed by the immense array of choices and challenges before them. The intuition that the "old" literacies are insufficient could be enough to discourage those who are already operating under a deficit. To Stuckey's premise that the change in work is a change in literacy, we can add: the change in communications technologies is a change in cognition. But there are other changes driving literacy as well. A global diaspora is creating dangerous and delicious cultural cacophonies. Biotechnology is forcing painful and exciting redefinitions of our bodies and minds. The distinctions between human, animal, machine, life, and death are increasingly blurred. Dualistic models will not explain away these paradoxes.

All this and more than this transform our epistemologies while the tail end of modernism reinforces racism, redefines sexism, and reinscribes classism under the rubric of post-capitalism. Modernism has eaten both communism and democracy, leaving us with a series of urgent questions. Who can supply the answers? Surely not the majority of Americans, who do not know the difference between a bacterium and a virus. How can an electorate ignorant of basic biology make decisions about health care alternatives? How can this same electorate cope with the issues surrounding AIDS, recombinant DNA, or similar threats? To repeat: nothing in this study is meant to suggest that what is termed "the literacy crisis" does not name something profound. The ideologies of literacy are cruel; their social results are deadly.

What ties together this text, this web? The realization that the "old" dualistic ideology of literacy is fracturing, even "fractaling," and that the plastic logic of the rhizome is more suited to the emerging epistemologies around us. Rhizomes make room for paradox; so should we all. Paradox has certainly found room for us.

An associative model for literacy enables flexibility and travel. Tricksters please us when we are musing this way because they make room for multiple meanings and contradiction. Tricksters signify fluency in multiple contexts; they not only acknowledge cultural mixing, they are able to warn us of the dangers ahead and demonstrate skills that can turn threat into opportunity. Trickster and ginger root literacy is a figuration alive in our days and nights.

What literacy *was* cannot save us, but newly emerging literacies have the potential to help us thread our way through postmodern life. Theorists like Gregory Ulmer attempt to discover alternate pedagogical practices appropriate to new modes of cognition. His experimental work, *Teletheory: Grammatology in the Age of Video,* looks strange (the first sentence, "This may not be a book after all," puts strange up front), just as many of the experiments in this text look strange.

It invites us to participate in the invention of "a style of thought as powerful and productive as was the invention of conceptual thinking that grew out of the alphabetic apparatus" (Ulmer 1989:ix–x). His numerous neologisms—teletheory, mystory, euretics, oralysis—all gesture toward a redefinition of cognition. This redefinition, along with one of his major assumptions, "that video is not something in need of explanation, but something whose operations have changed the conditions of explanation itself," echoes the subtext of this thesis. Ulmer ties his suggestions for a new pedagogy to teletheory, an experimental "academic discourse that could function across all our media—voice, print and video" (1). The practices of a literate education need teletheory, which Ulmer identifies as including the poetic or associative modes of composition alongside the narrative and expositive modes more typical in academic writing (15). Teletheory turns academic discourse from the largely hermeneutic—the interpretive and the definitional—toward euretics—invention. *Teletheory* invents a new genre, mystory, inspired by Hayden White's call for a new historiography. Ulmer's "mystory" relies on a new style of thought called "oralysis," which is "writable in video, in the same way that analysis is writable in alphabetic literacy" (44). Mystory plays with my story, history, herstory, mystery, what Ulmer calls paganism and what Silko calls the storyteller. For Ulmer, "the joke can replace the riddle as the simple form organizing the drive of research" (81).

Umberto Eco, Ulmer notes, describes metaphors and jokes as shortcuts through the encyclopedic networks, the labyrinth. The nonsense generated by the joke is the result of what Arthur Koestler terms "the bisociation of ideas." Nonsense is "generated by the violation of boundaries." Jokesters, tricksters are intrinsic to mystory.

He has created a dense text, one that is open, endlessly suggestive and repeatedly concatenating knowledges. *Teletheory* courageously ventures beyond the edge. This text stops short of that edge; it gestures toward the field of possibility; its author is all too aware that "there be" tigers "in them there hills." Remembering that the trope, imagining literacy, is a utopian term, that it is meant to encourage us to invent multiple exits, this study optimistically affirms invention as a catalyst for hope.

While respecting dragons and tigers, individuals must be taught, cajoled, even tricked into weaving their own webs of understanding in response to other webs, whether this takes place in response to an isolated printed text or a concatenated set of texts. To ask for less is to ask readers to remain crippled by a mono-cultural, one-dimensional vision. This limited vision has already led to dire consequences. We have no choice. Reimagining literacy is central to our survival in a postmodern cacophony of mixed cultures, transmuting technologies, and constantly transmogrifying threats to individuals, communities, nations, and the planet.

NOTES

INTRODUCTION: TO READ OR NOT

1. The Spanish version of this poem, "El Guardián de los Libros," is available in *Selected Poems: Jorge Luis Borges,* edited by Alexander Coleman; however, both the Spanish and the English translation that I have used are from *In Praise of Darkness,* translated by Norman Thomas di Giovanni (Dutton 1974). Regrettably, permission could not be obtained to reprint this translation in toto as originally intended. Borges served as director of the library from 1955 to 1973. His blindness was inherited from his father, whose literary ambitions were cut short by the condition. He was advised to discontinue reading and writing in 1956. His mother served as his secretary until her death in 1975 at the age of ninety-nine.

2. See especially "The Wall and the Books" in *A Personal Anthology,* "The Total Library" in *Borges: A Reader,* and "The Library of Babel" in *Ficciones.*

3. Toni Morrison's "rememory" has given us an important signifier.

4. For an explanation of how standards of literacy have consistently escalated throughout American and European history from the most basic form, the ability to write one's name to a 1990's standard, which requires increased comprehension skills and the ability to problem-solve, see Miles Meyers, "Shifting Standards of Literacy—The Teacher's Catch-22"; Daniel Resnick and Lauren Resnick, "The Nature of Literacy: An Historical Exploration"; Carl F. Kastle, "Literacy and Mainstream Culture in American History"; and Robert Reich, "The Education of the Symbolic Analyst," in *The Work of Nations,* 225–242. Reich's discussions of literacy and work are interesting.

5. See the National Commission on Excellence in Education publications *A Nation at Risk: The Imperative for Educational Reform,* and *Meeting the Challenge: Recent Efforts to Improve Education across the Nation;* the United States Department of Education's *The Nation Responds: Recent Efforts to Improve Education;* and the National Endowment

for the Humanities publication *Humanities in America: A Report to the President, the Congress, and the American People.*

6. This study by the International Association for the Evaluation of Educational Achievement based at The Hague, Netherlands, did not test for depth of understanding, the higher standard increasingly demanded by governmental and business groups. "U.S. Students Rank among World's Best Readers," *San Jose Mercury News*, October 4, 1992, 8L.

7. During the 1992 presidential campaign, Bill Clinton repeatedly cited estimates that the average worker will need to be retrained eight times during his/her working lifetime in order to remain employable. Dan Quayle began echoing similar statistics. Tom Peters, author of *In Search of Excellence* and other pop-business, self-help titles, insists that individuals must reeducate themselves approximately every six years for life. As the economy improved, this rhetoric disappeared.

8. William H. Davidow and Michael S. Malone have supplied the most recent exhortation on this matter in their new book, *The Virtual Corporation*, excerpted in "Perspective," *San Jose Mercury News*, October 11, 1992, 4P: "We need an educational system that teaches children not just soon-to-be obsolete knowledge, but prepares them to be lifelong learners, with the flexibility to deal with rapid and perpetual change."

9. See Edward Yordon, *The Decline and Fall of the American Programmer* (1–12), for an interesting review of the job prospects of computer programmers. Undergraduate computer science course enrollment peaked in 1983, but in 1984 universities turned out 50,000 computer science graduates, who competed for 25,000 jobs. Enrollment in computer science has decreased continuously since that year. Industry wants more highly trained programmers but is unwilling to train them on the job. In 1987 the United States produced 466 Ph.D.'s in computer science, but an estimated 1,000 a year are needed by academia and industry. Clearly, minimal levels of computer literacy are as problematic as minimal levels of general literacy. Yordon predicts that "the American programmer is about to share the fate of the dodo bird . . . international competition will put American programmers out of work, just as Japanese competition put American automobile workers out of work." Well-educated foreigners will be able to undercut American programmers because their wage requirements are five to six times less and their education and experience are fully comparable. See also Davidow and Malone, *The Virtual Corporation*, for an interesting theory of how material production is changing rapidly to allow for the rapid manufacture of physical products and services tailored to the specifications of individual buyers and requiring completely different management techniques and teams. Even production lines must be flexible; this means workers must be able to respond to a constantly changing work environment.

10. See the AFL-CIO's Workplace literacy programs described in Anthony R. Sarmiento and Ann Kay, *Worker-Centered Learning: A Union Guide to Workplace Literacy*, which defines literacy as a union issue.

11. See note 2 and also the 1953 science fiction classic "The Nine Billion Names of God," by Arthur C. Clarke, in which Tibetan monks utilize a computer to system-

atically record all the possible names of God. This project is named as blasphemous by a character before he knows that at its completion the universe will come to an end.

12. It is no accident that the spread of literacy in the United States is directly connected to Protestantism's injunction to read the Bible without an intermediary priest or pastor.

13. The Puente Project, a college program aimed at providing Mexican American and Latino students with role models during their initial college writing courses, is one such example of this trend.

14. Chapter 2, "Whose Encyclopedia?," will examine autobiographical testimonies of acquisition.

15. Those children who are not attracted to such games are probably without role models who display an enviable literacy.

16. Again, this was not the case in oral cultures.

17. This term is borrowed from Claude Lévi-Strauss, who begins his discussion in *The Savage Mind* (16–18) with a reference to the French term *bricoleur,* signifying an individual who undertakes odd jobs and is able to do what needs to be done by resorting to a collection of tools and materials that have been assembled over time. These tools bear no relation to the current project or to any other particular project, but are nevertheless brought to bear by the *bricoleur* out of the necessity of the moment. These tools and materials have been collected over time as a result of circumstance. Literacy can indeed be thought of as a *bricoleur*'s skill.

CHAPTER 1: THE SEMIOSIS OF LITERACY

1. See also Jameson's *Political Unconscious,* 165 ff. and 253 ff., and "After Armageddon: Character Systems in *Dr. Bloodmoney.*" In the foreword to *On Meaning,* Jameson maps Hayden White's *Metahistory: The Historical Imagination in Nineteenth-Century Europe* on a semiotic square.

2. See Umberto Eco's notions of infinite semiosis for a description of this process.

3. "Looking" in expositions and museums is discussed as an aspect of literacy in chapters 4 and 5.

4. His 1967 book was titled *Validity in Interpretation* and his 1976 book was *The Aims of Interpretation.*

5. In *Literacy in Theory and Practice,* Brian Street goes on to make a case for understanding the development of more sophisticated literacy as rooted in the commercial needs of the community (168 ff.).

6. See the lists at the end of his 1987 book and two subsequently published works: E. D. Hirsch Jr., Joseph F. Kett, and James Trefil, *The Dictionary of Cultural Literacy: What Every American Needs to Know,* and E. D. Hirsch Jr., *A First Dictionary of Cultural Literacy: What Our Children Need to Know.*

7. This is Secretary of Labor Robert Reich's position in his book *The Work of Nations,* which contains two interesting chapters on education.

8. Check Ong, "Reading, Technology, and Human Consciousness." Stuckey (1991:73) discusses Ong's ideas about interiority and silence. Silence, privacy, and interiority allow spirituality. Writing and print allow the interiorization of consciousness.

9. See chapter 5 for a discussion of synesthesia and literacy.

10. Again, chapters 4 and 5 explore these other modes of reading/writing.

11. *Gesture* here refers to signals that do not correspond to any natural language. Sign language may be spoken of as gestural, but each hand movement corresponds to an identifiable phoneme or morpheme. Sign language is not body language.

12. See note 17 in the introduction.

CHAPTER 2: WHOSE ENCYCLOPEDIA?

1. Encyclopedia, or reasoned dictionary of the sciences, arts, and crafts, published by a society of men of letters.

2. See the *Oxford English* and *American Heritage* dictionaries and Hankins (1985): 163–170.

3. A Porphyrian tree is a Manneristic maze.

4. This maze is a trap in which you continually repeat mistakes without exit (Eco 1984b:81).

5. Hirsch's 1987 *Cultural Literacy: What Every American Needs to Know* was preceded by a series of articles and followed in 1988 by *The Dictionary of Cultural Literacy: What Every American Needs to Know,* coedited by Hirsch, Joseph F. Kett, and James Trefil, and the children's version, *First Dictionary of Cultural Literacy: What Our Children Need to Know.* These volumes were followed by another series of articles defending the Cultural Literacy program. The 1987 dictionary was updated in 1993.

6. The best comprehensive critique I have uncovered is Stanley Aronowitz and Henry A. Giroux's "Schooling, Culture, and Literacy in the Age of Broken Dreams: A Review of Bloom and Hirsch."

7. Voodoo is, of course, one local knowledge that is almost always denigrated in Western cultural ideology.

8. See Gregory G. Colomb, "Cultural Literacy and the Theory of Meaning: Or, What Educational Theorists Need to Know about How We Read"; E. D. Hirsch Jr., "From Model to Policy"; and Colomb's "Response." See also Hirsch's "A Postscript: Cultural Literacy, What Every American Needs to Know"; "Hirsch Responds: The Best Answer to a Caricature Is a Practical Program"; "The Primal Scene of Education"; and "'The Primal Scene of Education': An Exchange."

9. Hirsch's publisher has "trademarked" the term *cultural literacy,* although I find no instances of the activation of this trademark. Perhaps they anticipated a series of competing products purporting to convey their own brand of cultural literacy. In any case, the construct *cultural literacy* provides a fascinating mantra.

10. Elsewhere this study discusses recent research suggesting that even successful schooling does not lead to improved economic conditions for the disenfranchised.

11. From the introduction to *Global Literacy,* in manuscript.

12. In "The Value of Narrativity in the Representation of Reality" (in White 1987), Hayden White reminds us that there are three basic kinds of historical representation—the annals, the chronicle, and the history proper—each generally thought to demonstrate a "higher" form of representation. Annals simply list events in chronological sequence. The earliest inventories are usually considered the historical catalyst for literacy. Commerce and taxation required not just lists of goods but also records of births, marriages, deeds, and wills. In other words, the most basic use of literacy—the inventory—is parallel to the most basic form of historical representation.

The second method of historical representation, the chronicle, is dependent upon a central organizing principle. Like annals, the chronicle supplies no closure. It undertakes to record relevant details concerning, for example, an individual, a town, an institution, or an undertaking.

13. As I first drafted these pages, a flawed survey suggested that about one-third of American adults believe that the Holocaust may never have happened. Later, as I revised, the survey was revealed to have been poorly devised. Meanwhile, the Bosnian holocaust continues. In a few years, students entering college will probably be unable to recognize the name Bosnia.

14. Hirsch claims that the list project came first and that what was meant as a short preface to what would become the cultural literacy dictionary grew into his 1987 book.

15. These three have been nicknamed "the killer bees" by their opponents.

16. The dictionary was used as a basis for the 1989 National Academic Decathlon Competition, conducted for American high school "whiz kids." (Thanks to Analisa Narareno's UCSC essay, "What Every Reader Should Know about *The Dictionary of Cultural Literacy,*" for this nugget.)

17. Sandoval's notion of oppositional consciousness has influenced the deep structure of my thinking. See her "Oppositional Consciousness in the Postmodern World: U.S. Third World Feminism, Semiotics, and the Methodology of the Oppressed."

18. "The Trope of the Talking Book," chapter 4 in Henry Louis Gates Jr.'s *The Signifying Monkey: A Theory of African American Literary Criticism,* points out the relationship between imagining freedom and imagining literacy in a number of examples: John Jea's "midnight dream of instruction . . . represents the dream of freedom as the dream of literacy, a dream realized as if by a miracle of literacy" (166).

CHAPTER 3: READING TRICKSTER WRITING

1. An encyclopedic entry is like an address without a map.

2. Of course, the writer's process is not ordinarily observable. Ethnographies of writers made visible practices ordinarily invisible to researchers and students of writing. In the same way, literary ethnographies of literacy may make visible literacies ordinarily invisible. Such description is necessarily tainted by interpretive bias, but description of the writing process is also tainted. Obviously, what the observer may

conclude is not necessarily what is taking place. In fact, the writer may not be able to consciously articulate his/her own process, although the attempt to do so can sometimes be very revealing and useful.

3. Cf. Michel Foucault, "What Is an Author?" (in Foucault 1977).

4. See chapter 4 below, "Disney's Labyrinth," and *The Woman Warrior:* "'You have to infer the whole dragon from the parts you can see and touch,' the old people would say. . . . The dragon lives in the sky, ocean, marshes, and mountains; and the mountains are also its cranium. . . . Sometimes the dragon is one, sometimes many" (28–29).

5. Raul Villa's point about the commodification and co-optation of some aspects of Chicano music needs to be addressed here, but I am talking about a sort of subconscious and conscious opposition. It is not that all minority voices are by definition oppositional. Rather they are by definition positioned oppositionally unless they lay down their swords by choosing to adopt an assimilationist voice that lacks a critical or political edge. Sometimes their choice is involuntary or unconscious. Sometimes it is the result of a calculated decision. See Villa's unpublished qualifying essay, June 14, 1990 and his dissertation, "Tales from the Second City: Social Geographic Imagination in Contemporary Urban California Chicana/Chicano Literature and Art."

6. I am reminded of not just the Nazi Holocaust but also "the Disappeared" in South America, who have spawned an entire political movement because the pathos of their missing bodies has stirred people worldwide.

7. Johnson's meticulous text has influenced my analysis in ways that cannot be made clear through citation alone.

8. See Tillie Olsen's *Silences* for multiple descriptions of other writers who have struggled with voice. Maya Angelou's silence during her childhood led to years of intense reading, which obviously resulted in a voice of considerable power.

9. Tayo uses the term *half-breed* as a self-description and notes that Betonie's hazel eyes are like his own. Tayo stares so intently into those hazel eyes that Betonie volunteers, "My grandmother was a remarkable Mexican with green eyes" (119).

10. It is worthy of note that Silko's sources were almost certainly written and in translation, and she insists that these myths and chants are of her own invention, though they are obviously based on some awareness of traditional myths and ceremonies. Since she implies in her formal presentation that what we are looking at on the page is poetry, the issue of "authenticity" is blurred by considerations of written text. Its relation to the oral is problematic. "If the song, the poem, the epic are incompatible with writing, if writing threatens them with death, how do we explain the coexistence of the two ages?" (Derrida 1976:269). Thanks to Gerald Vizenour for these thoughts.

11. The Latino comedy group Culture Clash smashes local knowledges against one another as a signature comedic style.

12. Kingston asks us: "How do we teach readers to have a tolerance for ambiguity? Some of my readers get so frustrated, they quit." One suggestion: teach them the value of ambiguity and expose them to many texts that force them to grapple with that value. Exposure is sometimes the best teacher.

13. Spiderwoman's consistent transformations are signified by her many names—Changing Woman, Yellow Woman, and so on.

14. Kingston notes that she uses math formulae, too, thereby concatenating science, culture, and the myth of science.

15. Encyclopedic competence is that fund of semiotic associations that every individual possesses in relation to every morpheme s/he possesses. From this competence comes a welter of associations that make interpretation of any utterance possible. See chapter 4 below, "Disney's Labyrinth," 58, and Eco's *Semiotics and the Philosophy of Language*, 46–86.

16. This term is from Bakhtin, *The Dialogic Imagination* (426–427): "A word, discourse, language or culture undergoes 'dialogization' when it becomes relativized, deprivileged, aware of competing definitions for the same things. Undialogized language is authoritative or absolute. . . . Everything means, is understood, as a part of a greater whole—there is a constant interaction between meanings, all of which have the potential of conditioning others. Which will affect the other, how it will do so and in what degree is what is actually settled at the moment of utterance."

CHAPTER 4: DISNEY'S LABYRINTH

1. Two hundred eighty-four miles of raw footage have been edited to fourteen. To see all the film in one day would require viewing a mile of film an hour for fourteen hours.

2. The term *culti-multural* is a coinage of "robo-raza II" Robert Sanchez, put into wide circulation by Guillermo Gómez-Peña. It attempts to name the problematics of multicultural discourses that seek to encapsulate issues of race and ethnicity in sanitized and static narratives of liberalism. See Gómez-Peña's "The New World (B)order." In the New World (B)order, all traditional borders and categories have been destroyed. "Culti-multural" is what came before.

3. By *simulacrum/simulacra*, I mean to conjure both the simple denotation of an image or representation of something and also the postmodern connotation of a representation that has been split from its original and has attained the status of "real" in and of itself. My use of this term follows Baudrillard: "Simulation is no longer that of a territory, a referential being or substance. It is the generation, by models, of a real without origin or reality: a hyperreal" (1988:166). For Baudrillard, "No longer does the code take priority over or even precede the consumer object. The distinctions between object and representation, thing and idea are no longer valid" (5–6). In their place, Baudrillard fathoms a strange new world constructed out of models or simulacra that have no referent or ground in any "reality" except their own (Mark Poster, Introduction to Jean Baudrillard, *Selected Essays*). I am not, however, as cynical about this phenomenon as is Baudrillard.

4. The hands-on exhibits at the Wonders of Life pavilion are labeled a "Sensory Funhouse."

5. The film *Jurassic Park* makes the connections between theme parks and bodies all the more explicit. While the body is pleasured at Disney World, it is ravaged at Jurassic Park. This is not as clear in the novel as it is in the film, largely because the bodies on the screen partake of virtuality. One subtext of this essay is the violence of exclusion. A favorite line from *Jurassic Park* illustrates this dichotomy: "When the 'Pirates of the Caribbean' breaks down, the pirates don't eat the guests." Perhaps more eating occurs at Disney than this essay makes explicit.

6. Disney was the son of a turn-of-the-century socialist. Utopian socialist sentiments in books like Edward Bellamy's *Looking Backward* probably influenced Disney's father. Interestingly, Michael Harrington has pointed out that such books not only contained notions about the underdog and social justice, they also contained a kind of "warmhearted, futuristic authoritarianism." This is replicated in the Disney parks (Fjellman 1992:115–116; Harrington 1979).

7. I agree with Cornel West that this phrase has become monotonous. It is, however, useful as a shorthand. Class, by the way, is entirely invisible at Disney World. Everyone—but everyone—is middle class in this universe. Somehow, even the Third World is represented as middle class. The problem of representing nonindustrialized countries and cultures is not just a problem of race, because for Disney the only imaginable life is a middle-class one punctuated by geniuses who make millions because they create valuable commodities.

8. Those who feel that Disney's ideology is unacceptably right wing might note that Christian fundamentalists find it objectionable. It depicts reproduction, evolution, science, and a secular lifestyle as "good" and "true." There is evidence that Jim and Tammy Bakker's Christian theme park was constructed as an alternative to Disney parks.

9. One example of ideology manifested in museum display and how an oppositional literacy can help us is surely the contrast between Henry Ford's representation by Disney and his representation at Los Angeles' Simon Wiesenthal Center (Museum of Tolerance), where he is notable for his circulation of the anti-Semitic tract *The Jewish Problem*. Ford is one of Disney's most persistent heroes.

10. It is important to remember that for Anzaldúa, *la conciencia de la mestiza* signifies not just the consciousness inhabiting the biological bodies of Chicanas, but a consciousness that is potential in those who inhabit similar borderlands of place, language, race, culture, and gender.

11. Open texts are defined by Eco as texts that require the reader to deal with "a maze of many issues. But in the last analysis what matters is not the various issues in themselves but the maze-like structure of the text. You cannot use the text as you want, but only as the text wants you to use it. An open text, however 'open' it be, cannot afford whatever interpretation" (Eco 1984a:9).

12. Sometimes the "ride" is replaced by a more standard theater production, but these pavilions seem dated, and they are surely less fun.

13. Except cars—you leave your car in the parking lot. Louis Marin accurately points out how this abandonment helps to construct Disneyland as utopia.

14. Stephen Fjellman has said, "I hope WDW becomes the most important museum representing the historical period when commodification ruled. People can bring their children to see what life was like in those dangerous days" (1992:17). He ends his book with this thesis: "The Critics Have Only Interpreted Walt Disney World, in Various Ways; the Point, However, Is to Make It into a Museum" (403). Disney paid Neil Postman and twenty-nine other consultants to make recommendations regarding improvements at EPCOT. He found the task hopeless but observed that EPCOT is perhaps America's most popular museum. The subtext of this essay is this: What does it teach and how can we read it?

15. Disney has taken special pains to attract African Americans in recent years. Special advertising in publications like *Ebony* has paid off. My last visit confirmed that African Americans are visiting EPCOT in greater numbers. They seem to enjoy it as much as anyone else. So, too, do all the vastly underrepresented people of color and females who visit. These groups have been trained to accept underrepresentation in their entertainments and educational materials. Disney is careful not to offend African Americans by releasing *Song of the South* in the United States, but that does not prevent the company from releasing it in Japan, where it fosters American-style racism abroad.

16. "The American Adventure" is the only pavilion that does not in its nomenclature metonymically confuse *pavilion* with *country.* All the other pavilions in World Showcase are called simply by the name of the country. Thus we do not visit the Canadian pavilion; we visit Canada.

17. "Audio-Animatronic" is one of the neologisms coined by the Disney organization. It names Disney's own brand of "robotic" figure. These simulacra are not robots; they are "lifelike" simulations that are part of numerous theatrical presentations at his parks. Most Americans have seen the figures on television even if they have not been to the parks.

18. Thanks to Ivan Karp for drawing my attention to the Muppets' self-referential criticality and Disney parody.

19. The World Showcase promenade is about 1.3 miles around its forty-acre lagoon.

20. A portrait of Einstein is on display in the pavilion's Heritage Manor gift store. Labeled "America's greatest scientist," his outrageous appropriation is embarrassingly counterpointed just three feet away by a racist display of knickknacks trivializing slavery.

21. It was replaced in 1994. This decision was made before Jackson's recent troubles. It replaces an earlier 3-D film, *Magic Journeys,* which is now shown in the Magic Kingdom and is itself due for replacement in 1994.

22. Jackson's personal obsession with the Disney parks is well known. He keeps a suite filled with his Disney memorabilia at Walt Disney World (Fjellman 1992:442).

23. The parallels between Michael Jackson and Mickey are substantial and are worthy of a separate essay. No doubt the Disney Corporation is aware of them. They include the white gloves, the benign tricksterism, the constant transformation of form

(Mickey's physical appearance has been constantly updated in subtle reconfigurations). Susan Willis has pointed out that Jackson moves like Mickey, that both are rubbery and seemingly without skeleton. And while Michael is a bad-boy trickster gone cyborg in many of his video productions, Captain E/O is introduced to the audience as simultaneously infamous and inept. "The Command considers us a band of losers. We're gonna show them we're the best. If we don't, we'll be drummed out of the corps." Shades of Mickey's understated and underrecognized competence. Jackson's affection for and identification with mice dates to his childhood when he turned a household rodent into a pet. Disney is said to have tamed a field mouse when he lived in Kansas City (Brockway 1989:26).

24. Thanks to Linda Haas for cueing me in to this while we watched it together.

25. It is not appropriate or even relevant to question Jackson's veracity regarding his descriptions of his illness or to consider his guilt or innocence regarding these legal matters. While important moral questions are at issue here and should not be minimized, what counts on the ground at EPCOT is Michael Jackson's cultural capital. As that changes, so do the meanings that guests make out of his figure.

26. These techniques are now well known under the term *morphing*. The pictures themselves have come to be called *morphs*. They are increasingly commonplace in our media environment.

27. In "Speed Demon," a particularly funny claymation sequence, Jackson is pursued by two nerdy and obese teenagers who ask him to autograph their tummies. An animated Statue of Liberty provides the commentary "America, land of the brave, home of the weird."

28. One of the most popular new attractions at Anaheim's Disneyland is "Fantasmic," which presents "Sorcerer Mickey" powers as emanating from his light-filled gloves.

29. The Artist Formerly Known as Prince is experimenting in much the same vein and continues to do so by playing with his multiple signifiers, adopting, rejecting, and readopting "names."

30. They are very similar in appearance to the Borgs in *Star Trek: The Next Generation;* also, an episode of *Babylon 5* included a cyborg woman visually encased and hanging from a ceiling just like Huston's character.

CHAPTER 5: THE SMITHSONIAN'S ENCYCLOPEDIA

1. Carol Duncan makes the point that Third World despots are enthralled with the creation of museums and the signal that they give to the Western powers that the regime is ready to adhere to Western cultural symbols and values. Michael Jackson's obsession with military dress and collection comes to mind as a bizarre counterpoint to this observation. MacDonald notes that the president of Indonesia championed a heritage theme park near Jakarta, costing close to $1 billion and causing university students

to riot. They wanted universities, not museums. Clearly, those students doubted the educational efficacy of museums.

2. Zahava Doering has observed that with the possible exception of the Met and the Getty, no institution is imagined separately from its contents. The SI is mythologized around the globe (Doering conversation 1994).

3. The bequest is cited in innumerable SI documents, catalogs, and brochures.

4. Most of the early history of the Smithsonian that is summarized here is taken from Geoffrey T. Hellman's eccentric but useful book, *The Smithsonian: Octopus on the Mall.*

5. Dr. Rush invented the "tranquilizing chair," a contraption that treated the mentally ill by immobilizing the entire body while bleeding the patient and administering purgatives. Rush made his eldest son, John, the beneficiary of his science. John died in his father's Pennsylvania hospital after twenty-seven years of such treatments (Takaki 1990: 16–35). Richard Rush went on to become ambassador to Great Britain, secretary of the Treasury under John Quincy Adams, and finally minister to France (Hawke 1971: 389–390).

6. Washington, D.C., covers sixty-nine square miles; Disney World covers forty-three. *Harper's* reports that while a remarkable 60 percent of Americans have visited D.C., 70 percent have visited Disneyland or Disney World.

7. Visitor statistics at the SI are counts made by security guards of individuals entering each museum. People come and go all day, so the same individual may enter a museum more than once, may visit more than one museum a day, or may return one or more times during a calendar year. Air and Space is visited approximately 7.5 million times a year; Natural History, 6.2 million times; American History, 5.7 million times. Total individual attendance is calculated from about 26 million separate visits by estimating that each visitor enters between two and three museums a day (Doering and Bickford 1994: iii–viii, 1–16).

8. I actually have not seen this at the SI. I saw one copy of the painting in question in Gallup, New Mexico, in 1970. The gallery told me the only other copy was at the Smithsonian. It is, however, buried in the archives and consistently unavailable when I visit, although I have contacted curators more than once on repeated visits. But like the keeper of the books, it comforts me to know that it is there.

9. Walter Benjamin's "The Work of Art in the Age of Mechanical Reproduction" (in Benjamin 1985b: 217–251) is often cited in museum studies, especially for its discussion of "aura."

10. See especially Haraway's "Teddy Bear Patriarchy" (in Haraway 1989) and James Boon's "Why Museums Make Me Sad" (1991).

11. I am reminded that it has been said that all writing is autobiography.

12. In *Synesthesia,* Cytowic takes pains to explain that he "does not want to be misunderstood as considering synesthesia to be vestigial, more primitive or atavistic. . . . *The neocortical mantle is not a higher rung on the ladder, completely suppressing everything below it,* but is built as a detour in the ladder, interposed between brainstem and limbic brain" (1989: 21).

13. Many thanks to my companions, Juan Carlos Garza, Mark Lawson, Sybil Santee, and Aaron Velasco, all Ford Foundation fellows who shared their experiences with me on October 16, 1993.

14. The original exhibition planned around the *Enola Gay* was withdrawn because of tremendous political resistance from the public and members of Congress.

15. Remember that the National Museum of the American Indian will be built to the immediate east of Air and Space.

16. In 1994 the Disney organization received so much unexpected, organized, and monied opposition to its proposed American history theme park in suburban Virginia just outside D.C. that it withdrew its plan to cash in on its rival's popularity. D.C.'s status as Disney's unique and separate competitor is safe for now; however, Michael Eisner insisted that another location just outside D.C. would eventually be determined.

17. I have heard tourists in D.C. comment on the scale. One savvy reader of public spaces declared it to be deliberately alienating. "They meant us to feel insignificant."

18. See the concept of *raza* or sentiments as discussed in Goswamny.

19. Falk and Dierking suggest that people remember the objects, displays, and architectural spaces of museums far more than the concepts curators embed in exhibits.

20. The Art/artifact exhibit organized by the Center for African Art in New York City is another example of an exhibit that took as its purpose the rhetoric of the museum. "Simulations" of different museum environments were meant to cause the audience to question how Westerners have displayed African art through their own cultural lens (Vogel 1991 : 191–204; Lavine and Karp 1991 : 8).

21. Many thanks to Lucy Fellowes of the Cooper-Hewitt for making this material available to me.

REFERENCES

Abrams, Roger D. 1970. *Deep Down in the Jungle* . . . : *Negro Narrative Folklore from the Streets of Philadelphia*. Chicago: Aldine.

Allen, Paula Gunn. 1988. "Who Is Your Mother? Red Roots of White Feminism." In *The Graywolf Annual Five: Multicultural Literacy: Opening the American Mind*, edited by Rick Simonson and Scott Walker, 13–27. St. Paul: Graywolf.

American Medical Association. 1988. *Journal of the American Medical Association* 260, no. 18 (November 18): 2776–2783.

Anaya, Rudolfo A. 1972. *Bless Me, Ultima*. New York: Warner.

Anderson, Benedict. 1991. *Imagined Communities*. London and New York: Verso.

Anzaldúa, Gloria. 1983. "Speaking in Tongues: A Letter to Third World Women Writers." In *This Bridge Called My Back*, edited by Gloria Anzaldúa and Cherríe Moraga, 165–174. New York: Kitchen Table, Women of Color Press.

————. 1987. *Borderlands/La Frontera: The New Mestiza*. San Francisco: Spinsters/Aunt Lute.

Appiah, Kwame Anthony, and Henry Louis Gates Jr., eds., and Michael Colin Vasquez, assistant ed. 1997. *The Dictionary of Global Culture*. New York: Knopf.

Arendt, Hanna. 1985. Introduction to *Illuminations*, by Walter Benjamin, 1–55. New York: Schocken.

Aronowitz, Stanley, and Henry A. Giroux. 1988. "Schooling, Culture, and Literacy in the Age of Broken Dreams: A Review of Bloom and Hirsch." *Harvard Educational Review* 5, no. 2 (May): 172–194.

Bakhtin, M. M. *The Dialogic Imagination*. Edited by Michael Holquist. Translated by Caryl Emerson and Michael Holquist. Austin: University of Texas Press, 1987.

Baudrillard, Jean. 1988. *Selected Essays*. Edited by Mark Poster. Stanford: Stanford University Press.

Benjamin, Walter. 1978. "Paris, Capital of the Nineteenth Century." In *Reflections*, translated by Edmund Jephcott. New York: Harcourt Brace Jovanovich.

———. 1983. "The *Flaneur*." In *Charles Baudelaire: A Lyric Poet in the Era of High Capitalism*. London: Verso.

———. 1985a. "Central Park." *New German Critique*, no. 35 (Winter): 28–57.

———. 1985b. *Illuminations*. Edited by Hannah Arendt. New York: Schocken.

Berman, Marshall. 1982. *All That Is Solid Melts into Air: The Experience of Modernity*. New York: Simon and Schuster.

Birnbaum, Steve. 1993. *Birnbaum's Walt Disney World*. N.p.: Hyperion and Hearst Business Publishing.

Bleich, David. 1978. *Subjective Criticism*. Baltimore: Johns Hopkins University Press.

———. 1988. *The Double Perspective: Language, Literacy, and Social Relations*. New York: Oxford University Press.

Boon, James. 1991. "Why Museums Make Me Sad." In *Exhibiting Cultures: The Poetics and Politics of Museum Display*, edited by Ivan Karp and Steven D. Lavine, 255–278. Washington, D.C.: Smithsonian Institution Press.

Borges, Jorge Luis. 1962. *Ficciones*. Edited by Anthony Kerrigan. New York: Grove.

———. 1967. *A Personal Anthology*. New York: Grove.

———. 1981. *Borges: A Reader*. Edited by Emir Rodriquez Monegal and Alastair Reid. New York: Dutton.

Brockway, Robert W. 1989. "The Masks of Mickey Mouse: Symbol of a Generation." *Journal of Popular Culture* 22, no. 4:24–34.

Brunner, John. 1975. *Shockwave Rider*. New York: Ballantine.

Buck-Morss, Susan. 1986. "The *Flaneur*, the Sandwichman, and the Whore: The Politics of Loitering." *New German Critique* 39 (Fall): 99–140.

Calvino, Italo. 1974. *Invisible Cities*. New York: Harcourt Brace Jovanovich.

Chicago Cultural Studies Group. 1982. "Critical Multiculturalism." *Critical Inquiry* 18 (Spring): 530–555.

Christian, Barbara. 1987. "The Race for Theory." *Cultural Critique* 6 (Spring): 52.

Clanchy, Michael. 1979. *From Memory to Written Record: England 1066–1307*. London: Edward Arnold.

Clarke, Arthur C. 1971. "The Nine Billion Names of God." In *The Science Fiction Hall of Fame*, vol. 1, edited by Robert Silverberg, 515–522. New York: Avon.

Colomb, Gregory G. 1989a. "Cultural Literacy and the Theory of Meaning: Or, What Educational Theorists Need to Know about How We Read." *New Literary History* 20, no. 2 (Winter): 411–450.

———. 1989b. "Response." *New Literary History* 20, no. 2 (Winter): 457–463.

Compute. 1988. 10, no. 7 (July): 86.

Csikszentmihaly, Mihaly, and Eugene Rochber-Halton. 1981. *The Meaning of Things: Domestic Symbols and the Self*. New York: Cambridge University Press.

Cytowic, Richard E. 1989. *Synesthesia: A Union of the Senses*. New York: Springer-Verlag.

Davidow, William H., and Michael S. Malone. 1992. *The Virtual Corporation*. New York: Harper Collins. Excerpted in *San Jose Mercury News*, "Perspective," October 11, 1992, 4P.

Deleuze, Gilles, and Felix Guattari. 1976. *Rhizome*. Paris: Minuit.

———. 1986. *Kafka: Toward a Minor Literature*. Translated by Dana Polan. Minneapolis: University of Minnesota Press, 1986.

Derrida, Jacques. 1976. "Of the Supplement to the Source: The Theory of Writing." In *Of Grammatology*, 269–316. Baltimore: Johns Hopkins University Press.

———. 1981. "The Law of Genre." In *On Narrative*, edited by W. J. T. Mitchell, 51–77. Chicago: University of Chicago Press.

Dick, Philip K. 1962. *The Man in the High Castle*. New York: Berkley.

Doering, Zahava D., and Adam Bickford. 1994 (February). *Visits and Visitors to the Smithsonian Institution: A Summary of Studies*. Washington, D.C.: Institutional Studies, Smithsonian Institution.

Doering, Zahava D., Audrey E. Kindlon, and Adam Bickford. 1993. *The Power of Maps: A Study of an Exhibition at Cooper-Hewitt, National Museum of Design*. Washington, D.C.: Institutional Studies, Smithsonian Institution.

Duncan, Carol. 1991. "Art Museums and the Ritual of Citizenship." In *Exhibiting Cultures: The Poetics and Politics of Museum Display*, edited by Ivan Karp and Steven D. Lavine, 88–103. Washington, D.C.: Smithsonian Institution Press.

Eco, Umberto. 1984a. *The Role of the Reader*. Bloomington: Indiana University Press.

———. 1984b. *Semiotics and the Philosophy of Language*. Bloomington: Indiana University Press.

———. 1986. *Travels in Hyperreality*. Translated by William Weaver. New York: Harcourt Brace Jovanovich.

———. 1989. *The Open Work*. Translated by Anna Cancogni. Cambridge: Harvard University Press.

EPCOT Center Guidebook. 1988. N.p.: Walt Disney World.

Falk, John H., and Lynn D. Dierking. 1989. "The Effect of Visitation Frequency on Long-Term Recollection." In *Visitor Studies: Theory, Research, and Practice*, 3:94–103. Jacksonville, Ala.: Center for Social Design.

Finch, Christopher. 1975. *The Art of Walt Disney: From Mickey Mouse to the Magic Kingdom*. New York: Abrams.

Fjellman, Stephen M. 1992. *Vinyl Leaves: Walt Disney World and America*. Boulder: Westview.

Foucault, Michel. 1977. *Language, Counter-Memory, Practice*. Edited by Donald F. Bouchard. Translated by Donald F. Bouchard and Sherry Simon. Ithaca, N.Y.: Cornell University Press.

Freire, Paulo. 1985. *The Politics of Education: Culture, Power, and Liberation*. South Hadley, Mass.: Bergin and Garvey.

———. 1993. *Pedagogy of the Oppressed*. New York: Continuum.

Gates, Henry Louis, Jr. 1984. "The Blackness of Blackness: A Critique of the Sign and the Signifying Monkey." In *Black Literature and Literary Theory*, edited by Henry Louis Gates Jr., 285–321. New York: Methuen.

———. 1988. *The Signifying Monkey: A Theory of African American Literary Criticism*. New York: Oxford University Press.

————, ed. 1984. *Black Literature and Literary Theory*. New York: Methuen.

Gee, James Paul. 1988. "The Legacies of Literacy: From Plato to Freire through Harvey Graff." *Harvard Educational Review* 5, no. 2 (May): 195–212.

Gómez-Peña, Guillermo. 1992. "The New World (B)order." *High Performance* (Fall): 59–65.

————. 1993. *Warrior for Gringostroika*. St. Paul: Graywolf.

Goody, Jack. 1977. *The Domestication of the Savage Mind*. Cambridge: Cambridge University Press.

————, ed. 1968. *Literacy in Traditional Societies*. Cambridge: Cambridge University Press.

Goswamny, B. N. 1991. "Another Past, Another Context: Exhibiting Indian Art Abroad." In *Exhibiting Cultures: The Poetics and Politics of Museum Display*, edited by Ivan Karp and Steven D. Lavine, 68–78. Washington, D.C.: Smithsonian Institution Press.

Graff, Harvey J. 1979. *The Literacy Myth: Literacy and Social Structure in the Nineteenth-Century City*. New York: Academic Press.

————. 1987a. *The Labyrinth of Literacy: Reflections on a Literacy Past and Present*. New York: Falmer Press.

————. 1987b. *The Legacies of Literacy: Continuities and Contradictions in Western Culture and Society*. Bloomington: Indiana University Press.

Greimas, Algirdas Julien. 1987. "The Interaction of Semiotic Constraints." In *On Meaning: Selected Writings in Semiotic Theory*, translated by Paul J. Perron and Frank H. Collins, 48–62. Minneapolis: University of Minnesota Press.

Hankins, Thomas L. 1985. *Science and the Enlightenment*. New York: Cambridge University Press.

Hansen, Miriam. 1993. "Of Mice and Ducks: Benjamin and Adorno on Disney." *South Atlantic Quarterly* 92, no. 1 (Winter): 27–61.

Haraway, Donna. 1985. "A Manifesto for Cyborgs: Science, Technology, and Socialist Feminism in the 1980s." *Socialist Review* 80:65–107. Reprinted in *Simians, Cyborgs, and Women*.

————. 1989. *Primate Visions: Gender, Race, and Nature on the World of Modern Science*. New York: Routledge.

————. 1991. *Simians, Cyborgs, and Women*. New York: Routledge, 1991.

————. 1997. *Modest_Witness@Second_Millennium. FemaleMan©_Meets_OncoMouse™*. New York: Routledge.

Harbison, Robert. 1977. "The Mind's Miniatures: Maps." In *Eccentric Spaces*. New York: Avon.

Harrington, Michael. 1979. "To the Disney Station: Corporate Socialism in the Magic Kingdom." *Harper's* 258, no. 1544 (January): 35–44.

Harris, Neil. 1986. "Museums: The Hidden Agenda." Keynote address, Midwest Museums Conference, September 24.

Hartsock, Nancy. 1983. "The Feminist Standpoint: Developing the Ground of a Specifically Feminist Historical Materialism." In *Discovering Reality: Feminist Perspectives on Epistemology, Metaphysics, Methodology, and Philosophy of Science*, edited by Sandra Harding and Merrill Hintikka, 283–310. Boston: D. Reidel.

Hawke, David Freeman. 1971. *Benjamin Rush: Revolutionary Gadfly*. New York: Bobbs Merrill.

Heath, Shirley Brice. 1983. *Ways with Words: Language, Life, and Work in Communities and Classrooms*. New York: Cambridge University Press.

Hein, Hilda. 1993. "Philosophical Reflections on the Museum as Canon Maker." *Journal of Arts Management, Law, and Society* 22, no. 4 (Winter): 293–309.

Hellman, Geoffrey T. 1967. *The Smithsonian: Octopus on the Mall*. New York: Lippincott.

Hirsch, E. D., Jr. 1967. *Validity in Interpretation*. New Haven: Yale University Press.

———. 1976. *The Aims of Interpretation*. Chicago: University of Chicago Press.

———. 1980. "Culture and Literacy." In *Toward a Literate Democracy*. Special Issue of *Basic Writing* 3, no. 1 (Fall–Winter): 27–47.

———. 1982. "Cultural Literacy." *American Scholar* (Spring): 159–169.

———. 1985. "Cultural Literacy and the Schools." *American Educator* (Summer): 8–15.

———. 1987. *Cultural Literacy: What Every American Needs to Know*. Boston: Houghton Mifflin.

———. 1988a. *Cultural Literacy: Let's Get Specific*, 15–21. Pamphlet. N.p.: *National Education Association*.

———. 1988b. "Hirsch Responds: The Best Answer to a Caricature Is a Practical Program." *Educational Leadership* 46, no. 1 (September): 18–19.

———. 1988c. "A Postscript: Cultural Literacy, What Every American Needs to Know." *Change* 20, no. 4 (July/August): 22–26.

———. 1989a. *A First Dictionary of Cultural Literacy: What Our Children Need to Know*. Boston: Houghton Mifflin.

———. 1989b. "From Model to Policy." *New Literary History* 20, no. 2 (Winter): 451–456.

———. 1989c. "The Primal Scene of Education." *New York Review of Books* 36, no. 3 (March 2): 29–35.

———. 1989d. "'The Primal Scene of Education': An Exchange." *New York Review of Books* 36, no. 6 (April 13): 50–51.

———. 1992. "Core Knowledge: Rx for Ailing Students." *Newsweek*, September 21, A8–9 (special advertising section).

Hirsch, E. D., Jr., Joseph F. Kett, and James Trefil. 1993. *The Dictionary of Cultural Literacy: What Every American Needs to Know*. 2d ed. New York: Houghton Mifflin.

Hoskin, Keith. 1981. "The History of Education and the History of Writing." Unpublished essay, Department of Education, University of Warwick.

———. 1984. "Cobwebs to Catch Flies: Writing (and) the Child." Unpublished essay, Department of Education, University of Warwick, January.

Humanities in America: A Report to the President, the Congress, and the American People.

1988. Washington, D.C.: National Endowment for the Humanities, Lynne V. Cheney, Chairman.

Hurston, Zora Neale. 1990. *Their Eyes Were Watching God.* New York: Harper and Row.

Jameson, Frederic. 1975. "After Armageddon: Character Systems in *Dr. Bloodmoney.*" *Science Fiction Studies* 2 (March): 31–42.

———. 1981. *Political Unconscious: Narrative as a Socially Symbolic Act.* Ithaca, N.Y.: Cornell University Press.

———. 1987. Foreword to *On Meaning: Selected Writings in Semiotic Theory,* by Algirdas Mulien Greimas, vi–xxii. Minneapolis: University of Minnesota Press.

Johnson, Barbara. 1984. "Metaphor, Metonymy, and Voice in *Their Eyes Were Watching God.*" In *Black Literature and Literary Theory,* edited by Henry Louis Gates Jr., 205–219. New York: Methuen.

Kaplan, Caren. 1987. "Deterritorializations: The Rewriting of Home and Exile in Western Feminist Discourse." *Cultural Critique* 6 (Spring): 187–198.

Karp, Ivan, and Corinne A. Kratz. 1993. "Wonder and Worth: Disney Museums in World Showcase." *Museum Anthropology* 17, no. 3 (October): 32–42.

Karp, Ivan, Christine Mullen Kreamer, and Steven D. Lavine, eds. 1992. *Museums and Communities: The Politics of Public Culture.* Washington, D.C.: Smithsonian Institution Press.

Karp, Ivan, and Steven D. Lavine, eds. 1991. *Exhibiting Cultures: The Poetics and Politics of Museum Display.* Washington, D.C.: Smithsonian Institution Press.

Kastle, Carl F. 1981. "Literacy and Mainstream Culture in American History." *Language Arts* 58, no. 2 (February): 207–218.

Kingston, Maxine Hong. 1977. *The Woman Warrior: Memoirs of a Girlhood among Ghosts.* New York: Vintage.

———. 1980. *China Men.* New York: Ballantine.

———. 1989. *Tripmaster Monkey: His Fake Book.* New York: Knopf.

Koran, John J., Jr., John Scott Foster, and Mary Lou Koran. 1989. "The Relationship among Interest, Attention, and Learning in a Natural History Museum." In *Visitor Studies: Theory, Research, and Practice,* 2:239–244. Jacksonville, Ala.: Center for Social Design.

Kowinski, William Severini. 1985. *The Malling of America: An Inside Look at the Great Consumer Paradise.* New York: William Morrow.

Lavine, Steven D., and Ivan Karp. 1991. "Introduction: Museums and Multiculturalism." In *Exhibiting Cultures: The Poetics and Politics of Museum Display,* edited by Ivan Karp and Steven D. Lavine, 1–9. Washington, D.C.: Smithsonian Institution Press.

Lévi-Strauss, Claude. 1962. *The Savage Mind.* Chicago: University of Chicago Press.

Lippard, Lucy R. 1990. *Mixed Blessing: New Art in a Multicultural America.* New York: Pantheon.

Lockridge, Kenneth. 1974. *Literacy in Colonial New England.* New York: Norton.

Lubiano, Wahneema. 1993. *America: Multicultural Education for the Twenty-first Century.* Minneapolis: University of Minnesota Press.

MacDonald, George F. 1987a. "Epcot Center in Museological Perspective." Paper presented at the CMA Annual Conference, May 26.

———. 1987b. "The Future of Museums in the Global Village." *Museum: The Museum and the Community* 155, no. 39: 209–216.

———. 1992. "Change and Challenge: Museums in the Information Society." In *Museums and Communities: The Politics of Public Culture*, edited by Ivan Karp, Christine Mullen Kreamer, and Steven D. Lavine, 158–181. Washington, D.C.: Smithsonian Institution Press.

MacDonald, George F., and Stephen Alsford. 1994. "Towards the Virtual Museum." *History News* 49, no. 5 (September): 10–18.

Malcolm X. With the assistance of Alex Haley. 1990. *The Autobiography of Malcolm X.* New York: Ballantine.

Marin, Louis. 1984. *Utopics: Spatial Play.* Translated by Robert A. Vollrath. Atlantic Highlands, N.J.: Humanities Press.

Mazón, Mauricio. 1984. *The Zoot-Suit Riots: the Psychology of Symbolic Annihilation.* Austin: University of Texas Press.

McLaren, Peter L. 1988. "Culture or Canon? Critical Pedagogy and the Politics of Literacy." *Harvard Educational Review* 58, no. 2 (May): 213–234.

Meeting the Challenge: Recent Efforts to Improve Education Across the Nation. 1983. A report to the Secretary of Education prepared by the staff of the National Commission on Excellence in Education, November 15.

Meyers, Miles. 1984. "Shifting Standards of Literacy: The Teacher's Catch-22." *English Journal* 73, no. 1 (April 1984): 26–32.

Mitchell, Timothy. 1989. "The World as Exhibition." *Comparative Studies in Society and History* 31, no. 2 (April 1989): 217–235.

Moore, Alexander. 1980. "Walt Disney World: Bounded Ritual Space and the Playful Pilgrimage Center." *Anthropological Quarterly* 53, no. 4 (October): 207–217.

Morrison, Toni. 1988. *Beloved: A Novel.* New York: Plume.

———. 1993. *The Nobel Lecture in Literature, 1993.* New York: Knopf.

A Nation at Risk: The Imperative for Education Reform: A Report to the Nation and the Secretary of Education. 1983. Washington, D.C.: National Commission on Excellence in Education.

The Nation Responds: Recent Efforts to Improve Education. 1984. Washington, D.C.: United States Department of Education.

The National Education Goals Report: Building a Nation of Learners. 1992. Washington, D.C.: U.S. Government Printing Office.

Newmann, Fred M. 1988. "Go for Depth." *Social Education* 52, no. 1 (October): 432–438.

Oates, Joyce Carol. 1972. "New Heaven and Earth." *Saturday Review* 55 (November 4): 51–54.

Olsen, Tillie. 1978. *Silences.* New York: Delacourt Press.

Ong, Walter J. 1982a. *Orality and Literacy: The Technologizing of the Word.* New York: Methuen.

————. 1982b. "Reading, Technology, and Human Consciousness." In *Literacy as a Human Problem*, edited by James Redmond, 170–201. University, Ala.: University of Alabama Press.

Pattison, Robert. 1987. "On the Finn Syndrome and the Shakespeare Paradox." *Nation* (May 30): 710–720.

Paz, Octavio. 1961. "The *Pachuco* and Other Extremes." In *The Labyrinth of Solitude*, translated by Lysander Kemp. New York: Grove Press.

Pearce, Susan M. 1989. *Museum Studies in Material Culture*. Washington, D.C.: Smithsonian Institution Press.

Pease, Donald A. 1990. "Author." In *Critical Terms for Literary Study*, edited by Frank Lentricchia and Thomas Mclaughlin. Chicago: University of Chicago Press.

Peters, Roger. 1978. "Communication, Cognitive Mapping, and Strategy in Wolves and Hominids." In *Wolf and Man: Evolution in Parallel*, edited by Roberta L. Hall and Henry S. Sharp, 95–107. New York: Academic Press.

The Power of Maps. 1993. Exhibition catalog. Washington, D.C.: Cooper-Hewitt, National Museum of Design, Smithsonian Institution.

Radin, Paul. 1956. *The Trickster: A Study in American Indian Mythology*. London: Routledge and Kegan Paul.

Reich, Robert. 1991. *The Work of Nations: Preparing Ourselves for Twenty-first Century Capitalism*. New York: Knopf.

Resnick, Daniel, and Lauren Resnick. 1977. "The Nature of Literacy: An Historical Exploration." *Harvard Educational Review* 47, no. 3 (August): 370–385.

Rickels, Laurence. 1989. "Mickey Marx." *Lusitania* 1, no. 4: 205–214.

————. 1991. *The Case of California*. Baltimore: Johns Hopkins University Press.

Robinson, Arthur H., and Barbara Bartz Petchenik. 1976. *The Nature of Maps: Essays toward Understanding Maps and Mapping*. Chicago: University of Chicago Press.

Rodriguez, Richard. 1982. *The Hunger of Memory: An Autobiography. The Education of Richard Rodriquez*. Boston: David Godine.

Rosaldo, Renato. 1987. "Politics, Patriarchs, and Laughter." *Cultural Critique* 6 (Spring): 65–86.

Ross, Kristin. 1987. "Rimbaud and the Transformation of Social Space." *Yale French Studies: Everyday Life*, no. 73. New Haven: Yale University Press.

Rugare, Steven. 1989 (March 20). "Towards a Poetics of Real Estate: Inhabiting Eschatology." Qualifying essay, History of Consciousness, University of California Santa Cruz, 67–72.

Rush, Richard. 1948. *The Autobiography of Richard Rush: His "Travels through Life" Together with His "Commonplace Book for 1789–1813."* Edited by George Corner. Princeton: Princeton University Press.

Russ, Joanna. 1978. "What Can a Heroine Do? or Why Women Can't Write." In *Woman as Writer*, edited by Jeannette L. Webber and Joan Grumman. Boston: Houghton Mifflin.

————. 1983. *How to Suppress Women's Writing*. Austin: University of Texas Press.

Sandoval, Chéla. 1993. "Oppositional Consciousness in the Postmodern World: U.S. Third World Feminism, Semiotics, and the Methodology of the Oppressed." Ph.D. diss., University of California, Santa Cruz.

Sarmiento, Anthony R., and Ann Kay. 1990. *Work-Centered Learning: A Union Guide to Workplace Literacy*. Washington, D.C.: AFL-CIO Human Resources Development Institute.

Sartre, Jean-Paul. 1964. *Nausea*. New York: New Directions.

Scarry, Elaine. 1985. *The Body in Pain: The Making and Unmaking of the World*. New York: Oxford University Press.

Schofield, Roger. 1968. "The Measurement of Literacy in Pre-Industrial England." In *Literacy in Traditional Societies*, edited by Jack Goody, 311–325. Cambridge: Cambridge University Press.

Scholes, Robert. 1988. "Three Views of Education: Nostalgia, History, and Voodoo." *College English* 50, no. 3 (March): 323–333.

Schulte-Sasse, Jochen. 1987. "Modernity and Modernism, Postmodernity and Postmodernism: Framing the Issue." *Cultural Critique* 5 (Winter): 5–22.

Scott, Patrick. 1988. "A Few Words More about E. D. Hirsch and *Cultural Literacy*." *College English* 50, no. 3 (March): 333–338.

Scribner, Sylvia, and Michael Cole. 1981. *The Psychology of Literacy*. Cambridge: Harvard University Press.

Sieburth, Richard. N.d. "Same Difference: The French *Physiologies*. 1840–42." Unpublished essay.

Silko, Leslie Marmon. 1977. *Ceremony*. New York: Viking Penguin.

———. 1981. "The Storyteller." In *The Storyteller*, 17–32. New York: Seaver Books.

———. 1991. *The Almanac of the Dead*. New York: Penguin.

Simonson, Rick, and Scott Walker, eds. 1988. *The Graywolf Annual Five: Multicultural Literacy: Opening the American Mind*. St. Paul: Graywolf.

Smithsonian Institution. 1994 (May). *Willful Neglect: The Smithsonian Institution and U.S. Latinos*. Report of the Smithsonian Institution Task Force on Latino Issues. Washington, D.C.: Smithsonian Institution.

"Society's Ills Hurt Reform of Education." 1993. *San Jose Mercury News*, 25 April, A1.

Street, Brian V. 1984. *Literacy in Theory and Practice*. New York: Cambridge University Press.

Stuckey, J. Elspeth. 1991. *The Violence of Literacy*. Portsmouth, N.H.: Boynton/Cook.

Takaki, Ronald. 1990. *Iron Cages: Race and Culture in Nineteenth-Century America*. New York: Oxford University Press.

Tanner, Nancy Makepeace. 1981. *On Becoming Human*. New York: Cambridge University Press.

Turnbull, David. 1989. *Maps Are Territories: Science Is an Atlas—A Portfolio of Exhibits*. Geelong, Victoria, Australia: Deakin University Press.

Ulmer, Gregory. 1989. *Teletheory: Grammatology in the Age of Video*. New York: Routledge.

Ventura, Michael. "A Report from El Dorado." In *The Graywolf Annual Five: Multicultural Literacy: Opening the American Mind*, edited by Rick Simonson and Scott Walker, 173–188. St. Paul: Graywolf.

Villa, Raul. 1990 (June 14). Unpublished qualifying essay, History of Consciousness, University of California, Santa Cruz.

———. 1993. "Tales from the Second City: Social Geographic Imagination in Contemporary Urban California Chicana/Chicano Literature and Art." Ph.D. diss., University of California, Santa Cruz.

Vizenor, Gerald, ed. 1989. *Narrative Chance: Postmodern Discourse on Native American Indian Literatures*. Albuquerque: University of New Mexico Press.

Vogel, Susan. "Always True to the Object, in Our Fashion." In *Exhibiting Cultures: The Poetics and Politics of Museum Display*, edited by Ivan Karp and Steven D. Lavine, 191–204. Washington, D.C.: Smithsonian Institution Press.

West, Cornel. 1993. "Malcolm X and Black Rage." In *Race Matters*, 93–105. Boston: Beacon Press.

White, Hayden. 1973. *Metahistory: The Historical Imagination in Nineteenth-Century Europe*. Baltimore: Johns Hopkins University Press.

———. 1987. *The Content of the Form*. Baltimore: Johns Hopkins University Press.

"Who Needs Great Works: A Forum including Jack Hitt, E. D. Hirsch Jr., John Kaliski, Jon Pareles, Roger Shattuck, and Gayatri Chakravorty Spivak." 1989. *Harper's* 278, no. 1671 (September): 43–52.

Willis, Susan. 1991. *A Primer for Daily Life*. New York: Routledge.

Wohlfarth, Irving. 1986. "Et Cetera? The Historian as Chiffonnier." *New German Critique* 39 (Fall): 143–168.

Yordon, Edward. 1992. *The Decline and Fall of the American Programmer*. Englewood Cliffs, N.J.: Prentice Hall.

Zihlman, Adrienne, and Nancy Tanner. 1978. "Gathering and the Hominid Adaptation." In *Female Hierarchies*, edited by Lionel Tiger and Heather T. Fowler. Chicago: Beresford Book Service.

INDEX

Calvino, Italo, 163–164, 170
—*Invisible Cities,* 132, 133, 163
Canada, 6, 34, 39, 40, 65, 121, 143,
150, 199
canon, vii, 2, 3, 18, 35, 62, 82, 88, 117,
125, 132, 158, 176, 184
cartography, 53
Cheney, Lynne, 37, 74
Chicago Cultural Studies Group, ix
Chinese bureaucracy, 12
chronotope, 96, 99, 120, 148, 153,
162, 174
Civil War, 31, 65, 162
Clanchy, Michael, 40, 41
—*From Memory to Written Record,* 40
Clarke, Arthur C., 192
class, 1, 2, 6–10, 12, 13, 28, 34, 35, 38–
44, 48, 76, 79, 114, 117, 123, 130,
134, 138, 154, 159, 165, 184, 198
Clinton, Bill, 8, 192
cognitive map(s), 165–168, 167, 175,
176, 179, 181, 182, 185
Cole, Michael, 42, 210
Colomb, Gregory G., 61, 66, 83, 194
community college students, 30, 31
comprehension, 30–33, 35, 54, 61, 64,
66, 68, 70, 167, 191
conceptual map, 53, 54
conquistadors, 12, 134, 156
Constitution, 13
culti-multural, x, 123, 146, 197
cultural difference, 35
cultural literacy, 9, 12, 13, 22, 30, 31, 35,
36, 44–45, 56, 57, 61–64, 66, 68,
70–72, 77–79, 82, 87, 92, 113, 117,
118, 158–160, 172, 193–195
curricula, x, 35–37, 43, 53, 54, 56, 57,
62, 64, 67, 70, 74, 77, 80, 118
Cytowic, Richard E., 167, 201

Davidow, William H., and Michael S.
Malone, 192
Davis, Angela, xiii

Declaration of Independence, 63, 78,
160
decode, 2, 30, 32, 85, 123, 165, 181
decoding, 5, 7, 30–33, 35, 76, 83, 84,
136, 159, 179, 181
definition, 4, 10, 17, 28, 33, 53, 55, 57,
58, 61, 62, 68, 72, 82, 143, 157, 174,
183, 184, 196
—differentia, 57, 58
—exclusion, 58, 72, 78, 88, 175–
178, 185, 198
—infer, 32, 58, 157, 196
Deleuze, Giles, and Felix Guattari, 59,
88, 100
democratic, 12, 21, 38, 48, 159
desire, 3, 14–16, 20, 77, 101, 124, 125,
129, 133, 136, 138, 156–158, 169,
170
Dewey, 61
di Giovanni, Norman Thomas, 191
Disney, iv, vii, 56, 72, 73, 79, 119–132,
134–140, 142–157, 162, 163, 172,
177, 198–203
Disney World, 56, 120–124, 126, 128–
132, 138–140, 146, 147, 149, 153–
157, 162, 198, 199, 201
Doering, Zahava, xiv, 162, 171, 183, 201
—and Adam Bickford, 162, 171,
201
dolphins, 50, 157
Domesday Book, The, 41
dragon, 87, 145, 146, 157, 196
dualism(s), 19, 21, 23–32, 41, 42, 45–
49, 114, 146, 186

Eco, Umberto, 52, 53, 55, 57–61, 66,
68, 69, 72, 81, 82, 85, 87, 105, 131,
132, 134–136, 159, 165, 170, 179,
180, 188, 193–194, 198
—on James Bond, 179
—on Superman, 136, 179
—open and closed texts, 159, 165,
179, 180

Laguna, 95, 99, 109, 111, 174
Latino, 28, 44, 114, 141, 152, 175, 176,
    193, 196
—*Willful Neglect,* 175, 210
Lavine, Steven D., 159
Lee, Robert E., 31, 72
Lévi-Strauss, Claude, 193
lexical lists, 32
library, iv, 1, 2, 4, 12, 51, 52, 74, 75, 120,
    123–125, 130, 142, 147, 149, 155,
    156, 158, 159, 161, 164, 191
Limon, Jose, xiii
Lincoln, Abraham, 84
Lippard, Lucy, x
list, 13, 22, 53–60, 62–64, 66–72, 74,
    76–79, 86, 87, 92, 118, 122, 171,
    186, 195
literacy, i, iii, vii, xv, 1–23, 26, 28–51,
    53, 56, 57, 59–64, 66–89, 92–94,
    96, 97, 99, 100, 112–118, 123–125,
    129–131, 134, 135, 143, 146, 149,
    155, 156, 158–160, 172, 173, 180,
    181, 183, 186–189, 191–195,
    198–210
—and slavery, 15
—Christian, 12, 45, 145, 198
—definition, 4, 10, 17, 28, 33, 53,
    55, 57, 58, 61, 62, 68, 72, 82, 143,
    157, 174, 183, 184, 196
—discourses, 7–9, 21, 23, 48, 49
—instruction, 29, 38
—narratives, 18
—proposals, 9
—rebellion, 15, 16, 30
—revolution, 15, 16, 78, 87, 89, 90,
    93, 94, 114, 115, 159
—skills, 3, 5–9, 11, 12, 15, 17–20,
    23, 30–36, 40, 48, 61, 65, 66, 69,
    74, 76, 79, 80, 83, 84, 86, 87, 90,
    107, 109, 112, 113, 115, 123–125,
    129, 131, 143, 159, 171, 180–183,
    187, 191

—standards, 10, 33–35
—violence, 8, 21, 22, 37–39, 42–
    44, 105, 118, 152, 156, 186, 198,
    210
—workplace, 8, 14, 192
Lubiano, Wahneema, ix
Luther, Martin, 65, 148

MacDonald, George, 159, 162, 200
Malcolm X, 75–77, 84, 141
mall, 73, 120, 123, 126, 129, 139, 146,
    162, 163, 171, 177, 178, 201
map and maps, xi, 23, 29, 49, 52–56, 60,
    62, 68, 71, 72, 74–80, 82, 84, 86–88,
    104, 115, 124, 128, 153, 155, 159,
    165–170, 174–175, 178–179, 183–
    186, 195
Marco Polo, 54, 132–134, 163, 169
maze, 47–49, 59, 67, 68, 130, 139, 180,
    194, 198
meaning, x, 8, 19, 23, 28, 30, 33, 35,
    45–49, 51, 53, 55, 61, 66–68, 72, 77,
    79, 82, 85, 100, 103–105, 107, 114,
    115, 125, 134, 136, 140, 150, 155,
    170, 174, 181, 182, 193, 194
melting pot, ix, 63
memorization, 33, 70, 120
Mestizaje, 175, 176, 185
mestizo, 26, 99, 103, 109, 110
metonym, 3, 199
Meyers, Miles, 191
mixed cultures, x, xi, 19, 82, 117, 186,
    189
model minority, 27, 35
Mongols, 3, 12
monocultural, 30–32, 36, 37, 74, 77,
    80, 82, 87, 88, 101, 109, 117, 118,
    189
monocultural knowledge, 36, 80, 118
Montesquieu, 52
morphemes, 30, 33
morphing, 200

Morrison, Toni, 88
—*Nobel Lecture in Literature,* 88
—rememory, 12, 191
multiculturalism, ix, x, 19, 35, 36, 56, 74, 78, 175, 185
museum, vii, 76, 124, 134, 136, 145, 158–163, 165–168, 171–174, 178–185, 198, 199
Museum of the American Indian, 163, 172, 179, 182, 202
Muslims, 33
mystory, 188

Narareno, Analisa, 195
—standpoint, 63, 69, 77
nation, 6–8, 11–13, 17, 22, 23, 28, 33, 53, 62, 65, 70, 72, 74, 76, 81, 100, 101, 121, 159, 162, 163, 165, 174–176, 191
Nation at Risk, A, 6, 7, 33, 191
National Commission on Excellence in Education, 6, 191
National Educational Goals Report, 6
Native Americans, 13, 28, 176
Navajo, 14, 169
net, 56, 59, 60, 67–69, 82, 84, 85, 88, 99, 115–117, 133–135, 157, 159, 170
nonaligned nations, 74
non-Christian, 45
non-literacy, 46–47
nonperson, 74
nonviolent resistance, 74
Normans, 40, 41
not-writing, 29

Olsen, Tillie, 196
Ommaya, 167
Ong, Walter J., 21, 45, 46, 49, 194
—*Orality and Literacy: The Technologizing of the Word,* 21, 22, 45
oppositional literacies, 20, 123
orality, 12, 21–23, 45–47, 49, 127, 186
—pre-Socratic, 45

oralysis, 188
Oxford English Dictionary, ix

paradox, 15, 50, 53, 60, 71, 74, 99, 107, 110, 112, 116, 118, 134, 135, 187
Patterson, Orlando, 63
pedagogy, 10, 22, 23, 29, 30, 33, 34, 42, 50, 56, 84, 131, 188
people of color, 7, 12, 27, 36, 75, 127, 142, 148, 154, 172, 182, 185, 199
perceptions, visual and kinesthetic, 47
Peters, Roger, 165
Peters, Tom, 192
philosopher of knowledge, 53
phonemes, 30, 33
Plato, 46
Porphyrian tree, 57, 58, 60, 194
postindustrial, 12, 16
postmodern, 7, 12, 13, 19, 88, 101, 110, 114, 117, 118, 120, 121, 126, 143, 150, 154, 172, 188, 189, 195, 197
preliterate, 4, 15, 16, 44
Puente Project, 193

race, 6, 13, 26–28, 38–40, 73, 78, 101, 102, 114, 120, 123, 150, 151, 159, 160, 184, 185, 197, 198
racism, 26, 28, 73, 94, 100, 151, 158, 184, 187, 199
racist discourse, 26, 27
—non-black, 26–28
radical literacy, 41, 42
Ravitch, Diane, 61, 74
raza, 184, 197, 202
reader/response criticism, 179
reader's block, 115, 116, 159, 165, 180, 182
reading, vii, ix, 3, 6, 11, 16, 17, 19, 20, 29–33, 35, 46, 48, 62, 64–67, 70–73, 75, 76, 79, 81–86, 88, 109, 113–115, 123, 125, 136, 143, 154, 155, 157, 159, 165, 167, 172, 179, 180, 182, 184, 186, 191, 194–196

DATE DUE

GAYLORD · · · · · #3522PI · · · · · Printed in USA